AMERICAN CATHOLICISM

American

THE CHICAGO HISTORY OF AMERICAN CIVILIZATION
Daniel J. Boorstin, EDITOR

Catholicism

By John Tracy Ellis

Second Edition, Revised

THE UNIVERSITY OF CHICAGO PRESS

CHICAGO AND LONDON

THE UNIVERSITY OF CHICAGO PRESS, CHICAGO 60637
THE UNIVERSITY OF CHICAGO PRESS, LTD., LONDON
© 1956, 1969 by The University of Chicago. Published 1956
Second edition, revised, published 1969
All rights reserved. Printed in the United States of America
82 81 80 79 78   9 8 7 6 5
ISBN: 0-226-20554-1 (clothbound); 0-226-20556-8 (paperbound)
Library of Congress Catalog Card Number: 69-19274

In Loving Memory of My Mother

IDA C. ELLIS

July 12, 1880—January 20, 1955

Table of Contents

Editor's Preface

The election of John Fitzgerald Kennedy to the Presidency in 1960 signaled a new era in American history, in the history of religions in America, and in the history of American Catholicism. Catholics, although for many years the largest single religious group in the United States, had suffered some of the disabilities of a "minority." After the defeat of Governor Alfred E. Smith in his candidacy for President in 1928, it had been widely assumed that to be a Catholic was to be disqualified from election to the nation's highest office. But after 1960 no one could any longer make that assumption, and this was another momentous step in the full assimilation of these millions of Americans into the mainstream of our political life. The story of recent American Catholicism, therefore, is a peculiarly significant and inspiring chapter in the growth and fulfillment of American institutions.

Because the Roman Catholic Church is more universal and more cosmopolitan than any other institution which has held a comparable place in American life, this volume offers a special opportunity to observe the shaping role of American ideals

Editor's Preface

and American circumstances. How "American" has Catholicism become in America? In what ways has American life been most intimately touched and most largely shaped by Catholicism? These are some of the questions which Monsignor Ellis tries to answer in this book. He tells the story so succinctly, so judiciously, and so reverently, that in the dozen years since its first appearance this volume has earned a place on the small bookshelf of standard works on the subject. In the present revision Monsignor Ellis brings the book up to date and incorporates into his story the complex interaction of Catholicism and the United States in recent years.

One of the virtues of Monsignor Ellis' book is that it is very much a view from the inside of the church. Readers who do not share his faith may not share some of his interpretations. But all of us will find his book wonderfully instructive. Not only because he tells us the too-little-known story of the growing group of Americans who remain steadfast in their Roman Catholic faith, and of how they have struggled to keep their religious faith and institutions while building American institutions. Even more because all of us—Catholics, Protestants, Jews, and non-believers—will incidentally discover from reading this book how narrowly Protestant has been the familiar interpretation of our history. In this way, Monsignor Ellis, by the very commitment and sharpness of his own point of view, helps us enlarge ours.

The "Chicago History of American Civilization" aims to make each aspect of our culture a window to all our history. This series contains two kinds of books: a *chronological* group, which provides a coherent narrative of American history from its beginning to the present day; and a *topical* group which

Editor's Preface

deals with the history of varied and significant aspects of American life. This book is one of the topical group. It complements two other volumes in the series: Nathan Glazer, *American Judaism*, and Winthrop Hudson, *American Protestantism*.

Daniel J. Boorstin

Preface to the Revised Edition

The 1960's have been the most eventful and tumultuous decade in the twentieth-century history of the Catholic Church, and the American branch of the Church has been as strong a witness to the universal phenomenon of change as will be found anywhere in the Catholic world with the possible exception of the Netherlands. To summarize fully and to interpret adequately the events that have swept through the Catholic community of the United States since 1956 in a single chapter is seemingly to attempt the impossible. Yet that is what the new chapter, "The Changing Church, 1956–68," has tried to do. Given the startling pace at which the Church is now moving, some portions of the chapter, written in the spring of 1968, may, indeed, seem dated by the early months of 1969. The historian must, however, eschew the role of recorder and commentator on current events, since he cannot serve both roles in a satisfactory manner. Besides the additional material which brings the narrative down to 1968, parts of the earlier work have been corrected or revised, the statistics have been brought up to date, and recent items have been added to the bibliographies and to the table of important dates.

Preface to the Revised Edition

If much of the story of the developments since 1956 involves internal tension and conflict within the American Church, it is but a reflection of the mood that has characterized the Church throughout the world since Vatican Council II. In that regard it is well to recall what Hubert Jedin, one of the greatest of living historians of the Church's ecumenical councils, has said:

Truth is reached in any community by means of an exchange of opinions, by arguments for and against, that is, by means of an intellectual struggle. At the councils, as in any other place where men contend with one another for the truth, fallen human nature exacts its toll: the former, that is the struggle, is ordained by God, the latter he permits. . . . The toll paid by human nature in the councils is the price which the visible Church has to pay for being in the midst of the human race [*Ecumenical Councils of the Catholic Church: An Historical Outline* (New York, 1960), pp. 234–35].

JOHN TRACY ELLIS

UNIVERSITY OF SAN FRANCISCO
October 21, 1968

xiv

Preface to the First Edition

The plan and execution of this slender volume are so simple and uncomplicated that very little is needed by way of introduction. When the writer was invited under the auspices of the Charles R. Walgreen Foundation for the Study of American Institutions to deliver a series of lectures on the history of the Catholic Church in the United States, he suggested two possible avenues of approach: the first, a topical one in which there was envisioned a fairly detailed presentation of four major movements or problems in American Catholicism; the second, a general survey with a view to offering a chronological sketch of the development of the Church in this country from the days of the colonial missions to the present time. The latter was chosen by those responsible for the Walgreen Lectures, and in that form they were delivered on January 24, 25, 27, and 28, 1955.

The student of American history will have no difficulty with the dates assigned for the first chapter. In the case of the second chapter, however, the year 1852 needs a word of explanation. It was in May of that year at Baltimore that the American bishops held the First Plenary Council, a meeting which the historian of the councils described as "the most important step so far made by the hierarchy for complete uniformity of Church life in the United States."[1] That event, therefore, offered justification for a choice that might otherwise seem to be an odd date. In the breaking point between the third and fourth chapters the year 1908 is perhaps a bit more arbitrary. But Pope Pius X's action on June 29 of that year in removing the Church of the United States from the jurisdiction of the Congregation de Propaganda Fide and elevating it to a status of equality with the other full-grown branches of the Church was thought to be sufficiently indicative of the growing maturity of American Catholicism to warrant its use.

No one is more aware of the limitations of brevity in this book than the writer. It is, indeed, only a sketch in which many interesting and worthwhile features of American Catholic history have had to be sacrificed, as, for example, more ample treatment of lay trusteeism in the early nineteenth century, of the role played by the American bishops in Vatican Councils I and II, of the relations between Catholics and their fellow citizens of other religious faiths, and of the wider implications of the controversies between clashing national groups within the Church, which in turn contributed a large share to the furor over the supposed heresy of Americanism at the end of the century. These and many other aspects of this broad subject would merit fuller treatment, but, if one were to attempt to do them justice, these chapters would lose much of their original character as lectures and defeat the purpose which the publisher of the book has in mind.

No book, however brief, can be written without its author incurring obligations, and the present volume is no exception to

Preface to the First Edition

that rule. The writer wishes at the outset to thank Professor Jerome G. Kerwin, former director of the Walgreen Foundation, for inviting him to deliver the lectures and for the generous hospitality which he extended to him during his stay at the University of Chicago. He is likewise grateful to Daniel J. Boorstin, editor of the "Chicago History of American Civilization" series, for his courteous and helpful suggestions in the preparation of the manuscript for publication. And in the matter of courtesies, no one could have been more mindful than Professor Kerwin's able secretary, Mr. Robert A. Kennedy. Staff members of the Library of Congress were always obliging in the many calls for help, and a debt of gratitude quite beyond what can be absolved by a mere formal mention was incurred by the writer to the people of the Mullen Library of the Catholic University of America. Their unfailing patience and kindly assistance made the task much lighter and more pleasant than it would otherwise have been. The writer's student and friend, Miss Margaret C. Carthy, formerly of the College of New Rochelle, kindly read the final draft and pointed out a number of needed corrections. To his former secretary, Mrs. James S. Boss, he is likewise under obligation for a cheerful response to every demand made upon her in typing the manuscript. Finally, special thanks are owed to two friends: to the Very Reverend Louis A. Arand, S.S., retired president of Divinity College at the Catholic University of America, for his sound and balanced judgments which strengthened the work, and to the Reverend Henry J. Browne, professor of history in Cathedral College, New York, for generously passing on references which he had met in his own research and for the constructive criticisms which he offered in his reading of the manuscript.

That the Walgreen Foundation should have sponsored dur-

Preface to the First Edition

ing the academic year 1954–55 three series of lectures on the history of Protestantism, Catholicism, and Judaism in the United States is in itself a reflection of the increased emphasis which religion has been receiving in all phases of American life since World War II. In fact, the future historian is likely to characterize these years as a period that had its own mid-twentieth-century variety of religious "awakenings." It is a movement in which the historian of religion should take his share by demonstrating to the best of his professional skill the major contribution which religion has played in the national life and the deep roots which it struck in American soil from the very beginning of white settlement on this continent. Some years ago Christopher Dawson remarked in a thoughtful essay on "How To Understand Our Past" that for too long a time there has existed a tendency to treat secular history and ecclesiastical history as two self-contained subjects. No serious historian should be satisfied with a division of that kind. As Dawson said, "It destroyed the intelligible unity of culture and left the history of culture itself suspended uneasily between political and ecclesiastical history with no firm basis in either of them."[2] If, therefore, this work will have made any contribution to a better integration of the story of the Catholic Church in this country with the general history of the nation, and if it will have put that story into sharper focus for readers of any or no religious faith, it will have accomplished its objective.

JOHN TRACY ELLIS

I

The Church in Colonial America
1492–1790

"Columbus' conversation with the friar at La Rábida is the starting point of modern history. The past had ruled the world till then—what began that day was the reign of the future."[1] Thus did Lord Acton characterize the fateful change of plans brought about by the Italian navigator's visit to the former confessor of Queen Isabella; for it was Fray Juan Pérez who convinced Columbus that he should await the results of another approach to the Spanish sovereigns before turning to France. With that change of plans the destiny of every one of us was in a remote way connected by the voyage of 1492 which opened the real history of the world we inhabit.

In this discussion of colonial America I should like to dwell upon several principal aspects of the threefold penetration of the Western Hemisphere by the Catholic Church in the two and one-half centuries before the United States was born. I say "several" for this reason, as the reader will understand: a brief survey of such a lengthy span of years can afford only a very restricted treatment. The development of the subject is determined by the association of the Church in three quite distinct relationships, that is, with the colonizing enterprises of Spain, France, and England. There were, moreover, differences as to time and place of colonization. Spain preceded France and England by almost a century in planting permanent settlements. The Spanish Empire embraced Central and South America, the French occupied what is today Canada, and all three powers ultimately assumed a stake in the islands of the Caribbean. But with the history of these distant outposts we are in no way concerned; our sole purpose here is to deal with certain features of colonial Catholicism that occurred within the borders of what is now the United States.

If we Americans of the later twentieth century do not understand as well as we should the varied pattern of our colonial past, the reason is not far to seek. Until about a half-century ago the *leyenda negra*, or the "black legend" of Spain, so completely possessed the national mind that pioneers like Adolph Bandelier and others who sought to win a hearing for the case of Spain were shouted out of court by those bred in the tradition of sixteenth-century England. The historians of that tradition succeeded to a remarkable degree in passing on to generations of Americans a thoroughly biased view of Spain's accomplishments in the New World. In spite of the recently increasing number of solid studies in American historiography, I should say that students interested in the history of ideas will still find it piquant to trace the manner in which the Whig approach to Spanish history captured the American historical profession and held it firmly in its grip until a generation or more ago.

The man to whom, above all others, the credit is owed for a broader and more enlightened view is Herbert Eugene Bolton, who searched restlessly in Spanish archives on both sides of the Atlantic until his death in 1953. As Bolton uncovered the documentary riches, he became more and more convinced, not only of the defective method of many who had preceded him, but of the necessity for Americans to know the history of Spanish America if they were fully to understand their own past. It was an approach that slowly won a considerable audience; and by the time Bolton delivered his presidential address before the American Historical Association at Toronto in 1932 on a subject he entitled "The Epic of Greater America,"[2] it was realized that this sympathetic yet objective treatment could serve a highly useful purpose for the Good Neighbor policy of the Roosevelt administration, for the world view of history that even then was beginning to force itself upon our notice, and, too, for the cause of true historical scholarship.

With regard to Catholicism in the Spanish colonies, there are, I think, certain prime postulates that one should keep in mind. First is the fact that at the dawn of colonization and for a century thereafter Spain was a nation more united in its religious faith, perhaps, than in any other single way. The recent conquest of the Moors, the concessions granted to the Spanish crown by the Holy See over the management of ecclesiastical affairs, and the fact that Spain was unquestionably the greatest Catholic power of Europe set in conflict with the rising Protestant states—all helped to stamp upon every Spanish enterprise the seal of Catholic energy. Such zeal appears, indeed, in the first entry that Columbus made in his famous journal, where he remarked that among the principal aims of his voyage one was to contact the native peoples so that he might observe what he termed "the manner in which may be undertaken their conversion to our Holy Faith."[3] It is likewise evident in almost every major patent granted by the crown for settlement in the New World; for example, when Charles V in June, 1523, outlined for Vasquez de Ayllón the objectives he was to pursue in his conquest of Florida, the conversion of the Indians to Catholicism was described as "the chief motive you are to bear and hold in this affair, and to this end it is proper that religious persons should accompany you."

Not only was the religious motive high among the objectives of Spanish colonization, as to a lesser extent it was with both the French and English, but in no other country was the State's control over the Church quite so complete as in the case of Spain. A decade before the discovery of America there had begun with Pope Sixtus IV a series of concessions to the kings of Spain which culminated in Julius II's bull *Universalis ecclesiae* of 1508, which made necessary the State's approval for every church, monastery, and religious house opened in the colonies and which gave to the state the right to nominate in perpetuity to every ecclesiastical benefice in the colonial empire.[5] This exceedingly close union of Church and State was, then, both the greatest strength and the predominant weakness of Catholicism in Spanish America. The interests of the political and ecclesiastical orders frequently clashed over control of the Indians, and as a consequence Spanish colonial records through the three centuries from Juan Ponce de León's entry into Florida in 1521 to the opening of the last California mission at San Francisco Solano in 1823 are filled with the strife between Church and State.

However, this combination produced more than sterile quarrels. Within the immense arc which the Spaniards gradually drew around the rim of the United States from Florida on the east to upper California on the west, they had to deal with primitive and savage peoples, and in so doing they found no

4

more effective instrument than the Catholic mission system. The missionaries, dependent upon the civil and military authorities for financial support and physical protection, likewise realized that they could never press their claims too far. As a result the *real patronato*, the term used to describe the State's control over the Church, continued to the end of Spanish rule with many a dispute referred to superiors in Mexico City and Madrid for lengthy adjudication that gave ample time for fiery Spanish tempers on the frontier to cool. No informed person would endeavor to maintain that the churchmen were always in the right, but by the same token no one can deny that they were generally on the side of the angels in their treatment of the Indians. It was the outraged voice of a friar, Bartolomé de las Casas, which first made Europe aware of the fate that had befallen thousands of the natives in enslavement by the Spanish conquerors. And it was the agitation aroused by Las Casas and his kind that prompted Pope Paul III in 1537 to issue the bull *Sublimis Deus* in which he declared: "The said Indians and all other people who may later be discovered by Christians, are by no means to be deprived of their liberty or the possession of their property, even though they be outside the faith of Jesus Christ."[6]

There was an element of compassion for the red man as a child of God in the ideology of the Spanish missionaries that was entirely lacking in the attitude of most of the English settlers along the Atlantic Coast. It was the conviction that he had a soul worth saving that inspired their extraordinary sacrifices in his behalf. That, and that alone, will explain the dogged persistence with which the missionaries pushed on in the face of repeated setbacks and tragedies such as the murder of Fray Juan de Padilla, their protomartyr, on the plains of Kansas in 1542. How otherwise can one account for the fact that so many highly gifted priests like the Tyroiese Jesuit, Eusebio Kino, and Junípero Serra, the Franciscan from Majorca, both university-trained men, should abandon their cultivated surroundings to dedicate their lives to the moral and material uplift of these savage people? Failure they knew aplenty, but they also knew success, as, for example, when the Franciscan' superior in New Mexico reported in 1630 that there were then 35,000 Christian Indians living in ninety pueblos grouped around twenty-five missions. Two centuries later when the blow of secularization fell upon the twenty-one missions of California, a like number of peaceful and diligent red men were in possession of nearly 400,000 head of cattle, over 300,000 hogs, sheep, and goats, 62,000 horses, and farms that yielded over 120,000 bushels of grain plus the products of orchards, gardens, wine presses, looms, shops, and forges. In California alone between 1769 and 1845, there were 146 Franciscans who gave all or a portion of their adult lives to this difficult task. There were contributions the like of which could be duplicated in no other area of colonial America, and it was no romantic impulse when Bolton spoke of the missions of the Spanish Jesuits and Franciscans as "a force which made for the preservation of the Indians, as opposed to their destruction, so characteristic of the Anglo-American frontier."[7]

In all these colonial missions—and there were at one time as many in Texas as in California, more than that number in Florida, and twice California's twenty-one in New Mexico—the Franciscans, Jesuits, and other priests were not only ministers of religion. They were agents of the Spanish crown, and as such they supported the policies of the government whenever those policies did not run counter to the principal business of the missionaries, which was to save souls. For example, the news of Spain's declaration of war on Great Britain in June, 1779, was long in reaching California, but when Serra learned of it, he dispatched a circular letter to all the missions on June 15, 1780, in which he informed the friars of what had happened, reminded them of the generosity of Charles III's government to their missions, and emphasized the interest which they should take in the matter. There was nothing that the Franciscans in California could do to hasten Spain's victory over England but to pray, and with that in mind Serra said, "Of each and every one of Your Reverences I most earnestly ask in the Lord that as soon as you receive this letter you be most attentive in begging God to grant success to our arms."[8] Little did the American rebels on the Atlantic coast realize that over 3,000 miles to the west a Spanish friar was ordering prayers to be said for the defeat of their common enemy!

As an important part of the colonizing methods of Spain in the New World, the numerous missionary establishments of the Church were, as has been said, closely linked with the civil and military administration. The missionaries were in every sense agents of both Church and State, for it was from the State that they received—if often irregularly—their annual stipends. It was likewise the State that furnished troops from neighboring presidios for the protection of the missions. The civil government usually paid an initial grant equivalent to $1,000 for equipping the missions with items such as bells, sacred vessels and vestments for religious services, and tools for the workshops. But the priests more than earned their keep by their disciplining and civilizing of the natives. It was the missionaries who taught the Indians the rudiments of learning within the mission compound, instructed the women how to

*this guy sucks!
is unreadable*

cook, sew, spin, and weave, and the men how to plant the crops, to fell the forests and to build, to tan leather, run the forge, dig ditches, shear the sheep, and to tend the cattle. It was they who introduced to these distant frontiers almost every domestic plant and animal then known in Europe, and it was they who taught the savages how to make the best possible use of husbandry for profit and enjoyment.

No one acquainted with the history of Catholicism in the Spanish borderlands will deny that there were at times defects and abuses. One of the chief sources for the defects in the system was the *real patronato*, a set of privileges that had been conceded to the Spanish kings by the Holy See almost a century before the establishment of the first enduring mission in the future United States. Out of the State's patronage of ecclesiastical affairs, there arose endless disputes between the two authorities, which in turn led to serious division in the Spanish settlements and to a general weakening of colonial government. The scandal given the Indians by these quarrels was real, for they often found themselves the bewildered victims of contests between the civil and military on the one hand and the missionaries on the other. Consequently, there ensued a demoralizing effect on the natives and a lessened respect for the Catholic faith which they had been asked to embrace. The differences arose at many points where the jurisdictional lines between Church and State were dim, and in one form or another they existed throughout the entire colonial period. The military, for example, often tried to win the natives for their selfish purposes by plying them with liquor, a practice which the missionaries fought vigorously, as they likewise resisted the civil officials' attempts from time to time to profit by Indian labor. On the other hand, from time to time a missionary would overstep the bounds of his jurisdiction and encroach upon the civil domain. Thus the friction was more or less constant, revolving, as a historian of New Mexico has said, around fundamental issues ever the same: "rivalry for control of the destiny of the Indians, problems of mission discipline, the conflict of economic interests, the question of ecclesiastical immunity, the authority of the custodian as ecclesiastical judge ordinary, the proper exercise of ecclesiastical censures, and interference of the clergy in strictly secular matters."[9]

Today hardly more than a chain of place names, stretching from St. Augustine, Florida, the first Catholic parish established in 1565 within the present United States, through San Antonio, Los Angeles, and on to San Francisco, remains to remind Americans of the three centuries of Spanish rule on the borderlands of their country. Yet the mission system was the most successful institution for dealing with the aborigines, and its builders gave a style of architecture to the Southwest and California that is as characteristic of those regions as the colonial design is to New England. It was likewise by virtue of elaborate accounts of explorations through uncharted areas and detailed maps made by missionaries like Father Kino that the cartography of the West was advanced. Through the missionaries' grammars and dictionaries of the native dialects and their preservation of Indian artifacts, which one sees in the museums of the Southwest, anthropologists were furnished with knowledge of the languages and customs of the Indians that would otherwise have perished. This old Christian civilization of the borderlands endured far beyond the age of Spanish greatness, and when the Americans arrived in those areas in the mid-nineteenth century, it afforded a link entirely absent from the plains and valleys to the north, with which to bind the old with the new order. It was facts such as these that Herbert Ingram Priestley had in mind nearly a half-century ago when he said, "It is of prime importance for the life of America today that the first white men to settle on these western shores were Spaniards and Roman Catholics, representatives of a powerful nation that was the citadel of a united faith."[10]

France

In the case of France, the other major power through whose agency Catholicism entered North America, many characteristics of its colonial missions resembled those of Spain. Here, too, Church and State were at the time united, and since the concordat signed by Pope Leo X and Francis I in 1516 the crown had enjoyed the right of nominating to vacant bishoprics and to newly established sees. But the Gallican tendencies which by the time of Louis XIV had brought about so tight a control over the Church in France were never able to effect quite the same results in North America. In no small measure this was due to the precedents set by the first bishop in New France, François de Montmorency Laval, a man of iron will and determination, who after his arrival in the colony in 1659 gave battle at every turn to the officials of the State when the rights of the Church were threatened. A recent writer has said of the bishop: "In all, Laval guided the destinies of the Church in New France for thirty-four years, ruling in a more authoritarian and absolute fashion than any representative of the all-powerful Sun King. He left more of a mark upon the colony than any governor except the great Frontenac, with whom he had quarreled violently."[11] The union of Church and State in New France was nonetheless real, and it was the basis for many a contest waged between the two throughout the

The Church in Colonial America

North American experience of France in the seventeenth and eighteenth centuries.

But apart from political matters, there were other similarities between Spain and France in the New World. The same concept, of the Indian as a man whose soul had equal value in the sight of God with that of the white man, motivated the French Jesuit and Récollet around the Great Lakes and through the Mississippi Valley as much as it did their Spanish brethren farther south. Father Jean de Brébeuf, for example, lived nearly three years among the Hurons for the sole purpose of learning their language and gaining a knowledge of their customs. Enriched with this background, he wrote out in 1637 a set of instructions for his confrères who were to evangelize the tribe, and if any of the future missionaries had thought that his superior education would impress the red men, Brébeuf was quick to disillusion him. "Leaving a highly civilized community," he said, "you fall into the hands of barbarous people who care but little for your Philosophy or your Theology. All the fine qualities which might make you loved and respected in France are like pearls trampled under the feet of swine, or rather of mules, which utterly despise you when they see that you are not as good pack animals as they are."[12] Fully cognizant as he was of what was in store for him, Brébeuf yet continued his Indian ministrations through the next twelve years up to that day in March, 1649, when he was captured by the Iroquois near Georgian Bay and submitted to a series of tortures that has made many a modern reader recoil in horror. Francis Parkman detailed his last hours and remarked of Brébeuf: "He came of a noble race,—the same, it is said, from which sprang the English Earls of Arundel; but never had the mailed barons of his line confronted a fate so appalling, with so prodigious a constancy. To the last he refused to flinch, and 'his death was the astonishment of his murderers.' "[13]

As Spain's high missionary zeal in the sixteenth century had been quickened by the triumph over the Mohammedans and the contest with the Protestant north, so a century later the compelling faith that carried the French missionaries to North America was fired by one of the most resplendent periods in the Catholicism of France, the age that produced a St. Francis de Sales, a St. Vincent de Paul, a Jacques Olier, a Cardinal Bérulle, and a host of other striking figures in religious thought and action. In France, too, the union of Church and State facilitated the arrangement for joint undertakings in the distant colonies, even if it later often hindered their execution. But there was a difference between the Spanish and French ecclesiastical regimes. After 1659 there was a bishop at Quebec in the person of the forceful Laval who, once admitted to the governing council of New France, powerfully barred the encroachments of the civil arm against the Church. Though distances were great and travel slow between the Great Lakes and Louisiana, the official position and high ecclesiastical rank of Laval and his successors told with more effect when disputes arose between the missionaries and civil officials than was true of the remonstrances of bishops in Mexico and Cuba.

For a century and a half, Jesuits, Récollets, Capuchins, and the diocesan priests of New France traversed the heart of the continent in pursuit of a goal that often eluded them. If the souls of these steadfast priests had not been kindled by a deep and abiding faith, they would soon have despaired; the story of the sufferings of the Jesuits alone during the 1640's at the hands of the savages remains one of the most heroic tales in our colonial past. From the time that Isaac Jogues, after incredible tortures, was felled beneath the ax of an Iroquois near the little village of Auriesville, New York, in October, 1646, to the murder of Brébeuf and Gabriel Lalemant on Georgian Bay in March, 1649, the slaughter continued. Then the insensate hate of the Iroquois against the Hurons and their friends seemed for a time to abate.

The Huron mission, it is true, had failed, but the Blackrobes did not quit New France. Instead they directed their eyes westward toward Lake Superior where Isaac Jogues had traveled as early as 1641. These were the years that saw a renewal of war in Europe and a more aggressive policy upon the part of France once Louis XIV had assumed personal control of the government in 1661. As rivalry for the mastery of North America intensified, Jean Talon, the royal intendant of New France, laid plans to forestall competition in the heart of the continent. On June 4, 1671, Simon François Daumont, Sieur de Saint Lusson, acting as Talon's representative, took formal possession of the entire western country in the name of God and Louis XIV. In this ceremony at Sault Ste Marie, to which the chiefs of all the neighboring tribes had been invited, Father Claude Allöuez, already a veteran in those parts, played a prominent role. After the cross and the standard of the king had been raised aloft as the symbols of the dual auspices of the undertaking, Allöuez preached a sermon in which he explained to the savages the doctrine of Christ's redemption of mankind on the cross. Then pointing to the royal banner, he said, "But look likewise at that other post, to which are affixed the armorial bearings of the great Captain of France whom we call King. He lives beyond the sea; he is the Captain of the greatest Captains, and has not his equal in the world."[14] Thus were

Church and State joined at that remote spot on Lake Superior to advance the policies of Louis XIV, Colbert, and Louvois.

The years that followed bore greater fruit for the Jesuits' missions than they had hitherto known, and by 1673 there were 1,800 refugee Ottawas and Hurons resident at St. Ignace Mission on the north shore of the Straits of Mackinac. South and west from these northern bases, the Blackrobes fanned out into the future states of Michigan, Wisconsin, and Illinois, and as the civil and military arms of France advanced upon the Mississippi they were either in the vanguard like Alloüez—tracking for thirty years over the prairies and through the forests of the Old Northwest—or like Jacques Marquette, in company with Louis Jolliet, reaching down to the borders of the Southwest. During the time that Marquette had spent at La Pointe de Saint Esprit on the south shore of Lake Superior, he had received visits from tribesmen, including the Illinois, who spoke to him of a great river and asked that he come among them. The thought of establishing a mission for these Indians was uppermost in his mind, therefore, when in May, 1673, he set out with Jolliet on their famous expedition. In the long and arduous months that lay ahead, the missionary was sustained by his hopes for the conversion of the Illinois and by his deep and abiding faith in God and the Mother of Christ. No one has written more majestically of this personal devotion of Marquette for the Blessed Mother than Parkman, who, although he in no way shared in the Jesuit's sentiments, appreciated the beauty and elevation of his thoughts. Parkman said of Marquette:

> He was a devout votary of the Virgin Mary, who, imaged to his mind in shapes of the most transcendent loveliness with which the pencil of human genius has ever informed the canvas, was to him

the object of an adoration not unmingled with a sentiment of chival-
rous devotion. The longings of a sensitive heart, divorced from
earth, sought solace in the skies. A subtile element of romance was
blended with the fervor of his worship, and hung like an illumined
cloud over the harsh and hard realities of his daily lot. Kindled by
the smile of his celestial mistress, his gentle and noble nature knew
no fear. For her he burned to dare and to suffer, discover new
lands and conquer new realms to her sway.[15]

Before this great missionary gave up his life in May, 1675, near
where the river that bears his name empties into Lake Michigan, he had the joy of opening the mission of the Immaculate
Conception for the Illinois near the present village of Utica.
Although his failing health permitted only a brief stay, others
came to spread a network of Jesuit stations on the shores of the
Great Lakes and the banks of the rivers of the Middle West.

Meanwhile, members of other orders appeared in these in-
land regions to supplement the Society of Jesus in affording
religious ministrations to the white settlers in the wilderness and
to seek converts among the red men. It was a Récollet, Louis
Hennepin, who explored the upper Mississippi in 1680 as far
north as the present site of Minneapolis and named the Falls of
St. Anthony. Hennepin's confrères, Gabriel de la Ribourde and
Zénobe Membré, who visited the tribes of northern Illinois,
met violent deaths, the former in September, 1680, at the hands
of the Kickapoo near Seneca, and the latter with a fellow religious, Maxim le Clercq, in January, 1689, as a member of
La Salle's ill-starred venture on the coast of Texas. Diocesan
priests trained at the seminary of Bishop Laval at Quebec also
played a part as missionaries to the Indians of the Middle West
and as pastors of the infant parishes in the frontier towns.
Authorized in May, 1698, to open missions for certain tribes
along the Mississippi, these priests often became pastors to the

French, as, for example, did Henri Rolleux de la Vente, who in September, 1704, was installed as first pastor of the Church of the Immaculate Conception at Fort Louis, the forerunner of the present city of Mobile. After the French had established the new colony of Louisiana in the early years of the eighteenth century, an agreement in May, 1722, brought the Capuchins, who endured throughout the century and beyond the time of Louisiana's purchase by the United States.

It was fortunate for Catholics that the Récollets, Capuchins, and diocesan priests had been enrolled, for the disaster which befell the Jesuits in the colonies of Spain had been visited even earlier upon their French brothers. When in July, 1763, the superior council at New Orleans ordered Jesuits banished from Louisiana and the Illinois country, a most dismal page was added to the history of the Church in colonial America. The harshness with which the civil officials acted and the manner in which they profaned even the symbols of religion justified the comment of the old Jesuit who described the episode: "One might have thought that it was the enemies of the Catholic religion who had caused it."[16]

To understand the persistence of the French missionaries in the face of so many apathetic or hostile Indians, one must remember that they not only were trained for hardship and disappointment but were schooled as well for failure in the sense that the world reckons failure. To the Jesuits, for example, it was not a failure for more than three hundred of the finest specimens of French manhood to expend their lives in converting a few Indians and in the end to be ruthlessly expelled from America by the government that had brought them here. To men imbued with a living faith in the supernatural and in the philosophy of the cross, this type of failure

The Church in Colonial America

was akin to that of the martyrs of the pagan Roman Empire out of whose sufferings in the first three centuries of the Christian era the Church of Europe was born. It is the kind of attitude toward failure that we heard almost monthly after 1950 as the missionaries expelled from Communist China reached Hong Kong only to declare that they would re-enter China at the first opportunity. It is an exceedingly difficult thing to convey a spirit of this kind to paper, but Parkman caught something of its meaning when he wrote of Father Marquette, and even such moderns as Charles and Mary Beard, to whom the New World empires were mainly predatory operations, remarked: "The heroic deeds of Catholic missionaries, daring for religion's sake torture and death, bore witness to a new force in the making of world dominion."[17]

French Catholics in colonial America were less successful than the Spaniards in converting Indians, but they were, perhaps, more successful in planting permanent settlements in the wilderness. At towns like St. Louis, Vincennes, Detroit, New Orleans, and Mobile the Church continued to play a leading part in the restricted lives of the inhabitants down to the time of the American Revolution. Amid the rough surroundings of the frontier the spirit of religion often burned very low, but it was never completely extinguished.

When these frontier posts were later engulfed in the stirring events of the Revolution and the War of 1812, the French Catholic population was found loyal to the American cause. George Rogers Clark and his Virginia militiamen experienced that loyalty at firsthand when they took Kaskaskia in 1778 and received aid from Father Pierre Gibault, the village priest. It was Gibault's influence that won Cahokia, and it was he, too, who tracked through the forests to help deliver Vincennes

and its Indians into American hands. Father Gabriel Richard at
Detroit was so noticeably attached to the United States in the
War of 1812 that the British ordered his house arrest.

Throughout the western expanse traversed by the missionaries of France and settled by its Catholic people before the
American nation was born, a litany of cities, towns, and rivers
tells of who once settled there. There is Vincennes, there is
Marquette, and there is St. Louis, named to commemorate the
saintly Louis IX. There is Dubuque, named for a Canadian descendant of the French. There is Louisville, called after Louis
XVI, and Marietta, Ohio, after Marie Antoinette. To these settlements certain refugee French priests fled after 1790 before
the whirlwind of revolution that had broken over France. In
the wilderness these priests kindled anew the fire of religious
faith and enriched the lives of all—Catholic and non-Catholic
alike—with their cultured manners and minds. D. W. Brogan
has said that the old towns of the Middle West are more American and more touching to the historical imagination than the
large cities. Vincennes and Bardstown were once, as Brogan
stated, "centres of civilization, of learning, of religion, of commerce."[18] In both Vincennes and Bardstown, a cathedral and a
college were staffed by bishops and priests from France before
the advancing frontier had passed their doors. Here, then, was
a significant stabilizing factor in the maturing process of the
newborn states, an ancient and fixed tradition to mellow the
rough and raw elements of the West.

What a different world one enters when he turns to the
English settlements along the Atlantic Coast! Within the areas
subjected to the rule of Spain and France no other Christian
belief than that of Catholicism ever held sway, for religious
freedom played no part in Spanish and French reckoning; Ca-

tholicism was unchallenged by any but pagan Indian cults. To the English colonists, however, a century of official hostility had made Catholicism more hated than any other Christian faith. In fact, so thoroughly had the job been done that, as a student of English expansion remarks, "With such conviction did they preach this doctrine that Englishmen at length accepted it as their imperial destiny."[19]

For present purposes the history of the Catholic Church in colonial English America may be reduced without too great simplification to four main points. First, a universal anti-Catholic bias was brought to Jamestown in 1607 and vigilantly cultivated in all the thirteen colonies from Massachusetts to Georgia. Second, the small body of Catholics, mostly English and Irish, who settled on the Atlantic seaboard after more than a century of active persecution and handicap clung to their religious faith. Third, the Catholic minority in their brief tenure of power in two colonies introduced the principle of religious toleration. Finally, the absence of domination by any one of the different Protestant churches fostered the principle of religious freedom for all, a principle to which the Catholics gave full assent.

The first point scarcely needs much documentation, since the proscription against Catholics in the colonial charters and laws is too well known to require emphasis, and the sermons, religious tracts, books, and gazettes of the period with monotonous regularity bore the same spirit and intent. The Anglican ministers of Virginia and the Puritan divines of Massachusetts Bay were often worlds apart in their theology, but there was nothing that would cause them to close ranks more quickly than a supposed threat from the Church of Rome. That is why one finds so much similarity between Virginia's law against

American Catholicism

Catholics of March, 1642, and the enactment at Massachusetts Bay five years later. It may be said that this transplantation of English religious prejudices to America thrived, though carried thousands of miles from its place of origin, and struck such enduring roots in new soil that it became one of the major traditions in a people's religious life. In one of his works Louis Wright states that, for better or for worse, Americans have inherited the basic qualities of their culture from the British. The thought prompted him to say: "For that reason we need to take a long perspective of our history, a perspective which views America from at least the period of the first Tudor monarchs and lets us see the gradual development of our common civilization, its transmission across the Atlantic, and its expansion and modification as it was adapted to conditions in the Western Hemisphere."[20] Apace with the influences exercised by other national strains in the generation of American civilization, the British has yet remained the strongest and has assimilated most of the others. Americans are not Englishmen, but, as Wright concluded, "we cannot escape an inheritance which has given us some of our sturdiest and most lasting qualities." Certainly the anti-Catholic bias brought to this country with the first English settlers has proved one of the sturdiest and most lasting of these qualities. The viability of that tradition would have astonished even Edmund Burke, who understood so well how the hatred of Catholics had operated in his native land. It was Burke who in a famous letter on the penal laws against the Catholics of Ireland remarked:

> You abhorred it, as I did, for its vicious perfection. For I must do it justice; it was a complete system, full of coherence and consistency, well digested and well composed in all its parts. It was a machine of wise and elaborate contrivance, and as well fitted for the oppression,

impoverishment, and degradation of a people, and the debasement, in them, of human nature itself as ever proceeded from the perverted ingenuity of man.[21]

That the penal codes of the American colonies did not reach the tyrannical perfection noticed by Burke elsewhere was no hindrance to holding the few colonial Catholics in thorough subjection.

What made the laws against Catholics in colonial America seem so absurdly harsh was the fact that at no time was more than an insignificant minority of the population Catholic. Protestants outnumbered Catholics among the 200 to 300 colonists who settled Maryland in 1634, and a census of that colony in 1708 turned up only 2,974 Catholics in a total population of 33,833. In Pennsylvania, the other colony where Catholics were concentrated, the census of 1757 recorded about 200,000 inhabitants, of whom 1,365 were Catholics. Even as late as 1785, when the new United States contained nearly four million people, there were scarcely more than 25,000 Catholics. Catholics were lost to the faith during these years by reason of the lack of facilities for the practice of their religion in many areas, but for the most part the colonial Catholics held tenaciously to their faith amid the most trying circumstances. There were even some conversions among the Protestants, as, for example, the Brooke and Taney families of Maryland from whom the later Chief Justice of the United States was descended.

Why did Catholics come to America in the first place? The predominant motive was the same as that which had prompted the Puritans to settle in Massachusetts and the Quakers in Pennsylvania, namely, the hope that they might worship God according to their consciences, free from the hampering restrictions of England's penal laws. As the penal code tightened its hold about the lives of the English Catholics in the last years of Elizabeth, several furtive projects were set on foot to find a haven for the Catholics abroad. After several abortive attempts by others, a convert member of the gentry offered the first viable plan to the oppressed Catholics for a home in the New World. That man was George Calvert, the first Baron of Baltimore, to whom Maryland owed its origins. Calvert was a man of real although not striking abilities. He was honorable and benevolent by nature, had a good eye for business, and the strength of his character may be measured by the fact that, when he became convinced in 1624 of the truth of the Catholic faith, he did not hesitate to resign his state office and surrender his seat in Parliament to follow his religious convictions. Calvert had enjoyed high favor with King James I, and even his change of religion did not cause him to lose entirely the advantageous position which his winning personality and social standing had earned him. His conversion to Catholicism had, however, focused his attention on the meanness of life to which the penal laws had reduced the Catholics, and he determined to employ his wealth and prestige in their behalf. Calvert's first attempt of 1627 to establish a colony in Newfoundland was wrecked by attacks from the French and the severity of the climate. In 1629 he turned to Virginia, of whose founding company he was a member, in the hope of better fortune. But on his visit to Virginia he was quickly disabused of the notion after being informed that Catholics were not welcome there. It was then that he decided to ask Charles I, the son and successor of his old patron, to grant a charter for a colony north of Virginia.

The first Baron Baltimore was an enterprising man, and the

The Church in Colonial America

commercial aspects of his American colony were never absent from his thoughts. But as Charles Andrews remarks, "He was under the impelling influence of motives and obligations that were more imperative than those of a mere colonizer—among which was the sacred duty of finding a refuge for his Roman Catholic brethren."[22] George Calvert himself died on April 15, 1632, just two months before the charter of Maryland was issued. The project then devolved upon his son, Cecilius, who like his father was anxious to draw the support of Protestants as well as Catholics. Loyal Catholic that he was, the second Baron Baltimore nonetheless saw no reason why men of different religious faiths could not join in a business of this kind if all practiced moderation and good will. Even if he had not been sincerely of this belief, and there is no evidence to doubt it, he was too much of a realist to think in terms of an exclusively Catholic colony. For that reason he raised no theological questions when the charter empowered him as proprietor to erect churches "to be dedicated and consecrated according to the Ecclesiastical Laws of our Kingdom of England."[23]

It was clear from the outset that Maryland was intended to be a colony where all Christians would find peace of conscience. Ten days before the colonists sailed in late November, 1633, the proprietor wrote out for his deputies a set of instructions by which he hoped to establish that as a permanent policy. He urged the leaders of the expedition to have all Catholic religious services conducted as privately as possible, both on board ship and on land, and to instruct the Catholics to be silent on occasions when religion was discussed, to which he added the wish "that the said Governor and Commissioners treat the Protestants with as much mildness and favor as Justice will permit."[24] It was an act of expediency, true, but it was

23

just as obviously an act of fairness and tolerance altogether unique at the time. Thus two years before Roger Williams fled the Puritan wrath of Massachusetts Bay to establish religious tolerance in Rhode Island, Baltimore had laid the groundwork for such a policy in Maryland. For the first time in history there was a real prospect for a duly constituted government under which all Christians would possess equal rights, where all churches would be tolerated, and where none would be the agent of government. Such, in fact, Maryland did become, for to the "land of sanctuary" came Puritans fleeing persecution in Virginia and Anglicans escaping from the same threat in Massachusetts. This policy of religious tolerance has rightly been characterized as "the imperishable glory of Lord Baltimore and of the State."[25]

After some delays caused by minor mishaps, the "Ark" finally put to sea on November 22, 1633, and was later joined at Barbados by the "Dove." On board the "Ark" were Fathers Andrew White and John Altham, two English Jesuits who managed somehow, like the Catholic laymen in the party, to set off without taking the customary oath that would have involved the denial of their religious faith. In all there were between two and three hundred persons, the Catholics among them including Leonard Calvert, brother of the proprietor, the two priests and a Jesuit lay brother, sixteen gentlemen adventurers with their wives, children, and servants, and a number of Catholic yeoman farmers and laborers. The remainder of the passengers on the "Ark" and the "Dove," a numerical majority, were members of the Church of England. On March 24, 1634, the colonists landed on an island in Chesapeake Bay which they called St. Clement's, and here Father White offered the first Mass for the Catholics. After the celebration of Mass they held a procession in which they carried a cross that had been hewn out of a tree, and at the appointed place, as White described it some weeks later, "we erected a trophy to Christ the Saviour, humbly reciting, on our bended knees, the Litanies of the Sacred Cross, with great emotion."[26] Meanwhile the Protestants held their own religious service.

The experiment in Maryland put Catholics and Protestants side by side on terms of equality and toleration unknown in the mother country. "In that respect," says one historian, "the settlement of Maryland holds a unique place in the history of English colonization."[27]

During the early years religious differences were regarded peacefully as the colonists went about the business of laying out their plantations and building their homes. But the favorable auspices under which the colony had begun were not to endure. The chief source of trouble arose from William Claiborne of Virginia, whose deep hatred of Catholics made him resentful of their proximity in Maryland, and who likewise harbored a personal grudge against the Calverts for their claim to Kent Island on which he had a plantation. As the Puritans became stronger in England and the shadow of civil war between Charles I and the Roundheads loomed, Claiborne and his kind grew bolder. The fact that Baron Baltimore had permitted several hundred Puritans, unwelcome in Virginia, to cross over into Maryland in 1648 added a further complication, since the newcomers soon showed how little they appreciated the proprietor's hospitality by making common cause with Claiborne.

The English civil war had begun at Nottingham in August, 1642, and the suspicions concerning the Catholic sympathies of Charles I led to renewed persecution in England, where in 1641–42 eleven priests were put to death. The smoldering resentment of some of the Protestants in Maryland against the Catholics for holding most of the leading offices and against the freedom with which the Jesuits evangelized the Indians and ministered openly to the white settlers, was now sharpened by the developments in the homeland. Where facts were missing to back up their grievances, rumor often supplied. In these years arose a campaign of suspicion against the Catholics that at intervals was to bedevil their lives up to the time of the Revolution. Waves of rumor and suspicion were a constantly recurring phenomenon of American colonial life, and in that respect "few colonies suffered more from innuendo and whispering manoeuvres than did Maryland."[28]

It was against a background of this kind that Baron Baltimore sought to save the internal peace of his colony by drafting and sending out to his assembly in America the famous Act of Toleration of April, 1649. In that measure, passed by a body composed of both Protestants and Catholics, blasphemy and the calling of opprobrious religious names were made punishable offenses. But the most important clause of the act read as follows:

> And whereas the inforceing of the conscience in matters of Religion hath frequently fallen out to be of dangerous Consequence in those commonwealthes where it hath been practised. . . . Be it Therefore . . . enacted . . . that noe person or psons whatsoever within this Province . . . professing to believe in Jesus Christ, shall from henceforth bee any waies troubled, Molested or discountenanced for or in respect of his or her religion nor in the free exercise thereof.[29]

This law, liberal for so early a date, introduced nothing essentially new into Maryland, for there had been toleration for all Christians since Cecilius Calvert had incorporated that prin-

ciple into his instructions of 1633, a principle that was confirmed in 1648 when William Stone, the first Protestant governor, took his oath of office. The religious strife had, indeed,
called the measure forth, but that fact in no way lessens the
significance or value of the act, coming as it did at a time when
the religious enactments of Maryland's sister colonies were
showing an increasingly intolerant spirit.[30]

In spite of this memorable action of Baron Baltimore's government, the effort proved vain; for in the ensuing struggle
the Puritan element overthrew the proprietor's regime, and
thereupon the assembly of October, 1654, repealed the Act of
Toleration and outlawed the Catholics. Once in power, the
Puritans wreaked a terrible vengeance on the Catholics by
condemning ten of them to death, four of whom were ex-
ecuted, plundering the houses and estates of the Jesuits, and
forcing the priests to flee in disguise into Virginia. It is true
that Baltimore regained control for a few years, but the sequel
to the "Glorious Revolution" of 1688 which had encompassed
the downfall of King James II also deposed the Catholic Calverts. In June, 1691, Maryland became a royal colony, and with
the accession of William and Mary the penal legislation of the
mother country soon found a counterpart in Maryland. The
Church of England was established by law in 1692, and the
Catholics were compelled to pay taxes for its support. From
the time that they were completely disfranchised in 1718 down
to the outbreak of the Revolution, the Catholics of Maryland
were cut off from all participation in public life, to say nothing
of the enactments against their religious services and the law
that forbade them to have schools for the Catholic instruction
of their children. Remarking the very small number of Catholics against whom these laws were directed, and the fact that

during the half-century the Catholics had governed Maryland they had not been guilty of a single act of religious oppression, it is not surprising that Cobb should have characterized this legislation as "specially unwarranted and base."[31]

A decade before the exclusion of the proprietor had ushered in the darkest years for the Maryland Catholics, a new colony had begun to form immediately to the north. The persecution that William Penn had already undergone for his Quaker faith prompted him in 1681 to launch his "holy experiment" with a broad grant of freedom of worship and civil rights to all who believed in God. Even though this policy was found much too liberal for the taste of the English government which forced restrictions upon Pennsylvania in 1705, the mild character of the Quaker regime attracted a number of Maryland Catholic families northward. In 1706 the Jesuits likewise acquired land in Cecil County near the Pennsylvania border, where they opened St. Xavier Mission and for a few years conducted a school. In fact, so tolerant was the government of the Quakers on religious matters that about 1734 Father Joseph Greaton, S.J., appeared in Philadelphia and opened a chapel, thus becoming the first resident priest in the colony. Soon other missionaries followed, and after Father Henry Neale had been there for some months he told the English provincial in the spring of 1741, "We have at present all liberty imaginable in the exercise of our business, and are not only esteemed, but reverenced, as I may say, by the better sort of people."[32] In the same year several German Jesuits arrived in Pennsylvania to minister to the German Catholic immigrants from the Palatinate who had settled in fairly large numbers in thriving rural communities around Goshenhoppen, Conewago, and Lancaster. Only once in the history of colonial Pennsylvania did the

The Church in Colonial America

Catholics experience a period of serious tension, and that was related to the renewal of war between England and France. Long before the outbreak of war the two powers had been preparing for battle. As a move in the game, England drastically forestalled possible trouble in one quarter by herding over 6,000 Catholic Acadians on board British ships and distributing them in the colonies from Massachusetts to Georgia. In November, 1765, Pennsylvania received 454 of these unfortunate people. Their arrival, coming as it did four months after the humiliating defeat which the French had inflicted on Braddock's army near Fort Duquesne, heightened suspicion and fear. Pennsylvanians in 1756 heard wild rumors of a "popish plot" in which the Acadians figured.[33] A census of the population to determine the number of men capable of bearing arms revealed that there were in the entire colony only 1,365 Catholics out of a total of about 200,000 residents. Extremists were eager for proscriptive legislation against the Catholics, but the Quaker officials refused to be stampeded into any violation of their traditional policy. Gradually, therefore, the Catholics had resumed an unharried life when in July, 1765, Father George Hunter, S.J., reported to his provincial in England that there were about 10,000 "adult customers" in Maryland, with nearly as many children who had not yet been admitted to the sacraments, while in Pennsylvania he counted around 3,000 adults, with approximately an equal number of children.[34]

Catholics in the other eleven colonies went uncounted and little known by the Jesuit missionaries for the very good reason that there were few if any living in those regions. Now and then, it is true, a Catholic name appeared in other colonies, but aside from a few Catholics in northern Virginia, the Abenaki Indians in Maine, and the special case of Father

Gabriel Druillettes, S.J., who came to Massachusetts Bay in 1650 on a diplomatic mission for New France, the only other colony that saw them in any numbers—and that only for a few years—was New York.

During the period from 1609, when Henry Hudson took possession of the area in the name of the Dutch, to 1664, when the colony of New Netherland was conquered by the English, about the only Catholic appearance of which we know anything was Father Isaac Jogues' visit to New Amsterdam in the fall of 1643 on his way to Europe after the Dutch had rescued him from the Iroquois.[35] The English occupation, however, brought the proprietorship of James, Duke of York, whose conversion to Catholicism in 1672 soon reflected itself in his American domain. In 1682 James appointed Colonel Thomas Dongan, a Catholic, as governor, and the colonel arrived in August, 1683, with an English Jesuit in his party, Father Thomas Harvey, who was later joined by two other priests and two lay brothers of his order. For some years there had been serious agitation in New York for a more representative government, and in an assembly which he had summoned in September, 1683, Dongan stood sponsor for a bill of rights which was adopted in late October. This document contained a guarantee of religious freedom which read in part:

. . . that no person or persons, which profess faith in God by Jesus Christ, shall at any time, be any ways molested, punished, disquieted, or called in question for any difference in opinion or matter of religious concernment, who do not actually disturb the civill peace of the Province, but that all and every such person or persons may, from time, and at all times freely have and fully enjoy his or their judgments or consciences in matters of religion throughout all the Province, they behaving themselves peaceably and quietly and not using this liberty to Licentiousnesse nor to the civill injury or outward disturbance of others. . . .[36]

The Church in Colonial America

Thus did New York's Catholic governor join the honorable company of Roger Williams, Lord Baltimore, and William Penn as the chief promoters of religious freedom in colonial America. The significance of Dongan's action is not in any way lessened by the fact that the events of 1688 brought reaction to New York in the form of rebellion which quickly blotted out his generous policy in religious affairs. In May, 1689, a German-born Calvinist, Jacob Leisler, overthrew the government and inaugurated a reign of terror against the Catholics. Dongan himself was hunted like a criminal, the Jesuits were forced to flee, and in September, 1693, the Church of England was established by law in the four leading counties of New York. In due course followed all the familiar English penal legislation against Catholics, a series of laws from which they were not entirely freed until 1806.

Here, then, was a minority second to none but Roger Williams in the broad toleration granted to men of other religious beliefs. Had the Catholics never held power in colonial America, it would remain a matter of speculation what they would have done on matters of religious policy. The half-century, however, of Baltimore's regime in Maryland and the five years when there was a Catholic governor in New York afford us two instances by which to judge them extraordinarily tolerant for the seventeenth century. Baltimore, Dongan, and their Catholic assemblymen were not philosophers or theologians, and they wrote no treatises on the theories of religious tolerance or intolerance. They were intensely practical men who found themselves confronted with the real problem of differing religious beliefs among those whom they governed. To that problem they applied a practical solution based upon experience, an experience reflected in the words of the Maryland act of 1649 which spoke of how "inforceing of the conscience in matters of Religion hath frequently fallen out to be of dangerous Consequence in those commonwealthes where it hath been practised." Their settlement of the question resembled the final solution of the Founding Fathers of the Republic. They were, of course, painfully aware of the disadvantages under which they labored by being Catholics, and both Baltimore and Dongan had seen in their native England and Ireland how their coreligionists had been made to suffer on this score. The memory of it made them all the more anxious, therefore, that this sort of oppression should not be visited upon others by the governments over which they presided in the New World.

By reason of the penal status in which the colonial Catholics were compelled to live until the American Revolution, there was obviously no hope of a normal government for their Church. The English Catholic hierarchy had become extinct in 1585, and not until 1688 was there a bishop at London who could even make pretensions to any jurisdiction over the Catholics in America. Consequently, Catholic affairs were almost entirely in the hands of the 186 Jesuit priests who worked in the colonies as missionaries between 1634 and the suppression of their order in 1773. These priests got their faculties for administering the sacraments either through the General of the Jesuits at Rome, who dealt directly with the Congregation de Propaganda Fide, or through the missionary bishop who functioned under the title of Vicar Apostolic of the London District after 1688. In neither case was it a satisfactory arrangement, but the general anti-Catholic bias—especially the bitter prejudice against bishops—made it unthinkable for a bishop to be appointed for the colonies by the Holy See.[37] Some 156 years passed between the coming of the first missionaries to

The Church in Colonial America

Maryland and the appointment in 1790 of a bishop for the American Catholics. This long period of abnormal rule not only deprived them of the sacraments of confirmation and holy orders but likewise left them with little or no knowledge of the traditional form of church government, an ignorance that caused some very strange notions among both priests and laity concerning the episcopal office and its functions.

In the political realm the friendliness which colonial Catholics had shown toward the principle of religious freedom during their tenure of power in Maryland and New York was, as might be expected, only strengthened by the long dark night of penal legislation which descended upon them during the eighteenth century. It was not until the 1770's that one hears prominent mention of a Catholic name in colonial America, since for the better part of a century they had been entirely excluded from public affairs. But as the tension mounted between the colonies and the mother country, life in America began to change in many ways. When Charles Carroll of Carrollton in February, 1773, launched a series of remarkable letters in the *Maryland Gazette* against the arbitrary actions of the royal governor, Robert Eden, he was not only listened to but won general acclaim. Carroll wrote under the pen name of "First Citizen" against the governor's protagonist, Daniel Dulany, who used the name of "Antillon." Realizing that he was losing the debate, Dulany resorted to an attack on his opponent's religion. Carroll put the issue straight when he replied:

What my speculative notions of religion may be, this is neither the place nor time to declare; my political principles ought only to be questioned on the present occasion; surely they are constitutional, and have met, I hope, with the approbation of my countrymen; if so Antillon's aspersions will give me no uneasiness. He asks, who is this Citizen? A man, Antillon, of an independent fortune, one deeply interested in the prosperity of his country; a friend to liberty, a settled enemy to lawless prerogative.[38]

It was the kind of talking Marylanders were prepared to hear in that exciting spring of 1773, and in the end Carroll's effective polemics not only vanquished Dulany but played a major role in swinging the Maryland election in May of that year in favor of the patriot party that opposed the royal governor. Moreover, the forthright manner in which he had met the attack on his religion gave heart to many of his coreligionists who for the first time had witnessed a Catholic defend his faith and win the respect of many non-Catholics for doing so. Even so prejudiced a spectator as Jonathan Boucher, one of the leading Anglican ministers of Maryland, and himself a loyalist, credited Carroll with settling the doubts of the Catholics who, he said, soon "became good Whigs, and concurred with their fellow-revolutionists in declaiming against the misgovernment of Great Britain."[39] Twenty years before, Dulany's appeal to religious prejudice would have clinched the argument, but by 1773 Americans were beginning to realize interests broader than that of nursing the traditional bias against Catholics. In the changing climate of opinion that permitted a Catholic patriot to speak in the name of his fellow countrymen, one detects the first break in the isolation that had sealed them off from other Americans. It was an initial step toward the dawn of religious liberty for Catholics, a step that would lead the same Charles Carroll three years later to Philadelphia where he would proudly affix his signature to the Declaration of Independence of his country.

Yet before the American Catholics were permitted finally to emerge from the catacombs in which the penal codes had buried them, they were destined to suffer further ignominy over the grant of religious freedom to their Canadian brethren. To counter the rising temper of the colonists, the English government was naturally anxious to assure the loyalty of the French Canadians to the crown. They accomplished this purpose by the Quebec Act of June, 1774, which extended the boundaries of the province to the west, restored French law, and, most important of all, guaranteed freedom to the Catholic Church. The measure raised a frightful tempest throughout the colonies. Protests from all sides influenced the Continental Congress to adopt on September 17, 1774, the Suffolk Resolves, which highlighted that body's dislike of the Church. A month later the congress addressed letters to King George III and to the people of Great Britain in which the Americans declared themselves to be astonished that Parliament should have established a religion "that has deluged your island in blood, and dispersed impiety, bigotry, murder and rebellion through every part of the world."[40] What made the tone of these words all the more extraordinary was the fact that five days later the same congress sent a letter to the Canadians in an effort to enlist their aid. The congressional penmen mentioned Switzerland as a country where Protestants and Catholics lived together in peace, held out the promise of religious freedom if the Canadian Catholics would join the American cause, and piously signed themselves "your sincere and affectionate friends and fellow-subjects."[41] The Quebec Act, however, had done its work well enough that the Canadians were not beguiled by the blandishments from Philadelphia.

If in times of stress it is often difficult to maintain sincerity, as the actions of the Continental Congress demonstrated, it is then just as difficult to adhere to old prejudices and principles.

General Washington—who was personally free from religious prejudice—made that evident to his troops encamped at Cambridge in November, 1775, when he discovered that they were once more preparing to burn the pope in effigy and insult the Catholics in the annual celebration of Guy Fawkes Day. He put an end to the nonsense at once, and in rebuking those who were planning the affair at a moment when the Americans still hoped to gain Canada, he remarked, "To be insulting their Religion, is so monstrous, as not to be suffered or excused."[42] That very month Congress had appointed a committee and appropriated funds for initial diplomatic and trade relations with foreign powers. It would ill become the Americans, then, to indulge their prejudices lest word of it reach Catholic countries like France and Spain which, it was hoped, might be of service to the revolutionary cause.

Congress decided in February, 1776, to send a commission to Canada in another attempt to win its support. Not only did Charles Carroll of Carrollton accompany Benjamin Franklin and Samuel Chase to Canada, but Father John Carroll, distant cousin of Charles, was also asked to go. Neither of the Carrolls had sought the appointment, and it took a great deal of persuasion on the part of Charles to secure that consent of his priestly cousin. John Carroll deeply feared the effect that the Canadian mission might have on his standing as a priest; for as he confided to a private memorandum on the subject, "I have observed that when the ministers of religion, leave the duties of their profession to take a busy part in political matters, they generally fall into contempt, and sometimes even bring discredit to the cause in whose service they are engaged."[43] It was an eminently sound view, and only the urging of his distinguished cousin and his own sincere patriotism overcame his reluctance. The mission to Canada failed, but it offered one more chance for the Catholics to escape isolation and serve honorably in the public affairs of their country.

By the time that the delegates returned from Canada, Virginians were in the process of passing their act of religious toleration of June, 1776, and Pennsylvania and Maryland followed suit before the year was out. The Catholics, sharing in the revolutionary struggle as equals once the legal barriers were removed, responded generously to the national crisis. Charles Carroll took his seat in Congress at Philadelphia as a delegate from Maryland, John Barry came forward to win fame as one of the chief founders of the American navy, Stephen Moylan joined Washington's staff as muster master-general, Daniel Carroll was named a member of Congress from Maryland, and Thomas FitzSimons represented Pennsylvania. Moreover, after the alliance with France was signed in February, 1778, units of the French fleet began to dock at Philadelphia, each with its Catholic chaplain. Soon, too, the first French minister, Conrad Alexandre Gérard, became one of the leading personalities in the capital city, and when he sent out invitations in 1779 to a *Te Deum* in St. Mary's Church to mark the third anniversary of American independence and two years later to commemorate the victory of Yorktown, members of Congress found it expedient to be present. It had now become unthinkable to offer public or official slights to Catholics with France so close and powerful an ally.

The patriotic part played by the Catholics during the war, the influence of the French alliance, and the growing consciousness of the extreme complexity of the American religious pattern—all helped to dilute the anti-Catholic bias. In fact, after the war was over and a number of states had acted on their own in granting full religious liberty, it became evident that toleration necessarily would be the ultimate policy of the national government. In the Constitutional Convention the two Catholic delegates, Daniel Carroll of Maryland and FitzSimons of Pennsylvania, were heartily in favor of the principle, as they were likewise outspokenly in favor of a strong national government in opposition to those who would restrict its powers. In 1784, Father John Carroll had been named by the Holy See as superior of the American Catholic missions, then staffed by about twenty-five priests. Carroll, too, shared the belief that the fairest settlement of the religious issue would be to declare all churches equal before the law and to have no ecclesiastical establishment of any kind. A brochure which he wrote that same year in answer to an attack upon the Church revealed his reluctance to engage in religious controversy lest it should disturb the harmony then existing between the various Christian churches. That Carroll wholeheartedly accepted the pattern of Church-State relations then emerging in the United States, and which in less than a decade would be incorporated into the Constitution, was clear when he alluded to the promise which civil and religious liberty held out, a promise which, he said, "if we have the wisdom and temper to preserve, America may come to exhibit a proof to the world, that general and equal toleration, by giving a free circulation to fair argument, is the most effectual method to bring all denominations of Christians to a unity of faith."[44]

The final solution to the perplexing problem of religion as embodied in the Constitution and Bill of Rights was received by no American religious group with more genuine satisfaction than by the Catholics. It was a boon appreciated by their oppressed coreligionists in England and Ireland as well, and as at the consecration of Carroll in August, 1790, in England as the first Catholic bishop of the United States, the preacher of the occasion, Carroll's old friend Father Charles Plowden, testified when he remarked of the American Revolution: "Although this great event may appear to us to have been the work, the sport of human passion, yet the earliest and most precious fruit of it has been the extension of the kingdom of Christ, the propagation of the Catholic religion, which heretofore fettered by restraining laws, is now enlarged from bondage and it is left at liberty to exert the full energy of divine truth."[45] It was a sentiment which Bishop Carroll fully shared with his priests and Catholic people in the new United States. They and their ancestors had experienced the humiliation of practical outlawry for a century or more, and the prospect of freedom to worship God according to their consciences was the most singular blessing which the new Republic had brought to them.

Some months before Bishop Carroll went abroad for his consecration, a group of the leading American Catholics had expressed their esteem for President Washington in a formal address. Washington replied that he believed that as men became more liberal they would be more likely to allow equal rights to all worthy members of the community, and in this respect he hoped to see America among the foremost nations of the world. He then stated: "And I presume that your fellow-citizens will not forget the patriotic part which you took in the accomplishment of their Revolution, and the establishment of their government; nor the important assistance which they received from a nation in which the Roman Catholic religion is professed."[46] The exchange of compliments between the chief executive and his Catholic citizens had been a pleasant and heartening experience, and the latter could thank God that their interests in Church and State were now in the hands of two such leaders as President Washington and Bishop Carroll.

Catholics as Citizens
1790–1852

In the New World possessions of Spain and France the dominant Catholic white population united Church and State, even though secular and ecclesiastical authorities were often at odds on matters of policy. In the English colonies, however, Catholics existed through a century and a half as an insignificant minority in a state of practical outlawry. Yet in retaining their faith until the revolutionary crisis ultimately won them religious freedom in states like Pennsylvania and Maryland, they seemingly developed latent strength. The favored position of Catholics in Spanish and French colonies was not the source from which the main stream of American Catholic life took its rise. Rather it was the minority group along the Atlantic coastline that set the pattern for future Catholic development, a development destined to reach out to the West and South in the early nineteenth century and there be joined by the descendants of the Spaniards and French where Catholic elements fused on the distant frontiers.

Several points about the English-speaking Catholics will bear repetition and will introduce us to the subject of the present discussion. It is well to remember that in the two areas where Catholics held political power in colonial America, namely, Maryland and New York, they inaugurated and maintained the principle of freedom of conscience for all Christians until their governments were overthrown in the aftermath of the English revolution of 1688. After that revolution the Church of England was established by law in both colonies, and the penal code which had oppressed the Catholics of England and Ireland for over a century was imposed upon their coreligionists in America. It was the declaration of religious liberty by Pennsylvania and Maryland in 1776 that equipped Catholics for service on a basis of equality with their countrymen. Another point worth recalling is this: When the Founding Fathers of the Republic determined that the only equitable settlement for the wide variety of American religious beliefs was the highly sensible and sound solution which they embodied in the First Amendment to the Constitution, no religious body in the new United States gave a more complete and unhesitating assent to this adjustment than Bishop Carroll, his priests, and the American Catholic laity.

In surveying the post-Revolution period I should like to treat certain aspects of Catholicism in the United States between the inauguration of the government of the Church under Bishop Carroll in 1790 and the year 1852, the date of the first national or plenary council of the hierarchy. One can, I think, acquaint one's self with the character of American Catholicism by the mid-century if he views it under the following four headings: (1) nationalism, (2) the Church as an Americanizing institution; (3) nativist opposition; (4) the role of Roman Catholics in public affairs.

"Of all historical problems," said Henry Adams, "the nature

of a national character is the most difficult and the most important."[1] No student who has essayed the task of delineating the national character of a people will quarrel with this judgment. Certainly the American of 1790 knew very little about what that character was, or what it would be; in fact, he had as yet scarcely begun to think of himself as an American. The inhabitants of the new nation had no clear idea of even their number until the first federal census in 1790 revealed that there were 3,929,214 Americans—white and black—scattered through the sprawling settlements from Maine to Georgia and in the wilderness to the west. Approximately 35,000 Catholics lived mostly in the Middle Atlantic states and in the French villages of the western country.[2] Socially speaking, the Catholics endured as a suspect minority, although the Carrolls of Maryland were an exception, since their wealth, public services, and superior breeding forbade denial. For example, like other leading Americans of his day, the first Bishop of Baltimore sat for his portrait by Gilbert Stuart, while the statesman, Charles of Carrollton, posed for Sir Joshua Reynolds and Charles Willson Peale. Daniel, the bishop's brother, represented Maryland in the first United States Congress, increasing the prestige of the family. Moreover, a few other Catholic families of the Maryland gentry, such as the Brookes, Taneys, and Brents, enjoyed a measure of local respect. But most of Bishop Carroll's charges were poor and humble folk tilling their Maryland and Pennsylvania farms or keeping shop and laboring in the large seaboard towns. In civil affairs Catholics had equal citizenship in only five of the thirteen states, a situation which left many of them as mere observers of the most exciting events of their time. When one keeps in mind the colonial background from which they had recently emerged, as well as the traditional attitude toward their religion on the part of the governing element in England and Ireland whence most of their ancestors had come, it is not surprising to find in the American Catholics of the early national period the odd mixture of shyness and occasional belligerency which so frequently characterizes minority groups. Protestants took themselves for granted; in the new United States the memory of the past was still too poignant and the uncertainty over the future still too real for Catholics to do the same.

If the inhabitants of the United States in the 1790's had not yet a very clear concept of what constituted an American, there was no doubt that many of them viewed themselves as quite superior to those who came among them from abroad. A French visitor to Pennsylvania in 1797, for example, told of meeting a miller who was convinced that nothing was of any worth except it was American and that the genius of Europe was already in decline. "This error," said the Duc de Liancourt, "is to be found in almost all Americans—legislators, administrators, as well as millers, and is less innocent there."[3] Uriah Tracy of Connecticut, traveling through Pennsylvania in 1800, wrote home, "I have seen many, very many, Irishmen, and with a very few exceptions, they are United Irishmen, Free Masons, and the most God-provoking Democrats on this side of Hell."[4] The outraged New Englander had added, it would seem, a political bias to his abhorrence of foreigners! The Duc de Liancourt's Pennsylvania miller and the Connecticut Yankee were probably more extreme in their expression than most of their fellow countrymen, but that there already existed in the new republic a rather marked xenophobia would seem to be certain.

Throughout the colonial period one meets with scarcely any

evidence of this kind of sentiment among the Catholics in the English colonies. Its absence is accounted for by the fact that the great majority of them had come from England and Ireland, and as far as the extant records show, they lived together in peace and harmony. Nor did the considerable number of German Catholics who immigrated to Pennsylvania in the 1730's seriously disturb this harmony. The first signal of trouble on this score occurred at Philadelphia in 1787 where a group of German-born Catholics, dissatisfied with the ministrations of the English-speaking priests at St. Mary's Church, proceeded to have themselves legally incorporated, and thus started the first American Catholic parish on a nationalist basis at Holy Trinity Church in that city. The remonstrances of Bishop Carroll against their engaging a wandering German-born priest without his authority proved vain, and the congregation was in schism until by 1802 more moderate counsels prevailed.[5] The strife at Philadelphia's Holy Trinity Church came as a rude shock to the Catholics generally, but, as we shall see, it was only an opening gun that heralded the injection of the virus of nationalism among American Catholics, the virus that was to be with them until well into the present century.

Those Americans who disliked Catholicism found one of their principal talking points in the form of government which the universal law of the Church demanded for the rule of its congregations. According to the provisions of canon law, the right of appointing and dismissing pastors was vested solely in the bishops. There was nothing in canon law contrary per se to a system of lay trustees, and, in fact, the temporalities of parochial administration were often left to the hands of the laity. As Archbishop John Hughes of New York said many years later, "Regarded *a priori,* no system could appear to be less objectionable, or more likely, both to secure advantages to those congregations, and at the same time to recommend the Catholic religion to the liberal consideration of the Protestant sentiment of the country."[6] But the trouble arose when lay trustees took upon themselves the episcopal prerogative of appointing and dismissing their pastors. For the quarter century of John Carroll's rule and for years thereafter, this attempt on the part of laymen to usurp these rights was, perhaps, the most harassing problem with which the bishops had to deal in the United States. The difficulty was greatly aggravated by the increasing number of foreign-born Catholics of various nations who arrived in this country during the first half of the nineteenth century, only to find themselves under the spiritual rule of clergy of a nationality different from their own. Canon law and the regulations of the bishops were openly derided, and in some congregations, those in New Orleans, Charleston, Norfolk, and Buffalo, for instance, schism lasted for years at a time.

Not infrequently the recalcitrant lay trustees appealed to the civil authorities, although generally the latter had the good sense not to intervene. One of the instances where the public officials sided with trustees in rebellion against the authority of a Catholic bishop was at St. Louis Church in Buffalo. That case led to the enactment of the Putnam Bill by the New York legislature in 1855 which would compel lay ownership of all church property and forbid a clergyman to hold property in his own name. It was a Know-Nothing triumph, and for some years it successfully blocked the efforts of the New York bishops to put their ecclesiastical properties on a secure legal basis. Although the Putnam Bill was not strictly enforced, it remained on the statute books as a threat until 1863, when the need for recruits for the Union Army caused its repeal. Bowing to necessity, the New York legislature thus cleared the way for the Catholic Church to legalize its position in relation to its property holdings, and from that time on there was relatively little trouble over the question of how Catholic parishes in the United States should be governed.

Meanwhile unfriendly critics made the most of the unseemly factional quarrels within certain congregations and used them as an example to emphasize the un-American character of Catholicism. The issue of lay trusteeism admirably served the purposes of groups like the Nativists and Know-Nothings, and most American Protestants were irked by what they regarded as the show of power by an authoritarian Church. To most Protestant minds the right of the laity to control ecclesiastical finances and to select their own ministers was beyond question. On the first count the Church could, and often did, yield; on the second it was adamant. The impression thus made on the general public was an unfortunate one, since they felt that the trustees—and the priests who threw in their lot with them— were being barred by arbitrary bishops from the exercise of a right to which every American was entitled. Religious strife undoubtedly was abetted by these disputes over trusteeism, and as one student has said, "The fact that such occurrences were by no means infrequent accounts in some degree for the steady increase of sectarian antagonism after 1815."[7]

The question of nationalist feeling among the American Catholics, often so closely related to lay trusteeism, can be studied within the Church's hierarchy of these years more closely than they can be studied within the numerous and widespread clergy and laity, for the difficulties to which it gave rise among the bishops were often but a reflection of the national differences among those farther down in the ranks. When the Holy See made Baltimore an archdiocese in 1808 and created four new suffragan dioceses that were subject to Baltimore as the metropolitan see, Archbishop Carroll recommended two French-born priests for Boston and Bardstown and an Irish-born Franciscan for Philadelphia. The fourth see, New York, was at first left vacant for want of what Carroll considered to be worthy candidates. Needless to say, the American Church owed an incalculable debt to the French clergymen who had fled the revolutionary disturbances in their own country after 1790. But the priests were not followed by a proportionate number of French Catholic laity. Rather it was Ireland that contributed the chief increase in the laity from abroad in these same years, and it was not long before many of the Irish became antagonistic to the idea of being ruled by French bishops and priests. In time the hierarchy, too, found itself divided rather clearly into a French party and an Irish party. For example, of the ten bishops in the United States in 1830, six were either French or French sympathizers, while two were Irish-born, and two were of American birth but Irish ancestry. The nature of their differences on the score of national feeling can be illustrated by an incident in the life of James Whitfield, fourth Archbishop of Baltimore. Whitfield was English-born, but he had been trained by the Sulpicians in France at their seminary of Lyons, had been brought to the United States by his old professor, Ambrose Maréchal, S.S., whom he succeeded in 1828 in the See of Baltimore, and his sympathies were, therefore, entirely with the French. Following the death of Bishop Edward Fenwick, O.P., of Cincinnati in 1832, it was necessary for the bishops to consult about a successor. Late that same year Archbishop Whitfield told his friend, Joseph Rosati, Bishop of St. Louis: "If possibly a good choice can be made, let an American born be recommended and (between us in strict confidence) I do really think we should guard against having more Irish Bishops. . . . This you know is a dangerous secret, but I trust it to one in whom I have full confidence."[8]

Fundamentally, the problem in the late eighteenth and early nineteenth centuries revolved in good measure around the fact that most of the badly needed priests were Frenchmen who had fled before the revolutionary attacks upon the Church in their native country. Generally, these men were of excellent quality, but their inability to preach well in English, at a time when sermons meant more than they do now, irked many of the Irish, who constituted the greatest number of Catholic immigrants in these years. The descendants of the traditional Catholic families of Maryland had a sufficient number of their own priests to care for their needs, but the rising Catholic populations of towns like Boston, New York, and Philadelphia had no such stable ministry, with the result that they had either to rely on French priests or, what in the end proved more unsatisfactory, to take up with a number of erratic Irish-born priests who had already had trouble with their bishops in Ireland and who had come to the United States to seek their fortune wherever they could find it.

Had Archbishop Whitfield lived another twenty years, he would probably have despaired of the future of the American Church, for by that time the Irish had vanquished the French and the contest of nationalities had shifted to other ground. These strains within the Catholic body constantly changed according to circumstances of time and place. As has been said, at first the French and Irish bickered in the East and in Kentucky, but as time passed it became a contest between the Irish and Germans in the East and the Middle West. In Louisiana the earlier clashes of French against Spaniards often gave way after the purchase of 1803 to a combination of the two against the more recent arrivals, the Americans and the Irish. In a major conflict in Buffalo at mid-century, French and Germans were arrayed against the Irish. It is unnecessary to emphasize here what European immigration up to 1850 meant by way of determining the character of the Catholic Church in the United States. By that date the federal census-takers reported 961,719 Irish in the country. Many of these, it is true, were north of Ireland Protestants, but the greater number had come from the famine-ridden counties of southern Ireland, which were largely Catholic. Germans constituted over 25 per cent of the foreign-born in the country by 1850. The best authority on Catholic immigration has estimated that between 1790 and 1850 a total of 1,071,000 Catholic immigrants landed in the United States, a figure which far outran the natural increase of the native-born Catholics.[9]

Here, then, was one of the principal determining elements in the character of American Catholicism. Had Archbishop Carroll and his native Maryland Catholics had their choice, they would have preferred to see the Church grow at a much more moderate speed, at a pace that would have given it time to absorb its gains in a more systematic and orderly fashion. But they were given no such choice.[10] Years before, Crèvecœur had remarked that the motto of every immigrant was "Ubi panis ibi patria."[11] For thousands of Catholic immigrants in these years, one might paraphrase the motto to read, "Ubi libertas cultus et panis, ibi patria," for the double incentive of freedom of worship and a chance to earn their bread was too strong to hold them back. They kept coming in such numbers that they soon completely overshadowed the native Catholics and gave to the Church a foreign coloring that at once baffled its friends and exasperated its enemies.

Other American churches, to be sure, had to meet problems of a similar nature, as, for example, the Lutheran Church with the great influx of German immigrants to its fold, and the Presbyterian Church with which so many of the Scotch-Irish were affiliated. Yet no American religious body had to contend with the number and variety of newcomers who entered the ranks of the American Catholics in the same period. An Irish Lutheran, a German Episcopalian, a French Methodist, a Swiss Baptist, and an English Mennonite might then have been thought something of an oddity, but no one thought it strange to see men of all five nationalities occupying neighboring pews in a Catholic church of New York, Philadelphia, or Baltimore.

Willy-nilly the American Church had become catholic in the broadest sense, and the problem of how best to mold the congeries of nationalities that composed its faithful into a stable element of the American population became its most pressing preoccupation. In spite of the varied racial strains and backgrounds of the Catholic population in the early national period, and the friction which they often engendered, progress was made in adjusting these conflicting elements to their new environment and in gradually evolving a Catholic pattern that was authentically American. The Church rendered a distinct service to the nation by the Americanization program which it fostered among its foreign-born members, even under persecution. Measured by modern standards, it was not a scientific program, but the quiet counseling of the immigrants by bishops and by the priests in the parishes, the instruction in Catholic schools, and the information imparted through the Catholic press once it got under way in the 1820's constantly assimilated newcomers to the American way of life. True, the Church's ingenuity was taxed to the utmost degree by the undertaking, and it never completely overtook the problem by reason of the tremendous numbers of its immigrant flock. In the final analysis, however, the Catholic Church proved to be one of the most effective agencies in turning this vast army of foreign-born into law-abiding citizens whose children in the second and third generations gave witness of how thoroughly American they were.

Before the American Revolution had yet been fought, Crèvecœur had written his famous definition of an American, in which he said: "He is an American, who, leaving behind him all his ancient prejudices and manners, receives new ones from the new mode of life he has embraced, the new government he obeys, and the new rank he holds. He becomes an American by being received into the broad lap of our great *Alma Mater.*"[12] On all counts of Crèvecœur's definition except that of leaving behind his ancient prejudices and manners, the Catholic immigrant could qualify as an American. But on that point, one may ask, what immigrants, Protestant or Catholic, could qualify? It was part of the general optimism and progressive spirit of the age for native sons to believe that the newcomers could and should undergo a complete transformation upon their arrival. Actually no such thing happened, for as one literary historian has said, "The melting pot merely obscures, it never obliterates traces of racial elements."[13] Ordinarily a person's thought processes and cultural patterns are not effaced or radically altered by transplantation and adoption

Catholics as Citizens

in a new locale, regardless of how loyally attached he may have become to the country that has adopted him. In many ways it is well for the United States that this is so, for the glory of the national heritage is in part due to its tremendous variety. The overwhelming number of immigrants of the period—Catholic and non-Catholic alike—clung to their ancient customs while simultaneously they became loyal citizens and contributed labor and ideas to the country. Few will deny that the American cultural pattern has been the richer for it.

How did the Church meet the delicate responsibility of converting its huge immigrant flocks to American ways, without at the same time depriving them of their cherished customs which they had a legitimate right to retain? We can answer that question, I think, by concentrating attention upon four of the principal means which the Church employed, namely, schools, institutions of charity, the press, and the personal counsel of the bishops and priests.

As to the schools, such a thing as a guiding local Catholic tradition or precedent was simply nonexistent. Because Catholics had been forbidden throughout the colonial period to maintain their own schools, the national period opened without a single Catholic educational institution. Moreover, there was virtually no literary tradition among them, and it would have been quite idle for them to look for one in ancestral lands; in both England and Ireland the penal age had thoroughly stamped out all but the last vestiges of what was once a proud Catholic tradition in letters and learning. There was, it is true, a handful of highly educated Catholics such as the Carrolls, the Brents, and the Neales, whose families had possessed sufficient wealth to send their children abroad to school before the Revolution. In the continental colleges, these favored

few received education equal or superior to that of their colonial contemporaries, but most of their coreligionists had little
or no education.

Yet the lack of an educated and literary elite among Catholics in these years was not exceptional, for the typical citizen
of the young United States was quite inarticulate, and, as
J. Franklin Jameson, who wrote on the Revolution as a social
movement, said, "The few who wrote were as likely to be
expressing thoughts which they had found in European books
as thoughts which originated or were current among American minds."[14] Henry Adams found the same thing to be true
of his native state, where "the names of half-a-dozen persons
could hardly be mentioned whose memories survived by intellectual work made public in Massachusetts between 1783 and
1800."[15] This being true of non-Catholic Americans, one might
well ask, "If in the green wood they do these things, what
shall be done in the dry?"[16]

The absence of a native educational tradition and of any
cultivation of literary talent among Catholics made the task
of the Bishop of Baltimore all the more difficult when he
thought in terms of establishing educational opportunities for
his people. After much effort, however, he finally succeeded
in September, 1791, in launching Georgetown Academy. The
scope of instruction was outlined in an early broadside as one
that would conduct the students through their classical subjects to the point where they would be fitted to proceed "with
Advantage to the Study of the higher Sciences in the University of this or those of the neighboring States." The spirit in
which the institution intended to handle the question of the
students' religious life was stated as follows: "Agreeably to
the liberal Principle of our Constitution, the Seminary will

be open to Students of Every religious Profession. They, who, in this respect, differ from the Superintendent of the Academy, will be at Liberty to frequent the places of Worship and Instruction appointed by their Parents; but with Respect to their moral Conduct, all must be subject to general and uniform Discipline."[17]

With Georgetown Academy a start had been made, and in the same year the misfortune that had befallen the Catholics of France redounded to the advantage of their American co-religionists when a group of French Sulpicians arrived in Baltimore in July, 1791, to open St. Mary's Seminary, the first institution in the country for the training of native American priests. The infant seminary was so close to the heart of Bishop Carroll that after about a year he told the Holy See, "All our hopes are founded on the Seminary of Baltimore."[18] True, the fulfilment of Carroll's hopes was for some time deferred by reason of the dearth of students and the struggle for survival through which the infant seminary had to pass; but at length the prospect brightened for St. Mary's. By 1829 the seminary had ordained fifty-two priests, of whom twenty-one were native-born Americans, thirteen were natives of Ireland and England, and eighteen were of French or German birth.[19] Moreover, when the long suppressed Society of Jesus was re-established in the United States in 1806, the Jesuits took over the management of Georgetown College. Two years later a second school for boys, Mount Saint Mary's College, was begun in the hamlet of Emmitsburg, Maryland. In the same year a young New York widow who had become a convert to Catholicism, Elizabeth Bayley Seton, founded the first native religious community for women, and in 1809 she opened a school for girls in Emmitsburg. Her Sisters of Charity became the first source of teachers for the parochial schools, a source augmented in 1812 by the founding in Kentucky of two more native sisterhoods. Before Archbishop Carroll died in 1815, therefore, his lifelong ambition to staff the schools was on the way to fulfilment.

Through the medium of Catholic parochial schools, which by 1840 numbered at least 200 with about half of these west of the Alleghenies, the children of the immigrants were mingled with the children of the native-born Catholics and thus were introduced to their first formal instruction in the new homeland. The curriculum of these schools was in large measure that of the standard curriculum of the private Protestant and early public schools, with the exception that they taught classes in the Catholic religion rather than the classes in the Bible and Protestant beliefs. Many teachers were native-born Americans who used English exclusively in their classrooms, and even in those parochial schools serving the non-English-speaking immigrants, notably the Germans, some English was used in the instruction. In the first half of the century the Church reached nowhere near a majority of its children through its own schools, but, as the years went on, a larger percentage of them was absorbed in the expanding Catholic system.

A second major means employed by Catholics in the United States to preserve the religious faith of the immigrant, and which also assisted him to adapt to his new environment, was the practice of charity, in which the Catholics set an example often imitated by Protestant citizens. In Catholic charitable institutions the immigrant found a welcome in time of illness or old age, or a place of refuge for his children when misfortune struck his family. It was in October, 1814, that three Sisters of Charity arrived in Philadelphia from the community at Emmitsburg to open St. Joseph's Orphanage, the first (there are now 239 in the United States) of a long line of Catholic homes for infants and children. Fourteen years later the generosity of a leading Catholic layman of St. Louis, John Mullanphy, enabled the same order to take charge of the first American Catholic hospital in that city, the original link in a chain of Catholic hospitals that now numbers 930. It was likewise in St. Louis in November, 1845, that the first American unit of the famous French Society of St. Vincent de Paul was introduced in the old cathedral parish, the forerunner of thousands of such parish societies organized throughout the land for the voluntary help of the Catholic poor. There is no need to demonstrate further the service rendered to the immigrant by the orphanages, hospitals, homes for the aged, and parish poor societies.[20] The role they played in befriending him in a strange environment when he most needed assistance was of incalculable value in adjusting him to his new homeland and in smoothing out many of the rough spots in his often bewildered and troubled life. Thus during a period marked by strong impulses of humanitarianism and the movement for social reform, the American Catholics made it clear that they were not insensible to the needs of their less fortunate brothers, even if they did not as a group share the confident belief of so many of their fellow citizens of other faiths in the current doctrines of human perfectibility and inevitable social progress.

It should be noted that the early institutions of Catholic charity were not confined to Catholics and that Americans of all religious faiths shared, and still share, in their beneficial acts. It was a policy that more than once won them public and official commendation. For example, when the cholera epidemic of 1832 reached Baltimore in August of that year, seven Sisters of Charity from Emmitsburg responded immediately to the call for assistance, as other sisters had done for Philadelphia a few weeks earlier. The spacious residence of the Archbishop of Baltimore at Charles and Mulberry Streets was turned over to the city officials as an emergency hospital for the stricken of all classes and creeds. After the scourge had passed, Mayor William Stewart expressed gratitude in his own name and in the name of the board of health. He stated that the sisters' essential utility in nursing the sick was surpassed by their clothing destitute orphans at their own expense, an act he termed "the purest system of unostentatious Charity that could have been devised." The mayor and the city's health officers deemed it "an imperious duty, in behalf of the citizens of Baltimore, to express our warmest gratitude and deepest sense of obligation for those services which were given without compensation—thereby leaving us doubly your debtors."[21] The conduct displayed by the clergy and the sisters in Baltimore in the summer of 1832 was duplicated throughout the country wherever the cholera struck, as it was during the visitations of yellow fever later in the century.

Another instrument used to instruct the immigrant in his religious faith and in the ways of American life was the Catholic press, even though in the first years it gave an excessive amount of attention to Ireland and its problems. It was John England, Bishop of Charleston, who first realized its possibilities by founding in June, 1822, the *United States Catholic Miscellany*, the first American Catholic weekly newspaper properly so called. England was a born journalist, and he responded with zest to the nativist attacks by using his paper as a medium to answer their charges and misrepresentations, as well as to enlighten his own people. Confronted with the familiar accusation that Catholicism was incompatible with republicanism, the bishop replied that to him republicanism meant that no set of men had any inherent natural right to take precedence over their fellow men and that all power to regulate the public affairs of individuals, united in a social compact, was derived from the public will freely expressed by the voice of the majority. "This is what we understand by *Republicanism*," said England, "and we know of no doctrine of *Catholicism*, if we must use the expression, opposed to this. . . ."[22] England's paper exerted a powerful influence on American Catholic thought during the early nineteenth century, and the effectiveness of his courageous stands in the face of strident opposition from the nativists emboldened Catholics elsewhere to avail themselves of the opportunities offered by the press. During the next two decades Catholic newspapers were established elsewhere in the country at the rate of about one a year.

It is a simple task to chronicle the growth of Catholic schools, institutions of charity, and the press as factors that had a part in the molding of American Catholic character before 1852. It is quite another matter to attempt to assess the value of private instruction and counsel from the bishops and priests in this process. Commonly in all religions the perplexed layman turns to his minister for advice, but it was especially true of the Catholics, for, as we have said, no other American religious body had to deal with such a complex foreign-born population that needed immediate help. As any Catholic priest will bear witness, the confessional is a place to which many penitents carry more than their sins; they frequently bring their personal and domestic problems. Thus the reception of the sacrament of penance afforded a natural channel for guidance and direction in the countless difficulties which the immigrant encountered. Beyond the matter of personal counsel, known only to the recipient, there were church services, Sunday sermons, and vespers with the occasional parish missions where visiting priests conducted scheduled instructions for a week. The beauty of the centuries-old Catholic liturgy—for the most part, it is true, in poor and simple churches and chapels—recalled to the transplanted immigrants the splendor of their spiritual inheritance.

To the balance of Catholics, who lived in the crowded, lower-class areas of the rising industrial towns, the parish priest was often the sole source of help, a fact which did not go unnoticed by outsiders. For example, Gustave de Beaumont, traveling companion of Alexis de Tocqueville, used his time in the United States after their arrival in May, 1831, for observation of various phases of American life besides the prison system which the two Frenchmen had come to study. He, too, later wrote a book on the United States, although it was so largely overshadowed by the famous work of his friend that it is now practically forgotten. De Beaumont had considerable to say about American religious life, and in contrasting the Protestant and Catholic congregations he remarked that while the members of the former were generally enrolled from the same rank or social class, the Catholic parishes received indiscriminately persons of all classes and all conditions of society. In his judgment Catholicism was "the religion of the masses" because in that Church the poor man was equal to the rich, the slave to his master, and the Negro to the white. One of the factors which he felt would necessarily have a strong influence on the destiny of American Catholicism was what he termed "the morality of the Catholic clergy in this country."[23] Six months after the arrival of de

Catholics as Citizens

Beaumont, an English Protestant traveler came to the United States for an extended visit which took him through a good part of the country. In a volume published two years later he took note of the work of the Catholic priests among the lower classes:

> I am not a Catholic, but I cannot suffer prejudice of any sort to prevent my doing justice to a body of Christian ministers, whose zeal can be animated by no hope of worldly reward, and whose humble lives are passed in diffusing the influence of divine truth, and communicating to the meanest and most despised of mankind the blessed comforts of religion. . . . The amount, and the success of their silent labours, is not illustrated in the blazon of missionary societies. . . . And yet we may surely assert, that not the least of these labours is forgotten. Their record is, where their reward will be.[24]

As these foreign visitors indicated, no one could calculate the amount and success of the spiritual life of Catholicism; yet to ignore it would be to omit a powerful factor in the molding of the character of both native-born and foreign-born Catholics of any country.

A third consideration which exercised a determining influence upon mid-century Catholicism was in nature a negative one, namely, the revival of active hostility to the Church in the movement known as nativism. We have already spoken of the xenophobia which became a feature of American life in the years after independence. It was not universal and constant, surely, for how otherwise account for the Francophile sentiments of so many Americans in the last years of the eighteenth century? But beneath the surface of this affection for things French, there lurked the deeper strains of native complacency, and it needed only the misbehavior of Napoleon Bonaparte to show how really American the Americans could be. Before the ugly aspects of the nativist movement of the 1830's had become manifest, most Americans had a second thought that overrode their prejudice about foreigners and Catholics: there was need of strong hands to man the rising mills and infant industries, to handle the bustling commerce of the expanding seaports, to build roads, canals, and new railways, and to till the soil of the limitless lands of the West. Once the specter of Napoleon was permanently laid to rest, prospects for business in the days of peace brought back this practical tolerance. Thus in the tug of war that went on within the minds of many Americans in the years after 1815, the attraction of profit won out over the repulsion for foreigners and Catholics, and the welcome accorded the newcomers was on the whole a generous and good-natured one.

And for what European people could the American promise have more appeal than for the Irish? Crushed by economic oppression and bedeviled for centuries by religious persecution, it was not surprising that by 1827 Irish immigrants should number 20,000 and that they should keep streaming into the country until there were nearly a million of them by mid-century. Nor did the attraction of the new republic fail to touch the German world. The Germans had not suffered to the same degree as the Irish, but the presence of unpopular governments, religious discrimination, and universal military service stimulated immigration years in advance of the abortive revolutions of 1848 which sent them westward in still greater numbers. In 1832 German immigration exceeded the 10,000 mark, and although many of the German immigrants were Protestants, the number of Catholics among them was very high. In fact, by 1840 the American bishops were sending repeated calls of distress to Catholic missionary societies like the Ludwigsmissionverein of Munich and the Leopoldinen Stiftung of Vienna for assistance in caring for them. It was estimated in the decade of the 1820's that 54,000 Catholics had entered the United States from abroad, a figure which rose steadily when the 1840's alone accounted for 700,000 more. It was evident that the Church had a major problem on its hands in ushering these newcomers into a settled life.

Those Americans who felt an intense dislike for foreigners and Catholics did not wait to witness the tremendous influx of the 1840's before they gave the cry of alarm. Circumstances such as a falling off in the American shipping trade, the tariff of abominations of 1828, and the growing scarcity of jobs—aggravated by the cheap labor of the foreign-born—played their part as causes of the storm that was brewing, but the mainspring of action was prejudice against the foreign-born, especially foreign-born Catholics. A certain group of Protestant ministers took the lead in crystallizing these unfriendly sentiments, and the signal for the campaign, one might say, was given with the launching in New York on January 2, 1830, of *The Protestant,* an openly anti-Catholic weekly newspaper. Gradually the movement was spread to all parts of the country by hundreds of local societies which were assiduous in their distribution of calumnies and threats against Catholics and the foreign-born. Every pretext was seized upon to demonstrate the aggressive tactics of the Catholics, and when in 1842 Bishop Francis Patrick Kenrick of Philadelphia submitted a respectful petition to the city officials asking for redress against the abuse of Catholic children being compelled to use the King James Bible in the public schools, it provided the occasion for a national organization. Ninety-four Protestant ministers joined in the formation of the American Protestant Association on

November 22 of that year, declaring in their constitution that the principles of popery were "subversive of civil and religious liberty" and that they therefore were uniting to defend Protestant interests against what they called "the great exertions now making to propagate that system in the United States."[25]

The constant agitation of groups of this kind inflamed the tempers of thousands of Americans who otherwise would probably have remained at peace with their foreign-born and Catholic neighbors. It was not surprising that violence ensued, as it did in August, 1834, when a midnight mob—incited by the harangues of the Reverend Lyman Beecher—burned the convent of the Ursuline Sisters at Charlestown, Massachusetts. Philadelphia rioters in May, 1844, were responsible for the burning of two Catholic churches, the loss of thirteen lives, and the wounding of many citizens. Citizens less impassioned than the nativists made little effort to check depredations or to compensate victims. While American Protestants generally avoided violence in itself, their latent suspicions were heightened when they swallowed the story of Maria Monk and similar propaganda. A notable exception to the general acquiescence with which most Americans stood by while the civil rights and properties of their neighbors were violated was that of a rising young lawyer in Illinois. At a meeting in Springfield on the night of June 12, 1844, Abraham Lincoln made plain his detestation of bigotry, as well as his concern for the future of the Whig Party, to which he then belonged. One of the resolutions he submitted that night read:

> *Resolved,* That the guarantee of the rights of conscience, as found in our Constitution, is most sacred and inviolable, and one that belongs no less to the Catholic, than to the Protestant; and that all attempts to abridge or interfere with these rights, either of Catholic

or Protestant, directly or indirectly, have our decided disapprobation, and shall ever have our most effective opposition.[26]

It was a sentiment not shared by the men of his party, and the success the bigots enjoyed in these years was in no small measure due to the sympathy which they garnered from the Whigs. Meanwhile, the Catholics were compelled to look to the defense of their rights. One of the first means they chose was to strengthen their own press. Many came to realize as never before the wisdom of Bishop England in establishing a newspaper that would explain the true doctrines of the Church and answer the calumnies of its enemies. His example was imitated by Catholics, for instance, in New York, Philadelphia, Louisville, and Cincinnati, and by 1842 there were about twenty weeklies for the English-speaking Catholics, as well as the *Wahrheitsfreund* of Cincinnati, initially published in July, 1837, as the first German Catholic newspaper in the country. Not only did the nativist attacks spur the Catholics to establish their own newspapers—after they discovered they could not hope for justice in either the Protestant or the secular journals— but they likewise gave rise to a series of religious debates throughout the land, these proving for a time to be a very popular form of entertainment, if not always of enlightenment. Thus Father John Hughes of St. John's Church, Philadelphia, the future Archbishop of New York, engaged the Presbyterian minister, John Breckinridge; Bishop John B. Purcell of Cincinnati took on the Baptist Alexander Campbell; in the South the Bishop of Charleston had an exchange with the Reverend Richard Fuller, a Baptist minister of Beaufort.

Officially the Church remained silent through the first years, but later the provocation had become so severe that the bishops assembled at Baltimore in April, 1837, for the Third Provincial

Council decided to speak out. That they did so with reluctance was evident from their pastoral letter, wherein they expressed themselves "painfully constrained to notice the misrepresentation and persecution" that had marked the years since they had last met. Because the committee of the Massachusetts legislature appointed to consider the petition for compensation to the Charlestown nuns had questioned the right of Catholics to claim protection, Catholics supposedly acknowledging what was termed "the supremacy of a foreign potentate," the bishops were at pains to set the record straight concerning what spiritual allegiance to the Holy See really meant. It was completely false, they avowed, to deduce from this spiritual allegiance the premise that Catholics' civil rights should be abrogated. In analyzing the civic loyalty owed to the government, the bishops dwelt upon the rights conferred on the Catholics born in this country, as well as the rights conferred on the foreign-born when they attained full citizenship with the oath to renounce all civil or political allegiance to a foreign power. As for the manner in which their people should take the abuse which was then being heaped upon them, the prelates counseled patience and urged the ultimate good that would result from Catholic citizens going quietly about their business and leading exemplary lives. It was, they thought, the best way to meet the opposition. "This, beloved brethren," said the bishops, "is the vengeance of christianity."[27] For the most part their advice was heeded, although smoldering resentment gave rise here and there to incidents which broke the peace of a number of communities in the years immediately ahead.

Individually, the American bishops in their respective dioceses reacted to the situation according to their own lights and temperaments, a fact which was strikingly illustrated by the opposite policies pursued by the Bishops of Philadelphia and New York. As has been said, it was the petition of Bishop Kenrick to the public school board of Philadelphia in November, 1842, remonstrating against the use of the Protestant Bible and Protestant prayers and hymns in public schools, that had set off a chain of unforeseen events. Kenrick had quoted the school law which stated that "the religious predilections of the parents shall be respected" and had asked that the proper adjustments be made.[28] It should likewise be noted that the bishop did not ask to have the Bible removed from the public schools, but merely that the Douay version should be substituted for the use of the Catholic children. In any case, the petition was entirely misrepresented by the nativists and became a major factor in the gathering storm which broke over Philadelphia on May 8, 1844, when for three days the city was given over to a series of destructive riots. Having tried and failed by persuasion and appeal for peace to prevent the outbreak of violence, Kenrick left the city for some days until public order had been restored. In doing so, he acted in what he believed to be the best interests of all concerned, since he felt that his presence might lend further provocation to the rioters.

In New York, matters took a quite different turn. There the forceful Bishop John Hughes was not minded to yield anything short of the full complement of civil rights for his people. When the thoroughly Protestant character of the privately operated Public School Society had been protested by the Catholics in the spring of 1840, and they petitioned for their proportionate share of the funds distributed by this society, it had at once become a *cause célèbre*. For the next two years New York politics was heavily weighted with the issue. All efforts to gain their point having failed, the Catholics entered their own ticket in the elections of November, 1841. In the end the legislature put through the Maclay Bill in April, 1842, which broke the monopoly of the Public School Society over the schools of the metropolis, but which also carried a provision forbidding any state aid to religious schools in the city. Hughes had both won and lost; won, in the sense that the Public School Society's stronghold on the city's schools was ended; lost, in that no financial aid was henceforth to be given to any religious schools.[29]

Needless to say, the issue over the schools provided the nativists with additional arguments against Catholics as enemies of public education, and long after the passage of the Maclay Bill the question remained a live one in New York. When the New York nativists threatened in the spring of 1844 to imitate the violence of the Philadelphia group, they quickly found out that they were not dealing with a mild Kenrick but with a bishop who would fight. Hughes took a bold stand from the very outset, and after learning that the public authorities refused to guarantee protection, he stationed armed guards around the city's Catholic churches. He publicly announced that if their churches were fired, the Catholics' resistance would turn New York into a second Moscow. The mayor and his council tried to shift the blame for the threatening situation on the Catholics and pleaded with the bishop to restrain his flock, to which Hughes retorted, "I have not the power; you must take care that they are not provoked."[30] In the end, New York's churches remained unharmed, and the uproar gradually subsided without loss of life or property. When a renewal of the Philadelphia riots occurred in July, Hughes's example was followed with similarly satisfactory results. Speaking of the conduct of the Bishop of New York, the principal historian of the movement has said, "Such an attitude, belligerent as it was, was necessary, for only through open threats could bloodshed have been averted in New York in those troubled days."[31]

The violence of 1844 marked the peak of the nativist persecution; the decline of the movement was hastened by the outbreak of war with Mexico in May, 1846. In that contest Catholic leaders like Hughes, Generals James Shields and Bennet Riley, and Major John P. J. O'Brien distinguished themselves by their patriotic action. Moreover, as a result of a specific request made by President Polk, two Jesuit priests, John McElroy and Anthony Rey, were appointed to serve as chaplains with the troops entering Mexico in order that they might help to disabuse the Mexicans concerning the truth of a widely spread report in the Mexican press that the war was being waged against their country by "heretics" bent on pillaging their churches and destroying their religion.[32] Yet in spite of wartime solidarity, the scars left by the nativist agitation were deep and lasting. The benefit that accrued from a growth in the Catholic press was poor compensation for the injury done to Catholic self-respect by the ceaseless attacks on their religious beliefs, on the institutions of their Church, and on their very right to exist in the United States as equal citizens. Inevitably, the campaign of bigotry tended to make the Catholics draw in upon themselves more than ever before. It enhanced their feeling of inferiority as a minority group and increased their sensitiveness concerning the attitudes of outsiders toward their affairs.

The frequently repeated accusation that their religious allegiance disqualified them as citizens who could be trusted was one which the Catholics found difficult to understand. In order to explain their role in public affairs during the first half of the nineteenth century, it is necessary to go back a bit to put the matter in proper perspective. In the first years of the early national period the Catholics had equal citizenship in only five of the thirteen states, a condition which left many of them involuntarily passive amid the crucial events of their communities. In Massachusetts the Puritan oligarchy looked with scorn upon the 200 or more Catholics of 1790, and in New York, where they numbered nearly 2,000, the oath which John Jay had succeeded in getting into the state constitution of 1777 demanding an abjuration of all foreign jurisdictions, "ecclesiastical as well as civil," made it impossible for them to aspire to public life. In seven states there was still an established church in one form or another, and when the Catholics observed what had happened to the Protestant Episcopal Church in Virginia after disestablishment, it confirmed their belief in the wisdom of separation of Church and State. Decline of the Episcopalian communion had become so marked in the Old Dominion by 1800 that Bishop James Madison, who had returned from his consecration on the same boat with Bishop Carroll, finally gave up his attempts to stir his flock to new life and retired to a teaching post at the College of William and Mary.

Once the legal barriers had been cleared away in Maryland and Pennsylvania, where the Catholics were most numerous, qualified representatives of that faith took their places in both national and state governments. The services of Charles Carroll to the Continental Congress, and of his cousin, Daniel Carroll, and of Thomas FitzSimons of Pennsylvania, as framers of the Constitution left nothing to be desired by way of loyalty to their civic responsibilities. Maryland had likewise found Thomas Sim Lee worthy of two terms as governor, as well as the offer of a third term and a seat in the United States Senate,

Catholics as Citizens

both of which he declined. In 1806 the election of a Catholic, Francis Cooper, to the New York legislature occasioned the repeal of the clause in the state constitution which had forbidden a man to hold office unless he would take the oath to forswear allegiance to a foreign ecclesiastical power. In 1831 Roger Brooke Taney entered Andrew Jackson's cabinet as Attorney General, later filled the post of Secretary of the Treasury, and in 1836 was elevated by Jackson to the supreme bench as Chief Justice of the United States. In 1853 President Pierce named James Campbell of Pennsylvania to be Postmaster General. Where in the official records of these public figures, asked the Catholics, had there been found warrant for the constantly repeated charge that a Catholic could not serve both his Church and his country without jeopardizing his loyalty to one or the other?

What those of nativist mentality failed to perceive was clearly understood by one who in many ways was the wisest philosopher of democratic government in modern times. In May, 1831, Alexis de Tocqueville arrived in the United States for an extended tour during which his acute intelligence regarded many more things than the prison system which he had come to study. The famous Frenchman gave considerable thought to the relationship of Catholicism to democracy, and it led him to state:

I think that the Catholic religion has erroneously been regarded as the natural enemy of democracy. Among the various sects of Christianity, Catholicism seems to me, on the contrary, to be one of the most favorable to equality of condition among men. In the Catholic Church the religious community is composed of only two elements: the priest and the people. The priest alone rises above the rank of his flock, and all below him are equal. . . .

If, then, the Catholic citizens of the United States are not forcibly

71

led by the nature of their tenets to adopt democratic and republican principles, at least they are not necessarily opposed to them; and their social position, as well as their limited number, obliges them to adopt these opinions.[33]

No Catholic then or since would gainsay the soundness of de Tocqueville's judgment, and the perfect ease with which Catholics participated—once the law permitted them to do so— in the processes of democratic government proved the point. If de Tocqueville had been wrong, one might expect to find some indication of attempts on the part of Catholics to change the character of the American government. Not only was such evidence entirely lacking, but they partook with zest in the party politics of their day without let or hindrance from the hierarchy which, the nativist enemies so often declared, controlled their votes.

Catholics, for example, found no obstacle in their religious faith to bar them from full acceptance and participation in the activities of the Federalist Party, as the careers of the Carrolls, FitzSimons, and others make clear. And when that party broke up, many were found giving their allegiance, without any interference from their Church, to the Jacksonian Democrats, as was the case of Taney. In fact, Bishop Hughes was often annoyed by the Jeffersonian partisanship shown by much of the Irish press in the 1840's, because he believed that the Democrats were using the Irish for their own selfish purposes. But he took no overt steps to intervene. Many Catholics preferred the Democrats because their nativist foes were aligned with the Whig Party which formed about 1834. The Catholics were thoroughly opposed to the abolitionists, and the latter's organization into the Liberty Party in 1839 received no backing from them. What Bishop England had said four years before concerning the abolitionists was altogether true. Denying that he or any other Catholic clergymen had been the recipient of abolitionist literature, he remarked, "Nor do I know a single Roman Catholic, clerical or lay, with whom I conversed on the subject, who is not fully determined to use his efforts to prevent the mischief of their interference."[34]

Among the many wise precedents set by that extraordinary man John Carroll, few proved of greater public benefit than his insistence that the Catholic clergy should hold themselves aloof from politics. We have already seen his reluctance to join the Continental Congress' commission to Canada in 1776 lest this political action should endanger his priestly office, for, as he said, when ministers of religion leave their professional duties for the realm of politics, "they generally fall into contempt, and sometimes even bring discredit to the cause in whose service they are engaged."[35] Archbishop Carroll followed that principle all through life, and his policy made a lasting impression on the Catholic clergymen of his own day and on those who followed. When, for example, the Protestant pulpits rang with denunciations of Jefferson in the campaign of 1800, there was no corresponding echo from Carroll and his priests. Good Federalists as most of these clergymen probably were in their conservative sympathies, there was no public pronouncement to lend Catholic sanction to John Adams and his friends. Moreover, there was no religious group in the United States more generally opposed than the Catholics to the suggestion made by the Reverend Ezra Stiles Ely, a Presbyterian minister, in an oration of July 4, 1827, at Philadelphia, where he called for the establishment of what was termed a "Christian party in politics."[36] Such an idea was entirely foreign to American Catholic thinking and practice.[37]

The policy of clerical aloofness from politics was in part induced by the shyness of an unpopular minority, but it was equally a policy born of the dual conviction that the clergy's principal business was their religious ministry and that it was improper to use their office for political ends. A quarter century after Carroll's death, when the country was on the eve of what turned out to be the most exciting presidential campaign to date, the Catholic bishops closed their Fourth Provincial Council in May, 1840, with a pastoral letter to the clergy and laity in which they touched upon the political scene. At the outset they stated, "We disclaim all right to interfere with your judgment in the political affairs of our common country, and are far from entertaining the wish to control you in the constitutional exercise of your freedom. . . ." They confined themselves to counseling the Catholics to retain their calm and charity during the coming campaign and to reflect that they were accountable to God for what the bishops called "the honest, independent and fearless exercise of your franchise." If any Catholic should yield to undue influence through motives of favor or dishonest gain, then, they said, "You have violated your trust, you have betrayed your conscience, and you are a renegade to your country."[38] No reasonable man could take exception to advice of this kind from his moral leaders, and in the light of the extravagances that were to follow between May and November of that year it was salutary counsel. Thus the pattern of Catholic clerical conduct in relation to party politics became fixed, and with no more than four or five exceptions it has remained the pattern to the present day.

As a consequence of this policy the Catholic laity were left entirely free to follow whatever party they pleased, so long as its principles, obviously the case with the nativists, were not harmful to religion. Indeed, Harriet Martineau was not far wrong when she commented in 1837: "The Catholic body is democratic in its politics, and made up from the more independent kind of occupations. The Catholic religion is modified by the spirit of the time in America; and its professors are not a set of men who can be priest-ridden to any fatal extent."[39] That the great majority of Catholics in the early national period consulted their own interests and found them best served by the Federalist Party was true, and after the breakup of the Federalists their choice lay between the Democrats and the Whigs. Ultimately it did not prove a difficult decision for most Catholics to make, for if at first some of them leaned toward the Whigs, they were quickly disillusioned when they discovered the flirtations of that party with the nativists. On the other hand, the Democrats were by far the stronger proponents of religious freedom, and it was that party—not the Whigs—which extended a welcoming hand to the foreign-born.

Yet one finds striking evidence that Catholic support of the Democrats was not unanimous and, too, that the widest variety of opinion could, and did, obtain among the Catholics in the careers of two prominent leaders of that faith in Philadelphia in these years. One of these, Robert Walsh, who in 1811 founded and edited the first standard quarterly journal in this country, the *American Review of History and Politics*, remained to the end of his life a Federalist at heart. Walsh's highly conservative and aristocratic turn of mind could not abide the philosophy of the party of Jefferson and Jackson, and during the War of 1812 there was no New Englander who fought the Madison administration more vigorously than he did. Meanwhile Walsh's fellow townsman, Mathew Carey, the nation's foremost publisher of the period, was an enthusiastic supporter of the War Hawks, and in later years Carey joined in almost every manifestation of the burgeoning humanitarian movement.[40] As for the fringe groups of the period, the generally conservative principles which marked their training made Catholics suspicious of people like the Owenites whose flair for agnosticism and socialism repelled them. Similarly, the Catholic theological distinction between slavery as such and its abuses, plus an insistence on respect for property and duly constituted authority, kept its members entirely apart from the abolitionists. Thus the overwhelming majority of the Catholics joined the Democratic Party, even if it meant that they found themselves in the company of such strange bedfellows as most of the declared infidels and agnostics of the day and that their titular leader, Andrew Jackson, publicly extolled Tom Paine. The Catholics, however, would explain that they were Democrats for other reasons than had motivated Abner Kneeland and the freethinkers.

In the period under discussion American Catholics were frequently the object of political abuse, a fact that became painfully evident during the presidential campaign of 1840. Excitement was running high throughout the country in the spring of 1840 when the bishops met in Baltimore for their Fourth Provincial Council. We have already seen what they had to say about the political situation in the pastoral letter of May 23 with which they closed the council. Two months later the campaign provoked the appearance in the *Boston Quarterly Review* of the first installment of Orestes A. Brownson's famous essay on "The Laboring Classes." By reason of their social and economic status, it was an essay that should have been of more than ordinary interest to most Catholics, even if they were then unaware that four years later its author would become a convert to their Church. But most of the literature of the campaign contained no such solid food for thought as was found in Brownson's article. On the contrary, no campaigners to date had circulated more nonsense than those of 1840. Bishop England, for one, had an especially lively time of it. In a speech in Georgia, John Forsyth, Van Buren's Secretary of State, fastened on Pope Gregory XVI's letter of December, 1839, on the slave trade to link the Catholics to the abolitionists who were then supporting Harrison. The Bishop of Charleston answered Forsyth in a series of eighteen articles in the *United States Catholic Miscellany* through 1840 and 1841, setting forth the Church's teaching on the slave trade and on the institution of slavery. As the campaign progressed, both parties sought to enlist England's support, but the bishop would not be drawn in. He declined an invitation to a dinner sponsored by the Georgia and Alabama backers of Harrison on July 26, and when the Van Buren forces invited him to a rally at Detroit in September, he did the same.[41] In the same summer John Hughes, Bishop of New York, confessed to his friend, William H. Seward, the Whig Governor of New York, that he was "not inattentive to the course of things" and that he had a deep interest in the character of the men who were running for office. But Hughes felt that he should keep himself aloof from the fray, for, as he remarked, "I am not a politician. My people are divided & my sacred office requires that I should be a father to all."[42]

In the fall of 1840 the Whigs were victorious after a campaign that had degenerated into an exhibition of misrepresentation, abuse, and irrelevancies on a scale hitherto unparalleled in American history. It is impossible to say with any exactness what part the Catholic vote played or how far opposition to them influenced the final result. But there was no doubt that the triumph of "Tippecanoe and Tyler too" and their nativist camp followers boded no good for the Catholics.

In spite of the unpleasantness resulting from the noisy agitation of the enemies of the Church in these years, and the temporary handicaps it created for Catholic citizens in many states, it in no way availed to stop the Church's expansion. In 1818 Connecticut surrendered the last vestiges of an established church, and in 1833 Massachusetts did the same. On a national scale the federal government promoted the same principle, a fact felt at a very early date by Catholics living west of the Allegheny Mountains. Even before the organization of the national government, there had been fairly numerous settlements of French Catholics in the western country where veterans like Father Pierre Gibault at Cahokia were in time supplemented by French émigré priests such as Benedict Flaget, Gabriel Richard, and Stephen Badin. As early as 1785 a number of Maryland Catholic families, subscribing to what Crèvecœur had said of the citizen of this new land, "Here the rewards of his industry follow with equal steps the progress of his labour,"[43] migrated to the West. By the time that Kentucky entered the Union in 1792, there were promising Catholic colonies in Nelson and Scott Counties, where religious life was quite unhampered by the remnants of colonial penal legislation.

The principle of religious freedom maintained by non-interference of the State in the affairs of the Church was well illustrated by a case that arose in Louisiana. With the purchase of Louisiana in 1803, 15,000 Catholics of French and Spanish descent had been brought under the American flag in an area where a diocese had been established as early as 1793. The request of the Holy See in 1805 that Bishop Carroll should assume

temporary charge of these distant Catholics put an added burden on the already harassed prelate in Baltimore. Carroll fully
understood the predominantly French character of the colony,
but he was also aware of the strained relations that had developed between the United States and France soon after
Louisiana's purchase. Anxious, therefore, to be relieved of the
new responsibility as quickly as possible, he inquired of President Jefferson before making any suggestions to Rome if there
would be objection from the government to his recommending
a French priest for the vacant diocese in Louisiana. Secretary
of State Madison replied in November, 1806, that since the
case was of an entirely ecclesiastical nature, the president and
he felt it would be more in keeping with what he called the
"scrupulous policy of the Constitution in guarding against a
political interference with religious affairs" to decline a commitment. Madison told Carroll, however, that Jefferson would
have returned the same answer regardless of legal considerations because, as he put it, of "his perfect confidence in the
purity of your views, and in the patriotism which will guide
you, in the selection of ecclesiastical individuals. . . ."[44] It was
an early instance of how the unofficial relations of Church
and State worked in favor of both, and of how the high prestige of Carroll was sufficient guarantee that he would act in
the country's best interests.

As the policy of manifest destiny sent Americans toward
the Pacific and the Rio Grande, it must have seemed to them,
if they adverted to it at all, that the Church had ever been
before them in many areas for over two centuries. In the
realm of the spirit none of the new settlers from the East felt
more at home than the Catholics. Here old Catholic institutions
of the Spanish and French regimes were links to bind them to

their own past; the descendants of the *conquistadores* and the *coureurs de bois* fused with the newcomers to create an often strange amalgam of Catholic life on the distant American frontiers. The Holy See sometimes preceded government in looking to the needs of the settlers, as, for example, in California, where the first bishop was appointed in April, 1840, eight years before the famous find at Sutter's Mill. In May, 1840, Father Pierre-Jean De Smet, S.J., left St. Louis for the first of his journeys to the Indians of the Far Northwest, and a year and a half before John L. O'Sullivan's *Democratic Review* coined the phrase "manifest destiny," the Vicariate Apostolic of Oregon was erected in December, 1843. The same was true in the Southwest, where a bishop was appointed for Texas in July, 1841, four years in advance of its annexation to the United States. Nearly two years before the Gadsden Purchase, John B. Lamy, the principal character of Willa Cather's charming novel *Death Comes for the Archbishop*, arrived at Santa Fe to begin his almost forty years as a missionary bishop in New Mexico. After 1848, problems involving ecclesiastical jurisdiction and transfer of church properties in these areas were settled peacefully by the Department of State and prelates like Archbishops Samuel Eccleston, S.S., and Hughes, although Hughes thought the Church would have fared better if an apostolic nuncio of the Holy See, accredited to the American government, had been present in Washington to handle the business.

The tremendous territorial expansion of the United States at the mid-century was likewise reflected in the Catholic hierarchy when the bishops assembled at Baltimore in May, 1852, for the opening of their First Plenary Council. Wise men already knew that Henry Clay's compromise measures of two years before had not permanently settled the slave issue, and since the previous March thousands of Americans had been gaining a new insight into the problem from Harriet Beecher Stowe's *Uncle Tom's Cabin.* The thirty-two bishops in Baltimore, however, pressed other matters during the ten days of their conciliar meetings. Nine of the prelates were native-born, sixteen had been born in France or Ireland, four in Belgium or Canada, and one each in Austria, Spain, and Switzerland. The Church of the immigrant was thus mirrored in the bishops who led it. The number of American Catholics was then close to two millions, and 1,421 priests spread through six archdioceses, twenty-five dioceses, and four vicariates apostolic had charge of the 1,411 churches and 681 mission stations that stretched from coast to coast. There had been seven provincial councils between 1829 and 1849, but now, with six metropolitan provinces each headed by an archbishop, the problems were more truly national than provincial. The twenty-five decrees framed during the council treated such subjects as parochial schools, uniformity of discipline, and administration of church property. The council was characterized by a church historian as "the most important step so far made by the hierarchy for complete uniformity of Church life in the United States."[45] The conciliar decrees took no cognizance of secular concerns, and the only political note in the customary pastoral letter to the clergy and laity with which the bishops closed the council on May 20—ten days in advance of the Democrats' arrival in Baltimore for the convention that would nominate Franklin Pierce—was to the allegiance which they owed to their country. With the coming campaign no doubt in mind, the bishops counseled their people:

Show your attachment to the institutions of our beloved country by prompt compliance with all their requirements, and by the cautious jealousy with which you guard against the least deviation from the rules which they prescribe for the maintenance of public order and private rights. Thus will you refute the idle babbling of foolish men, and will best approve yourselves worthy of the privileges which you enjoy, and overcome, by the sure test of practical patriotism, all the prejudices which a misrepresentation of your principles but too often produces.[46]

In summary of what has been said in this chapter we can, I think, draw certain conclusions concerning the character of American Catholicism at the midway point of the nineteenth century. First, it was, and continued to be from 1790 to 1852, the religious faith of a small minority of the population. Second, its adherents suffered from the traditional prejudice which most Americans entertained for the Catholic Church. Third, the quite American complexion with which the Church had begun its organized life in 1790 had by 1852 been overshadowed by the predominantly foreign cast given the Church by the tremendous immigration of Catholics from Europe. Fourth, the organized attacks upon the Church gave rise, in turn, to an increased separateness of Catholics from their non-Catholic fellow citizens, to a further drawing in upon themselves in such ways as establishing their own newspapers when they found they could not expect justice from the Protestant and secular press, by increasing the number of their own schools when petitions for the use of the Douay Bible in the public schools were denied them, and to a general aloofness from their neighbors, which is a familiar characteristic among minority groups. Fifth, most of the Catholics by 1852 were Democrats in their politics, since that was the party friendliest to their vital interests. In spite of the opposition of nativists and other Americans, they participated actively in political life, as de Tocqueville had observed, without the least embarrassment from their religious convictions. Catholics generally belonged to the poorer classes employed in the rising industrial towns of the East and Middle West. Finally, the growing reality of American religious freedom enabled the Church to expand across the continent without interference from government so that by 1852 it had organized in every corner of the land. By the time the United States entered the second half of the century, the most disliked and suspect of all the American churches was on the way to becoming the largest and strongest single denomination in the land. With certain aspects of that seeming contradiction we will be concerned in what follows.

III

Civil War and Immigration
1852–1908

In the previous chapter we spoke of certain events and movements of the first half of the nineteenth century which conditioned the character that American Catholicism had assumed by 1852. The nature of history being what it is, namely, a series of continuing developments rather than static phenomena occurring in a fixed period, some of the features current in the years before 1852 were still prominent in the Church by the time the century closed. But there was this difference: in the second fifty years American Catholics had more experience to draw upon, and as a consequence their handling of the problems that confronted the Church showed a steadier, more mature approach. The question of the parochial schools is a case in point. On the other hand, in the later period entirely new situations arose in America, situations centered mainly around the tremendous industrialization that followed the Civil War. It was as a result of this industrialization that one of the present-day features of Catholicism in the United States became a permanent thing, that is, its predominantly urban character.

It was symptomatic of the intrenched bias against Catholics

that, in the month before the First Plenary Council convened, the secret Order of the Star-Spangled Banner passed into the hands of an expert new management that won for it a significant showing in the municipal elections of 1852. Two years later a national organization had emerged and the Know-Nothing Party, as it came to be called, was from that time to the Civil War a force which no Catholic or foreign-born citizen could afford to ignore. It is a dreary tale which we need not enter upon in detail, but it is important to remember that as a result of the ceaseless outpouring of books, pamphlets, and newspapers from sources of this kind the minds of thousands of Americans were irrevocably fixed in the traditional dislike of Catholicism which had been part of their intellectual heritage. Mark Twain testified to what this influence had meant to him during his youth in Missouri. Because he had grown up in an atmosphere where Samuel F. B. Morse's *Foreign Conspiracy* and similar tracts were read as gospel truth, it was not surprising that Twain should later say, "I have been educated to enmity toward everything that is Catholic, and sometimes, in consequence of this, I find it much easier to discover Catholic faults than Catholic merits."[1] How many Americans could have testified to the same fact! The enduring effect which an inculcation of religious prejudice has on men's minds was noted by John Henry Newman in his famous *Apologia Pro Vita Sua*, where he told of having read at the age of fifteen Newton's book *On the Prophecies* in consequence of which, as he remarked, "I became more firmly convinced that the Pope was the Antichrist predicted by Daniel, St. Paul, and St. John. My imagination was stained by the effects of this doctrine up to the year 1843. . . ."[2]

And yet some non-Catholics were not prepared to deny the

principle of religious freedom by thinking the worst of Catholics. In 1855 Abraham Lincoln was asked by an old Kentucky friend where he stood in politics. Lincoln replied that he thought he was a Whig, to which he added, "I am not a Know-Nothing. That is certain." He then asked:

How could I be? How can any one who abhors the oppression of negroes, be in favor of degrading classes of white people? Our progress in degeneracy appears to me to be pretty rapid. As a nation, we began by declaring that *"all men are created equal."* We now practically read it, "all men are created equal, *except negroes."* When the Know-Nothings get control, it will read, "all men are created equal, except negroes, *and foreigners, and catholics."* When it comes to this I should prefer emigrating to some country where they make no pretence of loving liberty—to Russia, for instance, where despotism can be taken pure, and without the base alloy of hypocrisy [*sic*].[3]

Catholics themselves felt keenly the injustice of the Know-Nothing campaign, and they were especially hurt at the support given to it by some Protestant ministers. In a moment of high triumph for the bigots, Chief Justice Taney commented sadly to his son-in-law, "In the eyes of the clergymen I am Mordecai the Jew sitting at the King's gate, and their zeal will hardly flag while I remain there."[4]

The Know-Nothing pursuit of foreigners and Catholics meanwhile ran its course and, as has happened more than once in the history of the United States, it was a national crisis which finally stilled the clamor. With the approach of the Civil War the outcry against the Church of Rome and the foreign-born seemed petty by comparison, and each section needed all the support it could muster for the struggle ahead. Many of the Know-Nothing gains were reversed, as, for example, when the New York legislature, which in the flush of a Know-Nothing victory in 1855 had passed the Putnam Bill forbidding the Catholic bishops to hold property in their own name, quietly repealed the measure in 1863 in response to the grave need for filling New York's quota in the depleted ranks of the army. For a generation thereafter Catholics were free from the embarrassment and hampering influences of an organized movement which challenged the validity of their citizenship. Not until 1887 was the third major wave of opposition whipped up against them, this time under the label of the American Protective Association, which carried on in nativist style until it diminished by the dawn of the present century.

It is part of the seeming contradiction to which we have previously alluded that the Church should grow and become strong in the face of the powerful opposition that was organized against it. But the contradiction is more seeming than real, and that for several reasons, beyond the good will and help from individual non-Catholics of prominence. First, the national government stood guard over the rights of conscience of Catholics and the citizenship of the foreign-born. Every effort made by the Know-Nothings and the A.P.A. to restrict these rights through a law of Congress was thrown back, and the gains that these organizations made through the legislatures of some states, although considerable, were not sufficient to withstand the test of time. A second reason lay outside the country. In spite of the ill repute which the United States had gained in European Catholic circles as a result of religious prejudice,[5] it in no way slackened the pace with which Catholic immigrants continued to seek these shores. The Irish potato famine of the late 1840's and the abortive German revolutions of 1848 were factors that far outweighed any misgivings the immigrant might have entertained concerning the future of his religious liberty in America. As a consequence of immigration and of a natural increase, therefore, the Catholic population of the country rose from 1,606,000 to 12,041,000 between 1850 and 1900, a total that was accounted for in good measure by the nearly 5,000,000 Catholics who arrived in the United States from abroad during those years.[6]

Moreover, if the Catholic immigrant after the mid-century found the nativist temper of the large eastern cities too hostile for his taste, he could go west with the help of the colonization societies that had been established by his coreligionists. It is quite true that these colonization societies never attained the success that they deserved, and later in the century Catholic leaders lamented the stand taken against them by Archbishop Hughes.[7] Yet as a result of such things as the Catholic colonization convention held in Buffalo in February, 1856, local societies in the West were stimulated to advertise the advantages of their regions for the immigrant. Thus the newcomer to cities like Boston, New York, and Philadelphia frequently found inviting prospects in his local Catholic paper. For example, an item from Dubuque in the *Pilot* of Boston on March 15, 1856, told him of the enthusiastic colonization meeting held some days before which, it was said, "afforded a cheering indication of the success that awaits the efforts that are now being put forth, East and West, North and South, on behalf of the poor Catholic immigrant."

Nor would the Catholic immigrant who took the westward trail generally be long out of reach of his Church. In the second half of the century almost every region of the country where settlement had been made in any numbers received the Church's attention without delay, and between 1852 and 1900 fifty-five new dioceses were erected in the United States. The geographical distribution of these new sees indicated the comparative strength of Catholicism in the principal sections of the country: Middle West, twenty-four; East, sixteen; Far West, eight; South, four; Southwest, three. The varied national backgrounds of the Catholic population likewise showed up among their bishops at the Second Plenary Council in October, 1866, where the forty-five prelates in attendance found fourteen born in the United States, eleven in Ireland, ten in France, three each in Canada and Spain, and one each in Austria, Belgium, Germany, and Switzerland. The native-born (about 33 per cent in 1866) gained slowly in representation, but the number of bishops born in Ireland, or of Irish descent, disproportionate to the general Catholic population and to bishops of German and other foreign strains, marked the period as one of an increasing Irish ascendancy in the American hierarchy, a fact which would bring severe internal tension before the end of the century.

The immense growth of the Church through immigration affected its attitude on more vital matters than the composition of its hierarchy, however, and one of these was the issue of slavery. Official Catholic doctrine held that slavery was not necessarily evil; it taught that slavery, thought of theoretically and apart from specific abuses to human dignity, was not opposed to the divine or natural law. Manumission was encouraged wherever circumstances would permit the slave to better his condition, and strong emphasis was always placed on the moral obligation of Catholic slaveholders to treat their subjects with justice and charity and to see that they received religious instruction. Moreover, the Church's condemnation of the slave trade was definite, something that had been reiterated more than once, and as recently as December, 1839, in the apostolic letter of Pope Gregory XVI.

In substance these were the views of the leading American Catholic theologian of the period, Francis P. Kenrick, when he treated the subject in 1841. The Church's decided opposition to the principles of the abolitionists was reflected in Kenrick's conclusion cencerning the slaves, in which he said, "Nevertheless, since such is the state of things, nothing should be attempted against the laws nor anything be done or said that would make them bear their yoke unwillingly."[8] Kenrick failed to make clear that his "slavery" was not the institution as it then existed in the United States. Rather it was the classical concept of slavery—which was preferable to the destruction of society—gained from the experience of the human race as defined by him and other theologians. In this sense the Bishop of Philadelphia made no contribution to the solution of the problem that so troubled his own generation.[9]

Catholic plantation owners—including the Jesuits—had held Negroes since the introduction of slaves into colonial Maryland, and their successors continued to own them in the nineteenth century. Archbishop Carroll, for example, directed in his will, written a month before he died in December, 1815, that his "black servant Charles" should be manumitted within a year after his death. The archbishop's cousin, Charles Carroll of Carrollton, who owned a large number of slaves believed strongly in the policy of gradual manumission, and at intervals he set many of his people free, manumitting thirty at one time in 1817.[10] Carroll was likewise an enthusiastic supporter of the American Colonization Society, organized in 1817 for the purpose of settling freed Negroes in Liberia, and after the death of Bushrod Washington he served as its president. Roger Brooke Taney was another who while he was still in middle life manumitted his Negro slaves. Many other Catholics retained their slaves until the emancipation. One such slave-holder, Michael M. Healy, Irish-born father of a future Bishop of Portland, Maine, and a president of Georgetown University, by 1831 had acquired a Georgia plantation of over 1,600 acres and owned seventeen slaves. Healy did the more extraordinary thing by marrying a mulatto slave girl who became the mother of his ten children.[11] Unlike Healy, most of the nearly 100,000 Irish in the South—many of whom, of course, were not Catholics—were engaged in business in the towns rather than on farms and plantations. But wherever they were, the Irish adopted the local point of view regarding slavery, an attitude which could probably be explained by the fact that most of them reacted favorably to a system which for the first time in their lives had placed others at the bottom of the social ladder.[12] Most of the French Catholics in Louisiana likewise had slaves on their plantations. All told, it was estimated that by the time of emancipation there were approximately 100,000 Catholic Negroes, free and slave, in the United States, Louisiana accounting for 62,500, Maryland for 16,000, and the remainder scattered throughout the country.[13]

More than once the Church had tried to improve the lot of the Negroes, but generally attempts to educate them had been frustrated through local pressure. For example, up to 1835 Bishop England conducted a school for free Negroes in Charleston, which the law of South Carolina still allowed at that time. But the public excitement over the anti-slavery riots of the previous year, plus the feeling against abolitionist tracts then inundating the state, was so great that within a brief period he was compelled to abandon it. Nine years later Peter R. Kenrick, Bishop of St. Louis, started a school for free and slave children in his see city, but after two years of rather promising results a combination of anti-abolitionism and anti-Catholic sentiment roused the populace to the point where in July, 1846, the sisters were threatened by a mob in the middle of the night. The superior later stated, "The day after our adventure the Mayor of St. Louis advised Bishop Kenrick to close that school for a time and he did so."[14] One gets a vivid impression of the burden placed on the conscience of the southern bishops by the presence of so many uninstructed Negroes, for the bishops described their problem in the communications which from time to time they sent to the foreign missionary societies. In a letter to the Society for the Propagation of the Faith, in France, William Henry Elder, Bishop of Natchez, whose diocese embraced the entire state of Mississippi, reported in 1858 that out of a total population of 606,526 persons in the state, 309,878 were slaves. Handicapped as he was by lack of priests, widely scattered churches, and great poverty, he confessed that the slaves were his principal anxiety; since they were not free to leave the plantations, the priests had to go to them. "Catholic masters," he said, "of course are taught that it is their duty to furnish their slaves with opportunities for being well instructed, & for practising their religion. And here is my anxiety, that I cannot enable these masters to do their duty because there are not Priests enough."[15] Conditions such as those mentioned in Charleston, St. Louis, and Mississippi were common throughout the South in these years, and it was out of the question, therefore, for the Church to attempt anything beyond the most elementary religious instruction for Negroes.

Insofar as general Catholic opinion was concerned, the issue that divided the nation along sectional lines divided the Catholics in precisely the same way. Catholics entered into the great debate that was then engrossing the entire populace, and editors of the Church's newspapers often aroused antagonism within Catholic ranks by their views. A few weeks after the Dred Scott Decision had provided a quickened tempo and material for renewed bitterness to the controversy over the slaves, an anonymous Catholic writer warned against the dangers to Catholic unity in this question:

> But have our remarks been suggestive of a Catholic political organization for the protection of Catholic rights, or the promotion of Catholic interests? God forbid that they should suggest such a thought in any one's mind. We leave Catholics, as men and American citizens, to avail themselves of such lawful and constitutional means of protection and defence as their own good sense, their charity, and their consciences may suggest and approve. We have no political course to propose, or political cause to promote.[16]

This statement, repudiating the notion of such a thing as a Catholic political party, represented not only the overwhelming sentiment of the Catholics of that day but of Catholics during the whole of American history. In fact, one may say that the idea has never been so much as seriously suggested by any reputable Catholic leader in this country. Meanwhile sharp exchanges continued between Catholic papers like the *Freeman's Journal* of New York and the *Catholic Mirror* of Baltimore. The student might, indeed, parallel the division between northern and southern Protestants with the differences that divided the Catholics of the North and South—with one notable exception. At no time did Catholics hint at desiring a break in the organizational bonds that linked the Catholics of the North to their coreligionists in the South. Their spiritual and organizational union was never in jeopardy, and in this repect they were quite a contrast to most of the Protestant churches which as early as 1845 had begun to break up into separate communions. To the very eve of the war Catholic bishops from above and below the Mason and Dixon Line continued to meet in councils of the Church with no attendant rift in their ecclesiastical deliberations by reason of sectional differences. This was true at the Ninth Provincial Council of Baltimore in May, 1858, where the bishops referred in their pastoral letter to the tension over slavery but forswore any interference with the judgment of the laity. Lay Catholics, they said, "should be free on all questions of polity and social order, within the limits of the doctrine and law of Christ."[17] The same situation obtained three years later among the bishops of the border Province of Cincinnati who two weeks after the firing on Fort Sumter stated in the pastoral letter of their Third Provincial Council, "While [the Church's] ministers rightfully feel a deep and abiding interest in all that concerns the welfare of the country, they do not think it their province to enter into the political arena."[18] Some might characterize this policy as an abdication of moral leadership, but with the Catholic faithful already aligning themselves on opposite sides of the barricades—and each claiming to be right—the bishops at Cincinnati acted with wisdom in the course that they pursued.

The complete freedom of political action which the hierarchy has left to the Catholic people was never better illustrated than during the Civil War. Upon the outbreak of hostilities Catholics at once enlisted in both the Union and Confederate armies and served as high officers, like Pierre Beauregard in the South and William Rosecrans in the North, and as marching privates. Forthright Catholic editors on both sides continued to give vent to their feelings. James A. McMaster, editor of the New York *Freeman's Journal*, was especially

vehement against the Lincoln administration in an editorial of
June 8, 1861, in which he exclaimed:

> Let those heed it who, one year ago, scoffed when we said that
> the election of Lincoln would cause civil war! We say, now, that if
> there be not conservatism enough in the country to stop and to re-
> buke the course of Lincoln and his Cabinet, we will have a bloody
> revolution and anarchy, resulting in a military despotism, with a
> different man from Lincoln at its head. We speak what we see and
> know. Our conscience forces us to speak, whether it please or offend.

It was scarcely a matter of surprise that language such as this—
which McMaster repeated week after week—offended Washington officials. In August, 1861, McMaster's paper was suspended, and he was arrested and imprisoned in Fort Lafayette
for nearly six weeks. McMaster's differences with the Lincoln
administration had been inspired by constitutional scruples
rather than by any deep sympathy with the South. But in
Baltimore another Catholic editor, Courtney Jenkins of the
Catholic Mirror, was an out-and-out southerner who went as
far as he dared in upholding the Confederate cause. Unlike the
strong-minded Archbishop Hughes, who had broken with Mc-
Master over the slavery question as early as 1856, the mild
Archbishop Kenrick of Baltimore, in spite of his disagreement
with Jenkins over the war, remained entirely aloof. In November, 1862, Kenrick told a friend: "The Catholic Mirror does
not reflect my sentiments or views. . . . I avoid interposing not
to give annoyance. I have had nothing to do with the controversies that have recently filled its columns."[19] Elsewhere in the
country similarly strong positions were taken by Catholic
editors. After the surrender of New Orleans to the Union
forces in April, 1862, Father Napoléon Perché, editor of
Le propagateur catholique and an ardent secessionist, kept up
his verbal warfare with the Yankees until his paper, too, was

suspended and he was put under house arrest. But if men like McMaster and John Mullaly of New York's *Metropolitan Record* were ranked with the Copperheads, their Catholic contemporaries, Patrick Donahoe of the Boston *Pilot* and Father Edward Purcell of the *Catholic Telegraph* of Cincinnati, fought just as vigorously with their pens for President Lincoln's conduct of the war. In a word, no pattern of general Catholic policy could be traced in the Church's press beyond the fact that practically all the southern journals sided with the Confederacy while a lesser majority of northern papers stood by the Union cause.

Similar differences obtained among the hierarchy. In Baltimore, the seat of the Church's premier see, Archbishop Kenrick found himself in the delicate position of being a northern sympathizer trying to rule a flock with decidedly southern views. Four months after the war began he remarked to a friend that Marylanders were generally with the South, especially since the occupation of the state by federal troops had made them feel like a conquered people. "I do not interfere," he said, "although from my heart I wish that secession had never been thought of. . . ."[20] It had been a custom at the Baltimore cathedral at the end of the Masses to read the prayer for civil authorities which Bishop Carroll had composed in 1791. But, once the war came, the priests of the cathedral household, who were all strong supporters of the Confederacy, refused to read the prayer because it contained a petition for the preservation of the American Union. Kenrick finally decided to read it himself. The result, as described many years later by Cardinal Gibbons, was that when he reached the offending phrase about the Union, "many people got up and publicly left the Cathedral, and those who remained expressed dissent from the Archbishop's petition by a great rustling of papers and silks."[21] Farther south in Tennessee a prelate with less discretion and forbearance than Kenrick openly expressed his northern sympathies by such actions as fraternizing with Union officers. Completely alienating the Catholics, James Whelan, O.P., second Bishop of Nashville, in May, 1863, resigned his miter and retired to a Dominican monastery in Ohio.

The most commanding Catholic figure of the day, John Hughes, Archbishop of New York, had wavered back and forth in his views on slavery, but once the shooting began he was thoroughly Unionist in sympathy, so much so, in fact, that in October, 1861, he was commissioned by Lincoln and Secretary of State William H. Seward to go to France in the hope that he might persuade Napoleon III to preserve neutrality. Hughes spent the better part of a year in Europe, where he was at pains to explain the issues at stake in the American conflict and to emphasize the righteousness of the northern cause. Early in June, 1862, Alexander W. Randall, American Minister to the Papal States, had an audience of Pope Pius IX in which the American diplomat paid tribute to the good accomplished by Hughes during the latter's lengthy visit to the Eternal City. In reporting the substance of the audience to Secretary Seward, Randall stated that he had told the pope of the important assistance rendered to the American government by the archbishop, and that he had remarked to Pius IX, "It is a source of regret, to thousands of good men, that the Government of the United States cannot, in any appropriate way, testify its appreciation of such services."[22] Not to be outdone by the North, the Confederate government later commissioned Patrick N. Lynch, Bishop of Charleston, to act in a similar capacity. Lynch sailed in the spring of 1864, but he was received in Rome solely as a bishop of the Church, and the desired diplomatic recognition of the Confederacy was not forthcoming.

Two months before the departure of Archbishop Hughes for Europe in October, 1861, he had an exchange of correspondence with Bishop Lynch on the subject of the causes for the war. Each prelate stoutly defended the action of his own section, Lynch contending that the election of Lincoln was a triumph for the Black Republicans who were determined to subjugate the South and insisting that the North should recognize the independence of the seceded states. Hughes, on the other hand, maintained that Lincoln's election had been caused by the disunity of the Democrats. He opined that, since the Constitution had been framed by the consent of all the states, no state had a right to secede except "in the manner provided for in the document itself."[23] Fundamentally at odds as the two bishops were on secession, they yet managed to keep their differences on a high level. The correspondence was later released to the press and was reprinted in practically all the leading New York papers with accompanying editorials. The *New York Herald* of September 4 had words of praise for the "statesmanlike views and admirable temper" of the correspondence, which, it was suggested, would receive "a widespread and attentive consideration both here and abroad." The dignified dispute was contrasted favorably with the conduct of certain Protestant ministers like Henry Ward Beecher and others who, said the editors, were dishonoring the pulpit by their fanatical outbursts about the war.

More than forty priests saw service as chaplains with the Union armies, and about thirty with the Confederate forces. James Parton, the famous biographer and himself a non-Catholic, stated three years after the war that a distinguished Protestant general, who had served in important commands during the entire conflict, had told him that the only chaplains who "*as a class*, were of such utility in the field," were the Catholic priests, which the general had attributed to the fact that they alone were accountable to ecclesiastical superiors.[24] Besides the regular chaplains, a number of priests without official status attended the troops. James Gibbons, the future cardinal, then a pastor in Baltimore, was one, and another was Abram Ryan, who not only braved the smallpox in Gratiot Prison in New Orleans when no other minister would accept the assignment but who gave spirit to the Confederacy both during and after the war by the poems and lyrics with which he commemorated the South's great struggle.

On the other hand, Ryan's fellow priest and fellow southerner, Adrien-Emmanuel Rouquette of Louisiana, remained unalterably opposed to the Confederacy. "Secession is rebellion," said Rouquette, "and armed rebellion is treason. The Seceded states are in war with the United States; they have, thereby, forfeited all their constitutional rights, and should be dealt with as enemies."[25] In Cincinnati Father Edward Purcell, editor of the *Catholic Telegraph*, who from the outset had backed the Lincoln administration—as had his brother, the Archbishop of Cincinnati—came out strongly for emancipation of the slaves and thereby alienated a number of Catholics of that borderline region. In a *Telegraph* editorial of April 8, 1863, three months after Lincoln's proclamation had freed the slaves, Purcell scored those among his fellow Catholics who were still opposed to emancipation, declared the door to freedom had now been thrown open to the slaves, and scorned those Catholics who wished to be "jailors of their fellowmen." They might go on trying to lock and bolt the prison, said Purcell, but "we take no part in any such proceeding."[26] Meanwhile Orestes Brownson, by this time a convert to Catholicism for nearly twenty years, silenced his criticism of Lincoln and the Republican Party. His *Quarterly Review* scolded high prelates and Catholic editors whose loyalty to the Union, he thought, left much to be desired. If, then, the student of American religious history were seeking to disprove what was once a widespread belief, that all Catholics think alike, he could hardly do better than to choose the Civil War as ground whereon to rest his case.

The Church in no way escaped the strain of a war that told so heavily on the personnel and resources of every institution in the land. Many of the schools in both sections were stripped of teachers when nearly 800 sisters went off as volunteer nurses to attend the wounded in hospitals, a self-sacrificing service which earned from President Lincoln, who met them at Stanton Hospital in Washington, the comment, "Of all the forms of charity and benevolence seen in the crowded wards of the hospitals, those of some Catholic Sisters were among the most efficient."[27] In the South the armies caused grave damages to property in towns like Beaufort, South Carolina, Winchester, Virginia, and Dalton, Georgia, where they either used the local churches for military storehouses or burned them to the ground. After a trip through his archdiocese in the last months of the war, Archbishop Jean Marie Odin of New Orleans told Archbishop Spalding of Baltimore, "Mourning is spread over every family, poverty extreme has replaced the ease and comfort of former days, [and] the crops will be almost an entire failure, as many of the servants, horses and mules have been taken from the inhabitants."[28]

In Mississippi Bishop Elder had a particularly hard time of it. Arbitrary Union officers interfered with his administration of

Civil War and Immigration

the Diocese of Natchez, going so far in July, 1864, as to expel the bishop from his see city and send him to Vidalia for a period of nearly three weeks because he had refused to allow the local commander to dictate the prayers said in the churches for the civil officials. Catholicism had always been weak in numbers and wealth in the southern states, and its poverty was, of course, greatly aggravated by the war. One gets a vivid impression of the universal havoc in the reports which the southern bishops made to the European missionary societies in these years, a source, incidentally, which has yet to be fully exploited by historians. For example, in June, 1867, Bishop Lynch gave an account of the Diocese of Charleston which pictured the ruin on all sides, and he remarked that his diocese then contained 750,000 emancipated Negroes of whom at most 20,000 were Catholics.[29]

What, in fact, was accomplished by the Church for the emancipated slaves? If one thinks in terms of the nearly 4,000,-000 Negroes involved, relatively little. Catholics had, indeed, preserved their organizational unity throughout the crisis more than any other religious body, a fact which was given striking proof when forty-five bishops from every section of the country met in Baltimore for the Second Plenary Council in October, 1866, a year and a half after Appomattox. Facing the problem squarely, the council decreed that every means be implemented for the religious care and instruction of Negroes. Anyone neglecting to provide these means for all, black and white, would, said the bishops, "merit the strongest reproach."[30] But it was far easier to exhort than to win effective action, as the Archbishop of New Orleans learned when he returned from the council. His appeal to the religious orders within his jurisdiction to open schools for Negroes went unanswered for months. So intense was southern feeling against educating the Negroes that the religious orders, some of whose members as southerners shared the sentiment, shied away from the task for fear of alienating white patronage. Finally in 1868, the Religious of the Sacred Heart agreed to open a school for Negroes at St. Michael, Louisiana. Resistance was still evident as late as 1889, when the Sisters of Divine Providence from San Antonio encountered trouble at Cloutierville, Louisiana, in starting a school for mulattoes and Negroes in St. John the Baptist Parish. A feud between the two groups forced out the Negroes in spite of the pleas of the sisters and of Bishop Antoine Durier of Natchitoches, who had asked them to undertake the work.[31] Similar instances could be cited in almost every diocese of the South.

Thus through a combination of racial prejudice, timidity, and scarcity of manpower and resources, the chance for large-scale conversion of the Negroes to Catholicism after the Civil War gradually slipped away. The situation vindicated the uneasiness expressed by Archbishop Spalding a year before the Second Plenary Council when he told the Archbishop of New York, "It is a golden opportunity for reaping a harvest of souls which neglected may not return."[32] And yet it would be a mistake to infer that the Church had done nothing in this regard. After the Civil War the southern bishops tried again and again by appeals for workers and funds to render the apostolate to the colored people effective, but their extreme poverty crippled most of the plans they set on foot. Meanwhile religious communities for colored women, such as the Oblate Sisters of Providence, founded in 1829, were multiplied and strengthened. Moreover, an increasing number of churches and schools were given over to Negroes. Groups like the Mill Hill

Civil War and Immigration

Fathers, introduced to Baltimore from England in 1871, devoted themselves exclusively to the Negro apostolate. But the startling increase in Catholic immigration in the closing decades of the century so dwarfed all other problems with which the Church had to cope that the conciliar legislation and high goal of 1866 were never carried out in force. The result may in part be measured by the fact that as of January 1, 1968, there were only 808,332 colored Catholics in the United States out of a Negro population of approximately 22,000,000.[33]

The question of American Catholicism and the Negro, like every other question relating to the Church in these years, can be properly understood only in the light of the spiraling Catholic immigration. If the Church after 1820 was looked upon as the Church of the immigrant, that characteristic became even more pronounced as the century grew old. In fact, for no national institution was the so-called "New Immigration" from southern and eastern Europe more a living reality. Thousands of Italians, Hungarians, Poles, and Lithuanians—to say nothing of additional thousands from Germany and Ireland—poured into the United States after the Civil War, and it should occasion no surprise that these varied national groups at times came into conflict with each other and brought on periodic crises within the American Catholic community.[34] Because of their religious faith these newcomers became the direct responsibility of the Church, a responsibility that taxed every bit of manpower and money in the parishes. These were the years—roughly from 1870 to 1900—which fixed the American Catholic pattern as predominantly an urban one with the immigration settling for the most part in the large industrial centers. Whereas many Protestant churches were abandoned in the old and crowded neighborhoods of the great cities, the

Catholic Church held on there and, as Arthur M. Schlesinger has said, "reared its edifices where humanity was densest, and thronged its pews three or four times each Sunday with worshippers whose hands and clothing plainly betrayed their humble station."[35]

Catholics felt no compunction that their Church should be thought of as the Church of the workingman, but their ingenuity was often stretched to the breaking point to provide the proper facilities and priests who could speak the many foreign tongues that the rough immigrant flocks demanded. They were hard put to furnish a guiding hand in American ways for those who, in the words of the ancient prophet, came as "the multitude of many people . . . the tumult of crowds, like the noise of many waters."[36] Earlier in the century churchmen had hesitated about how to handle the problem, but the experience of their predecessors made the bishops of the 1880's and 1890's surer of their footing. In their minds they were accountable before God for the religious training of both the native and immigrant Catholic children. They knew that earlier bishops had tried to reach an understanding with the public school system and had failed. If they would still their conscience, therefore, there was but one recourse left to them, regardless of what other Americans might think of the parochial school. That was to make the parochial school almost mandatory upon their priests and people, and this they did for the first time in the Third Plenary Council of Baltimore in 1884 with the result that by 1900 the number of such schools had been increased to nearly 4,000.

In addition to the parochial schools, the Church stepped up the establishment of parishes for the various nationalities and multiplied and widened the scope of its general agencies of charity. It founded hospitals, orphanages, and homes for the elderly where the infirm, orphaned, and aged immigrant found a friendly welcome in the religious atmosphere he had known from his earliest years. These institutions, as has been said, served the dual purpose of preserving the faith of the immigrant and of adjusting him to American ways. In that connection Henry Steele Commager, speaking of the years after 1880, remarked:

It might, indeed, be maintained that the Catholic church was, during this period, one of the most effective of all agencies for democracy and Americanization. Representing as it did a vast cross section of the American people, it could ignore class, section, and race; peculiarly the church of the newcomer, of those who all too often were regarded as aliens, it could give them not only spiritual refuge but social security.[37]

If, therefore, one does not find Catholics active in the social gospel movement that so deeply stirred American Protestants in these years, it was due in great measure to the fact that through voluntary offerings they were preoccupied in erecting an ever increasing network of enterprises that by 1900 totaled 827 institutions of private charity, to say nothing of the person-to-person efforts channeled through local groups like the Society of St. Vincent de Paul in the more than 6,400 parishes of the land.

The Church's efforts in behalf of training and adjustment for the foreign-born were not carried out without pitfalls and anxieties. As the bishops watched the increasing number and influence of the secret societies with which the country became honeycombed in the late century, and as they saw the spread of Marxian socialism in Europe and in this country, their uneasiness deepened for the religious faith of those committed to their care. The Freemasons had, of course, been repeatedly condemned by the Holy See since the early eighteenth century, and certain other and newer secret societies had likewise fallen under the Church's ban. The American hierarchy in the 1880's was particularly disturbed by those societies which appealed to workingmen, so many of whom were Catholics. And yet they indulged in no wholesale condemnations, for as early as the Second Plenary Council of October, 1866, the bishops had stated that they saw no reason why the Church's prohibition against certain societies should be extended "to those associations of workmen which evidently have no other purpose than mutual help and protection in exercising their trade."[38]

The most famous case of the Church and a suspect American society involved the Knights of Labor, the first major American labor organization. In its early years as a highly secret society, it had aroused the suspicion of a number of bishops who wished to have it condemned. Fortunately, the counsels of these prelates did not prevail, for at the head of the hierarchy at that moment there stood probably the greatest single figure the Church in the United States has produced, James Cardinal Gibbons. It was the foresight and wisdom of Gibbons, expressed in a remarkable document which he submitted to the Holy See in February, 1887, that convinced the Roman officials that it would be a fatal mistake to condemn the Knights of Labor, who were, as the cardinal said, merely seeking redress of just grievances from capitalists whose power and wealth had subjected them to abuses which only their united strength could remedy. Having previously been shown the constitution and bylaws by Terence V. Powderly, the Grand Master Workman, Gibbons knew whereof he spoke when he insisted that the Knights were in no way inimical to the interests of either Church or State. He contrasted the alienation of the masses from religion in other countries with the respect which it enjoyed among American workingmen, among whom, he remarked, there existed "not a democracy of license and violence, but that true democracy which aims at the general prosperity through the means of sound principles and good social order."[39] The cardinal emphasized the numerous proletarians who composed so large a part of the American Church and what such a condemnation would mean to them. There was no doubt about where he thought the Church's sympathies should lie, for he told Giovanni Cardinal Simeoni, Prefect of the Congregation de Propaganda Fide, "To lose the heart of the people would be a misfortune for which the friendship of the few rich and powerful would be no compensation."[40]

Here was the social gospel proclaimed in a new way, yet in a way that Washington Gladden and Walter Rauschenbusch would approve. And during the same visit to Rome, Cardinal Gibbons performed a similar service when he convinced the Holy Office that it would be futile to issue a public condemnation of Henry George's *Progress and Poverty*, a step which some American bishops had urged in their belief that George's teaching would undermine the right of private property. In all of this, Gibbons met vigorous opposition from some of his fellow bishops of a more conservative bent of mind, prelates who had as their titular leader Archbishop Michael A. Corrigan of New York. But he also had staunch friends in the hierarchy, men whose views on social questions were very much his own, and among these associates John Ireland, the forceful Archbishop of St. Paul, John J. Keane, first Rector of the Catholic University of America, and John Lancaster Spalding, Bishop of Peoria, were pre-eminent. These men felt a certain vindication when Pope Leo XIII in May, 1891, issued his encyclical *Rerum novarum* on the relations of capital and labor and gave his high sanction to the broad and enlightened principles for which these Americans had been contending. At the same time Corrigan and his followers found satisfaction in the encyclical's defense of private property.

In March, 1925, when he received Monsignor Joseph Cardijn of Belgium, Pope Pius XI lamented that the loss of the working classes of Europe had been the Church's principal tragedy in the nineteenth century. It was a calamity that never befell the Church in the United States, where in a certain sense there were even greater reasons for defection among the multitude of foreign-born. That tragedy was averted in the critical years of the century by men like Gibbons who were convinced that the workman should find a friend in the Church. A bond was then forged between the Catholic clergy and laity which repeated attempts of certain recent enemies of the Church have failed to break. Now that the American Church has become rich and powerful, the rank and file of Catholic men in the labor unions still feel spiritually at home within its portals.

It was to be expected that this rising success, increasingly apparent after 1880, would draw down upon the Church the ire of its enemies. The allegiance which American Catholics owed to the Holy See, the teaching of theologians on relations of Church and State, the insistence of American bishops on the necessity for religious education and the failure of the public schools to supply that need, and the protests of Catholic leaders against the mounting divorce rate and unnatural methods of birth control—all these beliefs and attitudes of Catholics, when added to their growing numbers and strength, made them appear to critical eyes as a menacing element which it behooved the Republic to halt. The new wave of bigotry crystalized in the American Protective Association founded at Clinton, Iowa, in March, 1887, by Henry F. Bowers and six associates, and for the next decade every corner of America rang with cries of warning against the Church of Rome. Religious hatred was rampant in the rural areas of the Middle West, where the Catholics had always been relatively few in number. What a writer in a Catholic journal had noted thirty years before was still true, namely, that people of an agricultural civilization were far more tenacious of their views and less liable to be acted upon by progressive ideas. "It is still the stronghold of anti-Catholic feeling," he said, "and that feeling would soon die out in the cities but for the periodical supply of country lawyers and ministers furnished to the cities."[41] The customary quota of ex-priests, whether real or bogus, and the so-called "escaped" nuns appeared to tour the land, and the old and familiar charges of Know-Nothing days now enjoyed a second spring. True, certain new elements entered each successive wave of bigotry, and the growing strength and numbers of Catholics and their increasing prominence in business and government offered to the A.P.A. campaign a seeming plausibility that predecessors had lacked. Analyzing these recurring outbursts of anti-Catholic sentiment, the historian is prompted to the conclusion of the old French axiom, *plus ça change, plus c'est la même chose!*

Catholics were not, therefore, particularly shocked at the mass support accorded to the purveyors of biased attacks against their Church, and they were gratified by the uncompromising opposition to the A.P.A. of such American Protestants as Theodore Roosevelt, the Reverend Washington Gladden, and Senator George F. Hoar of Massachusetts. Nevertheless, they were discouraged by the sentiments of some highly placed men whose patronage of movements like the A.P.A. helped to keep bigotry alive. Where, for example, could one find a better educated or more widely honored American of that generation than George Bancroft? And yet some years before the rise of the A.P.A., in a comment on what he called the "Roman clerical party," Bancroft told his friend the Reverend Samuel Osgood: "No band of conspirators was ever more closely welded together. The one will of the Pope rules the creed, the politics, the conduct of all. The selfsame malign influence is at work in Spain, in France . . . and in Austria. Nay it extends to England . . . and the United States."[42] If the American Minister to Berlin, and the man who was regarded by many as the greatest living historian of the United States, could honestly believe that the pope ruled the politics and conduct of Catholics throughout the world, it was easy to see how the errant nonsense of the A.P.A. persuaded many.

Of all the controversial issues stirred up between Catholic and non-Catholic Americans in the days of the A.P.A., that concerning the schools was probably the most bitter. It was—and it remains—a fundamental axiom of Catholic teaching that the child should be instructed in religion from his earliest years. It was true, as the Church's enemies declared, that Catholics felt entitled to financial aid from the state for their schools since they looked upon the double taxation for their own and the public schools as unjust. The efforts that Catholic leaders made to explain their position, such as the papers of Cardinal Gibbons and Bishop Keane, Rector of the Catholic University of America, read at the convention of the National Education Association at Nashville in July, 1889, in no way stilled the clamor. The chief emphasis of the two prelates was placed upon the necessity for religious training of the young. They had no quarrel, as they said, with the public schools, but they asked that room be made in their curricula for the teaching of religion. When in the following summer the N.E.A. invited John Ireland, Archbishop of St. Paul, to address the convention in his see city, he made clear from the outset that the desirability of public schools was beyond discussion. Admitting the differences between the public and parochial schools, he offered the following compromise proposal:

> I would permeate the regular state school with the religion of the majority of the children of the land, be this religion as Protestant as Protestantism can be, and I would, as is done in England, pay for the secular instruction given in denominational schools according to results . . . . This is not paying for religious instruction, but for the secular instruction demanded by the State, and given to the pupil as thoroughly as he could have received it in the state school.[43]

It was a sincere attempt to bridge the gap between the two school systems, and, true to his word, Ireland set in operation a plan of renting out several of his parochial schools to local school boards for $1.00 a year. But between the opposition which he encountered within the Church from conservative fellow bishops, who maintained that he was endangering the character of the religious schools, and the attacks of those outside the Church, who contended that he was entering a wedge whereby the Catholics would try to absorb the public schools, the Minnesota experiment was brought to a speedy and inglorious end, although in other areas of the country it worked to the satisfaction of most of those concerned.[44]

There had never been a real chance for Ireland's compromise of 1890 to be adopted on a national scale: the positions of the adversaries were utterly contradictory. The Catholic demand for religion in the public schools appeared to most Americans as the stratagem of a minority to foist its views on a majority content with matters as they stood. To this majority, the periodic demands of Catholics for state aid for their own schools seemed even more objectionable. Until the 1930's the demand for state aid had been spasmodic; most Catholics took the position that financial assistance from the state would create more problems than it would solve. During the last generation, however, the previous irregular character of these demands has given way to a more or less fixed policy.[45] In all that related to their schools thoughtful Catholics recognized the complications which their demands involved and they appreciated, too, the sincerity with which many outside the Church opposed their views. But what they found difficult to understand, and still do, is why so many non-Catholic Americans refused a solution along the lines of that reached in 1918 in so thoroughly Protestant a country as Scotland. The British education act of that year provided for the Local Educational Authority, the equivalent of the American school board, to appoint the teachers in Catholic schools after the Church had been given a chance to pass on the candidate's religious qualifications. In return, the Catholic schools were transferred to the L.E.A. and became a part of the general state system, thus freeing the Scottish Catholics of the unusual financial burden which they had previously borne.[46] It is a curious fact that the most equitable and mutually satisfactory arrangements between the state and Catholic schools are to be found in Scotland and the Netherlands, two countries with as strong, if not stronger, Protestant traditions than the United States. Why, then, Catholics asked, should it be thought impossible to effect a similar arrangement in this country without endangering the integrity of the public schools or the religious character of Catholic schools?

A new factor has brought a sobering second thought to many Americans on this critical problem. It is the alarming increase of juvenile delinquency, which threatens to become a national menace. In the light of this situation, men who a generation or two ago were more or less indifferent to the question of religious education now have come to believe that some kind of moral training is imperative for the young. This change of attitude has been reflected in various ways. It has shown itself, for example, in the widespread discussion within national educational bodies of the place of religion in the schools, in the increased emphasis among some denominational groups, like the Lutherans and Episcopalians, upon the need for their own schools, and in the plans of President Pusey of Harvard for the expansion of the Divinity School. The Supreme Court decision of April, 1952, in the case of released time in the schools of New York State was more sympathetic to religion than the decision in *McCollum* v. *Board of Education* four years before. The McCollum decision barred all religious instruction within public school buildings, but the New York decision sanctioned the release of students at a stated time each week that they might receive religious instruction elsewhere. Nor has the situation failed to bring a change within Catholic circles as well. In the years after the Third Plenary Council parents gradually came to look on the parochial schools as an accepted American Catholic tradition, and the mounting tide of juvenile delinquency since World War II has served to place a higher premium on the religious school than ever before in the minds of Catholic parents. Where bishops and priests once struggled to convince their own people of the necessity of parochial schools, many of the laity are found urging the clergy to multiply and enlarge the parish schools. It is possible, therefore, that in time necessity may once more prove to be the mother of invention, and that from a public opinion aroused to the indispensability of religious training for the young there may evolve a solution to a problem that has baffled generations of Americans of all religious beliefs.

A further point touching upon the intellectual life of American Catholics has to do with the meager contributions made by them to American thought and culture in the last half of the century. What, in brief, were the causes for this so-called cultural lag? First, the Church was so absorbed in providing religious training and elementary education for the stream of immigrants which never seemed to slacken that it found neither the means nor the leisure to foster literature and the arts in more than a perfunctory way. An ancient intellectual tradition it did, indeed, possess, far richer and of more enduring value than many a literary and philosophical fad that then passed across the American scene. But to the intellectual elite of the period, captivated by the dawn of realism in literature and by the exciting prospects of Darwin's theories of evolution and the higher criticism of the Scriptures, Catholic efforts such as Leo XIII's attempt in the encyclical *Aeterni patris* of August, 1879, to revive the study of scholastic philosophy seemed sadly out of date when it was implemented in such centers as the Catholic University of America in the 1890's.

The whole temper of American life was, in fact, clearly opposed to many of the fundamentals of Catholic thought. James Parton, the most successful biographer of his generation, found this out when he published a sympathetic article on the American Catholics in the *Atlantic Monthly* in the spring of

1868. Parton felt that there was a serious need for training leaders who showed a special aptitude for discerning what was right so that they might, in turn, inform the general conscience of the nation. In this he believed that the United States had much to learn from the Church with a wisdom based on the experience of centuries. He said: "If the same office is still to be performed for mankind, I think the organization that performs it will have to study deeply and long the Roman Catholic Church, and borrow from it nearly every leading device of its system, especially these three—celibacy, consecration for life, and special orders for special work."[47] The views of this reputable non-Catholic writer were greeted with scorn by most of those who troubled to notice them at all. To men immersed in the philosophy of pragmatism and liberalism which gave birth to the Gilded Age, the *Syllabus of Errors* of Pius IX was a scandal only a little less shocking than the definition of papal infallibility by the Vatican Council in 1870, a gathering attended by forty-nine prelates from the United States. An age that prided itself on its freedom from dictation of any kind thus viewed the Church, holding tenaciously to the principle of authority in dogma and morals, as a threat to modern progress. Most Americans would have echoed George Bancroft when he said of Catholicism and the Jesuits a year after the Vatican Council: "To carry out this system civilisation must go back; the beams of the state must decay from dry rot; and the eyes of the people must be put out. I adhere to the protestant doctrine, the great teachings of Luther, that every man is his own priest; and this is but the statement in respect of religion of the principle which divides ancient civilisation from modern. . . ."[48]

In an intellectual climate like that, it would have been futile for Catholics to expect their ideas to win a widespread hearing, even if expressed by original thinkers. A generation before, Robert Walsh, a Philadelphia Catholic who lived until 1859, had established a national reputation with the first quarterly in the United States, the *American Review of History and Politics*, begun in 1811. His reputation was enhanced by a later journal, the *American Quarterly Review*, one of the best publications of its kind in the country during the 1830's. Actually, however, there were conspicuously few first-class Catholic writers at the mid-century, and even the principal work of the most famous among them, Brownson's *American Republic*, was neglected by Catholics and non-Catholics alike until recent students of American government began to appreciate its worth. Meanwhile another convert, Father Isaac Hecker, began in April, 1865, the *Catholic World*, which developed into an able monthly journal; then in 1876 two learned priests, James A. Corcoran and Herman J. Heuser, launched the *American Catholic Quarterly Review*, which continued till 1924 to publish creditable articles and reviews. Poets John Boyle O'Reilly and Father Abram Ryan wrote verse of a high quality, and Catholic artists, John LaFarge and George P. A. Healy, were commended, the former for masterpieces like the murals and stained glass windows of Trinity Church, Boston, and the latter for his excellent portraits of famous men on both sides of the Atlantic. Patrick C. Keeley, the architect, designed more than a hundred churches in the United States, most of them in the neo-Gothic style prevalent at the time.

Generally speaking, however, superior attainments of American Catholics in the realm of culture were rare. Nor was Catholic leadership in education any more distinguished. The absence of a viable intellectual tradition at once Catholic and

American, the lack of any serious cultivation and patronage of the intellectual vocation, the absorption of the overwhelming majority of Catholics of the middle and lower classes in making a living, and the well-nigh universal unfriendliness to Catholic ideas among the general population—all these combined to make it uncommonly difficult for the few who sought to lift the level of Catholic thought. The most articulate contemporary voice in Catholic education was that of Bishop Spalding of Peoria. In numerous thoughtful essays and lectures he revealed himself as fully abreast of the time, and he showed, too, how intent he was that his coreligionists should break the isolation that surrounded them and meet the challenge of the age. To Spalding the Catholics were like men in a besieged fortress who talked largely to each other in accents that the world around them seldom heard.[49] But the ideas of the Bishop of Peoria were at the time by no means common in Catholic circles, and even Bernard J. McQuaid, Bishop of Rochester, a far from benighted prelate, was opposed to this policy of going out, as it were, to meet the world in which Catholics lived. In 1890 he prevented Bishop Keane, Rector of the Catholic University of America, whose ideas along these lines he did not approve, from addressing the Catholic students enrolled at Cornell University in his diocese.[50]

Dissatisfaction with the poor showing made by Catholics in national leadership and intellectual life had been voiced at an early date. In a commencement address at Mount Saint Mary's College, Emmitsburg, Maryland, in June, 1853, Brownson had deplored the national ethos which, he said, made an aristocracy out of "bankers, sharpers, brokers, stock-jobbers ... and in general worshippers of mammon."[51] Four years later an anonymous writer, who urged upon his fellow Catholics a policy of identification with their countrymen rather than isolation, was puzzled by the failure of the graduates of Catholic colleges to make a name for themselves. He asked: "Why do we not hear from them after the 'happy commencement day' has passed? Why is it, that from the obscurity, into which so many gifted and accomplished young men, fresh from the collegiate course, sink, that many practical men have been confirmed in their doubts of the expediency and sufficiency of classical and scholastic learning?"[52] There could be no question that the supreme American desire to make a fortune had captivated many of the Catholics along with their countrymen of other faiths and that this emphasis had caused them to undervalue intellectual pursuits. But Bishop Spalding, for one, was not content to let the matter rest there. For years he conducted an almost solitary crusade for an American Catholic university for graduate study in theology and other disciplines, and when he preached his famous sermon on the subject at the Third Plenary Council of Baltimore in November, 1884, he said: "When our zeal for intellectual excellence shall have raised up men who will take place among the first writers and thinkers of their day their very presence will become the most persuasive of arguments to teach the world that no best gift is at war with the spirit of Catholic faith. . . ."[53]

It was due largely to Spalding's persistence, intelligence, and resourcefulness that the Catholic University of America opened at Washington in November, 1889, and became in the years thereafter the center of much that was best in Catholic thought and scholarship.[54] In that major undertaking the Bishop of Peoria had the warm support of men like Gibbons, Keane, and Ireland once they were convinced that it could be done. Archbishop Ireland needed little urging, for as he said in his sermon at the centennial of the American hierarchy a few days before the university opened: "This is an intellectual age. . . . Catholics must excel in religious knowledge. . . . They must be in the foreground of intellectual movements of all kinds. The age will not take kindly to religious knowledge separated from secular knowledge."[55]

Thus as the century drew to a close, these bishops continued to do all within their power to heighten the intellectual tone of Catholic life and to encourage in every possible way a friendlier understanding with Americans of other religious faiths. In the former endeavor they never attained the success which their efforts deserved, and the failure of American Catholics to achieve distinction in the world of scholarship and learning still remains the most striking weakness of what is otherwise, perhaps, the strongest branch of the universal Church. No well-informed Catholic will, therefore, seriously quarrel with the judgment expressed by Professor D. W. Brogan, of Cambridge University, when he stated: ". . . In no Western society is the intellectual prestige of Catholicism lower than in the country where, in such respects as wealth, numbers, and strength of organization, it is so powerful."[56]

The general progress of American Catholicism by the end of the nineteenth century, however, was undeniable; as Catholics in France and less favored countries beheld the strides made by the more than 12,000,000 Catholics of the United States, a number of their progressive thinkers sought to imitate the American pattern. Foreign observers overlooked the absence of Catholics from key positions of leadership and influence, impressed instead by numerical growth, increasing prosperity, and complete freedom which Catholics enjoyed in America. To many French Catholics, especially harassed by the anti-clerical laws of the Third Republic, the American Church appeared a worthy object for emulation. But there were powerful conservative forces within the French Church that frowned upon what they regarded as American departures from traditional Catholic mores, men who saw, for example, in Father Hecker's methods of winning converts by emphasizing partial agreement rather than disagreement with Protestants a watering down of Catholic doctrine. Some Catholics in the United States felt that such things as the participation of Catholic churchmen in the World Parliament of Religions at Chicago in 1893, the broad approach of men like Gibbons, Ireland, and Keane to the problem of secret societies, and the efforts of Archbishop Ireland to find a compromise between the public and parochial schools fostered liberal tendencies which would imperil the integrity of the Catholic faith.[57] At the head of these Americans stood Archbishop Corrigan of New York, who found support from fellow members of the hierarchy, particularly among those of German descent.

As a result of these differences, what Bishop Keane characterized as "the war of ideas" grew more intense, and when a careless French translation of Walter Elliott's *Life of Father Hecker* appeared in 1897, it proved the occasion for an angry outburst that filled the columns of Catholic journals in the Old World and the New for several years. The controversy over what some termed the heresy of "Americanism" became so heated that finally Leo XIII appointed a commission of cardinals to study the entire question and report to him. The result was the papal letter *Testem benevolentiae* of January 22, 1899, addressed to Cardinal Gibbons wherein the pontiff summarized certain false doctrines which, as he was careful to say, were imputed to some within the American Church through the translation of a book in a foreign tongue. The errors amounted to this: that the Church should adapt itself to modern civilization, relax its ancient rigor, show indulgence to modern theories and methods, de-emphasize religious vows, and give greater scope for the action of the Holy Spirit on the individual soul. These tendencies, said the pope, would restrict the Church's right to determine questions of a doctrinal and moral nature, and if this was what was meant by Americanism, then it stood condemned. But Leo XIII was at pains to distinguish, for he said: "If, indeed, by that name be designated the characteristic qualities which reflect honor on the people of America, just as other nations have what is special to them; or if it implies the condition of your commonwealths, or the laws and customs which prevail in them, there is surely no reason why We should deem that it ought to be discarded."[58]

With the publication of *Testem benevolentiae* each side maintained that it had been vindicated. More conservative prelates like those of the Provinces of New York and Milwaukee thanked the Holy Father for saving the American Church from the danger of heresy, while their liberal colleagues agreed with Cardinal Gibbons when he told Leo XIII: "This doctrine, which I deliberately call extravagant and absurd, this Americanism as it is called, has nothing in common with the views, aspirations, doctrine and conduct of Americans."[59] From the perspective of over a half century it is evident that the sometimes careless expressions in the writings and speeches of men like Hecker, Keane, and Ireland were not heresy in the theological sense. Not a single American Catholic was known to have left the Church because he refused to give up the errors which the pope had reproved, even if several American priests took their departure a decade or so later as a result of the Modernist movement with which some associated Americanism.

Three years later Leo XIII celebrated the silver jubilee of his pontificate, and in response to a letter of congratulations from the American hierarchy he sent an extended reply. Poignantly conscious as he was of the trials through which the Church was then passing in France and other countries, the pope made it clear that, far from suspecting the Americanism of Catholics in the United States, he found conditions there a source of consolation. On that occasion he said: "Our daily experience obliges Us to confess that We have found your people, through your influence, endowed with perfect docility of mind and alacrity of disposition. Therefore, while the changes and tendencies of nearly all the nations which were Catholic for centuries give cause for sorrow, the state of your churches, in their flourishing youthfulness, cheers Our heart and fills it with delight."[60]

We have brought the story of American Catholicism to the opening of the twentieth century. The years between 1852 and 1900 were a period when the growing pains of the Church in the United States seemed at times that they might prove fatal: the immigrant flood, the lack of American Catholic intellectual achievement, and the bigotry of groups like the A.P.A. seemingly represented differences between Catholic belief and the dominant national mores that would forever stamp the Church as an institution alien to America. And yet the unity of no American religious body better withstood the strain of the Civil War, nor did any other group display more generosity in its service. If at times there was an excessive amount of protest of patriotism from Catholics, and there is little doubt of it, it was not because they felt any less at home in the

Civil War and Immigration

United States, but because their enemies so consistently emphasized a "Catholic threat" to the Republic, that they were constrained to assert their loyalty in defense. Meanwhile far from the public eye millions of Catholic Americans lived out their lives in a peaceful and law-abiding fashion, enriching the land with the products of their industry and toil. If Americans at the end of the nineteenth century justly gloried in the diversity and variety of their national heritage, it was a heritage that included the rich ceremony and liturgy, the flourishing institutions, and the deep religious faith of approximately one-sixth of the population enrolled in the ancient Church. These, too, were part of the American pattern. As the nation matured, children born to the rough and tumble crowd of Catholic immigrants were second to none in their true American character and spitrit.

IV

Maturing Catholicism in the United States, 1908–56

On June 29, 1908, Pope Pius X issued the apostolic constitution *Sapienti consilio*, which declared, among other things, that the Church in the United States had been removed from the jurisdiction of the Congregation de Propaganda Fide and had been placed on a basis of equality with such ancient churches as those of Italy, France, and Germany. In other words, America was no longer regarded by the Holy See as missionary territory. For that reason, and for others that will be mentioned, there is warrant for speaking of the period after 1900 as one in which the American Church came of age. In the present chapter nearly a half-century of Catholicism in this country will be reviewed under two broad headings: (1) what may be termed the factual history of those years which bears witness to the adulthood of the Church as an American institution; (2) an interpretation of certain more recent aspects of the relations of Church and State.

First, a word about the numerical increase of American Catholicism in the twentieth century. The best estimate we have of the Catholic population in 1900 fixed the number at

12,041,000,[1] whereas the *Official Catholic Directory* gave the number for 1956 as 33,574,017. In reckoning the number of its faithful, the Church counts all baptized persons, children as well as adults. It is generally agreed, however, by those who have made a scientific study of American Catholic population trends that the actual figures are far above those reported. For example, in May, 1944, two priests with special training for this kind of work published an article in which they concluded that the Catholic population for 1940 was much closer to 30,000,000 than the 23,000,000 reported for that year in the *Catholic Directory*.[2] The Catholic population of the United States in 1956 may, indeed, have been nearer to 40,000,000 than it was to the figure announced in that year.

To say this is by no means to convey the impression that the Church has not suffered serious losses. On the contrary, since 1836 when Bishop England sent his famous letter to the Society for the Propagation of the Faith with the startling guess that 3,750,000 Catholics had already been lost to the faith in the United States, few problems have been more widely discussed and controverted among Catholics themselves than that of the so-called "leakage." The principal areas of loss in the nineteenth century were the rural districts, especially in the South and West, in which many Catholics settled only to find that there were no churches or priests to serve them. Nor has the Church of the twentieth century succeeded in overtaking the slight impression made by the Catholic faith of an earlier day in the rural areas. True, the National Catholic Rural Life Conference organized in 1922 by Edwin V. O'Hara, the late Bishop of Kansas City, performed valuable service from the outset, and under the intelligent and energetic leadership of its first executive director, Monsignor Luigi G. Ligutti, and his successors, it has continued to strengthen the rural Church and to right the balance to some extent between the heavy concentration of Catholics in urban districts and their relatively few coreligionists in the countryside and the small towns. But over 80 per cent of the Catholics live in cities at the present time, a proportion 10 per cent higher than the urban part of the general population. As recently as 1953 there were 819, or about 26 per cent, of the counties of the United States that had no priest, 644 counties with no priest in the rural areas, and 73,000 small towns and hamlets where no priest lived.³ The conditions conducive to Catholic leakage in many rural sections of the country with few Catholics are, therefore, not greatly improved over those of the nineteenth century.

In our own century, however, the largest losses have been sustained in the region of the Church's greatest strength, namely, in the urban districts where parishes of 10,000 or more parishioners are not uncommon. The extent to which Catholics are concentrated in the large cities and their environs may be illustrated from the current figures for three ecclesiastical provinces in different parts of the country, three provinces which also offer an interesting illustration of the varied nationality groups of which the American Church is composed. For example, the Province of Chicago embraces the entire state of Illinois with its 55,947 square miles and comprises the Archdiocese of Chicago and the five suffragan Dioceses of Belleville, Joliet, Peoria, Rockford, and Springfield. In the Archdiocese of Chicago there are 2,343,000 Catholics, the largest jurisdiction in the country in point of numbers, although its area covers only 1,411 square miles in two counties. In the rest of the state there are only 976,099 Catholics in the five suffragan sees with a combined area of 54,536 square miles. In other words, the metropolitan see contains nearly three times the number of faithful as all of its five suffragan sees combined. Among the Chicago Catholics there is about as great a variety of national backgrounds as one will find anywhere in the country. For instance, there are at present fifty-six parishes in Chicago and its suburbs for those of Polish descent, a concentration which, it has been said, at one time helped to make Chicago the largest Polish city in the world outside Warsaw.

In the northeastern section of the country the Province of Boston includes the states of Massachusetts, Maine, New Hampshire, and Vermont with a total of 57,249 square miles of territory. In the 2,465 square miles covered by the Archdiocese of Boston there are 1,843,490 Catholics, whereas the six suffragan Dioceses of Burlington, Fall River, Manchester, Portland, Springfield, and Worcester—54,784 square miles in all—have a total of 1,689,691 Catholics. The urban-rural discrepancy in this case is less marked only because there are large industrial cities in Massachusetts outside of Boston. Within the Province of Boston the representation of nationalities is likewise highly mixed. There are many Armenian and Syrian Catholics, there are French Canadians throughout New England, and there are Portuguese in and around Fall River.

In the West the Province of Los Angeles takes in the southern halves of the states of California and Arizona, an area totaling 141,470 square miles. In the Archdiocese of Los Angeles, with but four counties and 9,508 square miles, there are 1,640,-167 Catholics, while the four suffragan Dioceses of Fresno, Monterey, San Diego, and Tucson, with almost 95 per cent of the territory of the province, have a combined total of only 1,185,587 Catholics. In this area one will find very few Catholics of Polish and French Canadian background, but one does find thousands of Mexicans and people of Mexican descent, as well as the increasing number of oriental Catholics.

Figures such as those given above for three widely separated sections of the country help to bring home the fact of how largely urban American Catholicism really is. As a consequence of conditions of this kind the limited number of priests often find scant opportunity to maintain personal contact with those who are inclined to drift away from their religious duties.[4] It is impossible to account with any degree of accuracy for the reasons why Catholics leave the Church. The impersonal character of the large city parish, the natural tendency of many people to shirk the obligations which religion imposes, the secularist spirit and alluring distractions of contemporary life, to say nothing of the current crisis of faith that has overtaken many Catholics—all play a part in the defection from the Church of numbers of its faithful. It is a phenomenon as old as the Church itself. There always has been—and there always will be—the type that cannot bear the burden, a type foreseen by St. Paul in the letter he wrote from his Roman prison about the year 67 to St. Timothy, wherein he sadly commented, "Demas has deserted me, loving this world, and has gone to Thessalonica."[5] One of the few scientific studies available on an area where the Catholics belong predominantly to the urban group concluded that the chief cause of leakage was marriage outside the law of the Church.[6] But whatever the reasons be, the fact remains that there have been substantial losses to Catholicism in the urban areas of the country.

Some Catholics have entered Protestant churches, of course, but one cannot take seriously the figure of 4,144,366 as published in the *Christian Herald* of April, 1954, for the previous decade. The fact that Will Oursler's poll used the figure of

Maturing Catholicism in the United States

181,000 to represent the Protestant ministers of the nation, whereas the statistical abstract showed 181,123 as the total for all American clergymen—including the more than 45,000 Catholic priests—was sufficient in itself to invalidate his conclusions. Moreover, in the ten years preceding 1954 there had been 1,071,897 converts to Catholicism in this country, a gain that made up for much of the Church's losses. In the final analysis, however, the exact extent of the leakage among American Catholics is known only to the recording angel, but there is no reason to question the conclusion reached by Shaughnessy, the best authority on the subject, when he stated, "There is no evidence to indicate that it is or ever has been abnormal. There is no evidence to indicate it is greater here than in other countries."[7]

A number of events relating to Catholicism and immigration in the present century merit at least a mention. Among them was the radical change that ensued for the Church with the passage by Congress in May, 1921, of the first of a series of immigration restriction laws which gradually closed off the greatest source of numerical increase among American Catholics. Simultaneously these laws made a direct contribution to the maturity of the Church in the sense that during the last generation its faithful has for the first time had an opportunity to become more or less stabilized. There was also the quarrel over control of church property and ecclesiastical jurisdiction which broke out among a group of Catholics of Polish birth and descent at the end of the last century. By 1907 these differences had developed into the only sizable and enduring schism in the history of American Catholicism, in what came to be called the Polish National Catholic Church, a body which today numbers around 250,000 communicants residing largely in New England, the Middle Atlantic States, Wisconsin, and Chicago, with its chief bishop located in Scranton, Pennsylvania.

At the close of the era of large-scale immigration, therefore, the Catholic Church in the United States found its racial and national strains the most varied of all the branches of the universal Church, while numerically it has since become the third largest body of Catholics in the world, exceeded only by those of Brazil and Italy. These were the years that witnessed a further influx of French Canadians into New England, a group which had begun immigrating in large numbers in the 1870's and which at the present time represents about as sharp a delineation along national lines as one will find among the Latin Rite Catholics of this country. Still another result of the late immigration was the appearance of Catholics of various Eastern Rites with their own liturgies, separate episcopal jurisdictions, and, in some cases, a married clergy. To accommodate these people the Ukrainian Greek Catholic Diocese of the United States was established in May, 1913, and in February, 1924, the Holy See erected the Greek Rite Diocese of Pittsburgh. By 1960, the representatives of about ten varieties of the Eastern Rite Catholics totaled approximately 800,-000. Finally, since World War II the most recent immigrant problem has been created for the Church by the entrance into this country of numerous Puerto Ricans, concentrated chiefly in New York and Chicago, for whose special care priests with a knowledge of the Spanish language have been assigned.

Among other signs of the Church having attained ecclesiastical adulthood since the turn of the century is its role in the field of foreign missions. In the century between 1822 and 1922,

Maturing Catholicism in the United States

Catholics in this country received immense assistance from missionary societies in France, Bavaria, and Austria, amounting in those hundred years to almost $8,000,000. Although the Society for the Propagation of the Faith had been set up in many American dioceses, and by the end of the nineteenth century Catholics here had become numerous and relatively well off, they had as yet done relatively little to repay these benefactions by way of help to less favored areas of the world. The American hierarchy were pointedly, if politely, reminded of this fact in 1889 on the occasion of their centennial. In a letter addressed to Cardinal Gibbons, Herbert Vaughan, the Bishop of Salford, England, who had already made a name for himself as a promoter of the missions, conveyed his congratulations to his American brothers, but he did not fail to ask: "Can you expect that the second century of your existence will be as blessed & magnificent in its religious history as your infancy has been, if you do not send forth your heroic missioners to bear the torch of faith into those dark regions which are now possessed by the enemy of man's salvation, & by over twelve hundred millions of pagans & unbelievers?"[8] Vaughan's call for American missionaries was not answered for many years, although the monetary contributions for the missions from American Catholics were steadily increased to the point where the annual sum passed $100,000 in 1904. It reached the million mark by 1919, and for some years now the American Church has been the chief contributor of funds to the international missions through organizations like the Society for the Propagation of the Faith.

But in the supply of personnel for the Church's far-flung commitments in mission lands the Americans were far more tardy. Fifty Marianists, several Franciscan friars, and a few

Sisters of Charity from this country were serving abroad before the end of the nineteenth century, but as late as 1906 the Americans in the foreign missions numbered less than a hundred. Not until 1909 was there opened at St. Mary's Mission House in Techny, Illinois, an American training school for this purpose. Two years later, however, the foundations were laid for the first distinctively American society for the Catholic foreign missions when Fathers James A. Walsh and Thomas F. Price secured the approbation of the hierarchy and in June, 1911, won the formal approval of the Holy See. Maryknoll, as it is familiarly known, got its start under humble circumstances at Hawthorne, New York, in January, 1912, but it grew slowly during World War I and by September, 1918, the first departure ceremony was held for the four pioneer priests who were leaving for China. During the last forty years the movement among American Catholics has flourished, and today Maryknoll alone numbers over 1,000 priests, about 1,400 sisters, and 100 or more brothers whose lives are devoted to this cause. Meanwhile other religious orders in the United States had entered actively upon the work, and by January, 1966, there was a total of 9,303 American priests, brothers, sisters, and lay missioners serving in Asia, Africa, Latin America, and the islands of the West Indies and the Pacific.

Two other indications of the maturing process within the American Church relate to the Catholic world in general. Beginning in 1881, a series of international eucharistic congresses, gatherings of Catholics who assemble for religious ceremonies and conferences honoring their belief in the presence of the Body and Blood of Christ in the Blessed Sacrament, had been held at intervals in various countries. But it was not until 1926 that American Catholics for the first time played host to thousands of their coreligionists from all over the world when the twenty-eighth International Eucharistic Congress was held in Chicago on June 20–24. The four-day sessions were broken up into twenty-two language groups which heard papers on different phases of devotion to the holy Eucharist and to the liturgical life of the Church. A gathering of this kind not only helped to impress upon the Catholics of this country a sense of international solidarity with their fellow Catholics of other lands, but it likewise gave to them, and to Americans generally, a better appreciation of the superior status that the American Church had by that time attained.

A similar fact may be noted in the increased American representation in the College of Cardinals and in the offices of the Roman Curia and the diplomatic service of the Holy See. Between 1875 and 1921, there was never more than one cardinal in this country, but since that date there have been as many as eight, a figure reached in May, 1967. The death of Cardinal Ritter on June 10 of that year meant that seven churchmen of the United States held this honor, a distinction, incidentally, which is often conferred as a compliment to an entire nation and its government, as well as to the Catholic faithful. Of late years a larger number of American priests have likewise been appointed to offices in the Roman congregations, and citizens of the United States have also served in the capacity of apostolic nuncios and apostolic delegates of the Holy See. The Apostolic Nuncios to Germany and Ireland and the Apostolic Delegates to Great Britain and South Africa have been citizens of the United States. Appointments of this kind clearly indicate the enhanced importance of Americans in the councils of the universal Church.

Among the symptoms of maturity in twentieth-century

American Catholicism

American Catholicism there is one which has surprised even Catholics themselves. It is doubtful if any other people in the world are more committed by nature and temperament to the active life, and less inclined to the arts of contemplation, than Americans. Yet there is no more unmistakable sign of spiritual maturity in the Catholic theology of asceticism than a flourishing contemplative life. The contemplative life is understood as a state in which souls devote themselves exclusively to the worship of God and aim at attaining through prayer, penance, and detachment from the external works of active life the closest possible union with God. Normally this religious dedication is to be found only in the strictest religious orders, although it is possible to practice divine contemplation outside their ranks. From the earliest days of the Republic there had been a small number of contemplative nuns in this country: a group of American-born Carmelites, trained in the English convent at Hoogstraet in Belgium, had made their foundation near Port Tobacco, Maryland, in October, 1790. But these women often encountered a cool reception even among many of their own coreligionists, who were too absorbed in the intensely active American atmosphere to have much time for contemplatives. A case in point was that of Mother Mary Magdalen Bentivoglio, who arrived from Italy in 1875 and had a long and difficult struggle before she succeeded in founding the first American convent of Poor Clares in Omaha.[9] Not until recent years, therefore, have the scattered communities of Carmelites, Poor Clares, and other contemplative orders for women experienced any marked growth in the United States.

Meanwhile the first male contemplatives, a band of Reformed Cistercians, or Trappists, had reached the United States in 1802 after a series of wanderings brought on by the disruption of their religious life during the French Revolution. For ten years or more these Frenchmen attempted to strike roots in various parts of the country, but a chain of misfortunes and the return of religious peace to France finally caused them in 1814 to quit the New World and return to their native land. But in December, 1848, a second group of French Trappists arrived in Kentucky, where about fifty miles southeast of Louisville they succeeded in making the first permanent American foundation. Later other Trappist houses were opened near Dubuque, Iowa, and Providence, Rhode Island. But they all passed through a long period of hardship, and for nearly a century few novices entered this order with its rule of perpetual silence and similar austerities that made it one of the strictest in the Church.

At the end of World War II, however, a startling development occurred when hundreds of young Americans began pouring into contemplative monasteries, many of the newcomers fresh from their service with the armed forces. The movement was broadcast by the autobiography of a young sophisticate who had vainly sought for peace in the haunts of Greenwich Village and finally found it amid the Trappist silence of the Abbey of Our Lady of Gethsemane. For months after its publication in 1948, Thomas Merton's *The Seven Storey Mountain* was a best-seller that gave many reading Americans of all creeds their first glimpse of the mysteries of a contemplative monastery. What is perhaps more remarkable is the fact that for a decade or more the trend showed no signs of abating, but the twelve Trappist monasteries in the United States have undergone a decline in the last few years from their over-all membership of more than 1,000 monks in 1956; by the end of 1966 they numbered 754. Moreover, ten years ago the first house of American Carthusians, the strictest of all the Church's religious orders, was opened near Whitingham, Vermont. This development of the contemplative movement, especially among men, has been not only a symbol of the adulthood of American Catholicism—and another indication of the widespread disillusionment of our time—but it has witnessed the fact that the arts of contemplation can flourish in the intensely active American environment, something which many of the Catholics' coreligionists in Europe and Latin America had thought impossible.

A final fact that should be mentioned among those which attest an increasingly mature outlook on the spiritual life by American Catholics is the growth of the liturgical movement. "The liturgy," as Louis Bouyer said, "is that system of prayers and rites traditionally canonized by the Church as her own prayer and worship."[10] In that system the Mass is paramount. Until some forty years ago, however, attendance at Mass on the part of many Catholics in this country was not performed with the fullness of understanding demanded by this unique act of worship. The absence of a meaningful participation in the holy Sacrifice was due in great measure to a lack of proper training and also to the lack of aids to assist the laity in following the divine service. The recitation of the rosary or the reading of certain types of prayer books during Mass answered the need for a devotional sense on the part of many. For others, however, these methods did not afford the deeper understanding and close participation they sought in their assistance at this central act of Catholic worship.

Certain American priests had meanwhile become aware of the liturgical revival going on in some parts of Europe, and these men took steps during the 1920's to remedy the situation by introducing the laity to the use of the daily missal and by publishing books and articles that explained for the general Catholic public the richness and significance of the liturgy. One of the most active of these leaders in the American liturgical movement was Father Virgil Michel, O.S.B., of St. John's Abbey, Collegeville, Minnesota. Through the initiative of Michel, and the active co-operation he received from others, *Orate Fratres* (now entitled *Worship*), a monthly journal devoted to the liturgy was launched in November, 1926. In time the dialogue Mass, where the people recite the prayers with the priest, was introduced in a number of parishes. This practice created a demand for missals, and from an estimated fewer than 50,000 copies in circulation throughout the United States in 1929, they multiplied to the point where by 1952 the publisher of one of the six daily missals then in use had sold over a million copies.

A further impetus was given to the movement by the Pius X School of Liturgical Music which was founded in 1916 at Manhattanville College, New York, for the serious study of Gregorian chant, and by the inauguration in 1940 of a series of annual Liturgical Weeks whereby those interested in problems relating to the Mass, the divine office, or the breviary recited daily by priests and many members of religious orders, and the other liturgical services of the Church could meet and exchange ideas. As a consequence of these efforts thousands of American Catholics today, unlike their parents and grandparents, have a much more intelligent grasp of the true nature of the acts of worship of their Church and the active participation which they should take in them. The liturgical movement, it is true, has not reached nearly all the Catholics in this country, but the progress made gives reason to hope that the liturgical revival will continue to spread and to make for a more enlightened practice of their faith by the Catholics of the United States. Meanwhile among the nonliturgical devotions that once enjoyed great popularity, the Forty Hours, the novena to Our Lady of the Miraculous Medal and to favorite saints such as St. Thérèse of Lisieux, there has ensued a decline.

Let us now proceed to a more detailed account of three interesting topics: (1) World War I and its aftermath; (2) the Church and social problems; (3) the status of Catholics in relation to other Americans in national leadership.

The day before Congress declared war on Germany in April, 1917, Cardinal Gibbons gave an interview to the newsmen in which he said:

> In the present emergency it behooves every American citizen to do his duty, and to uphold the hands of the President . . . in the solemn obligations that confronts us.
>
> The primary duty of a citizen is loyalty to country. This loyalty is manifested more by acts than by words; by solemn service rather than by empty declaration. It is exhibited by an absolute and unreserved obedience to his country's call.[11]

This statement from the dean of the American hierarchy, which one can scarcely conceive a Catholic bishop of the United States making today without serious challenge, was indicative of two things: first, of the manner in which the Catholic Church has reacted to every national crisis, and second, of the kind of leadership that the cardinal had given to American Catholic affairs for the previous forty years and would continue to give up to his death in March, 1921. That Catholics responded to the call of their country and their Church was evident from the high proportion of men of that faith who were members of the armed forces during World War I. Six months after war had been declared, Newton D.

Maturing Catholicism in the United States

Baker, Secretary of War, in a letter concerning the religious agencies which were principally responsible for the welfare work in the camps, mentioned the Knights of Columbus as representing the Catholics who, he said, "will constitute perhaps 35 per cent of the new Army." It was a very high estimate for a religious group who at the time were only one-sixth of the total population.[12] That the role of Cardinal Gibbons is not exaggerated will be obvious to all who know anything of his career. After his leadership in the war had been observed for some months, former President Theodore Roosevelt wrote to him in January, 1917, "Taking your life as a whole, I think you now occupy the position of being the most respected, and venerated, and useful citizen of our country."[13] If at times it may seem to those outside the Church that Catholics like Huguet, the officer of Richelieu's guard in Lytton's play, are "half suspect—they bow too low," it is simply because their loyalty has so consistently been one of the principal targets of the Church's enemies. In that connection Bishop Spalding expressed the mind of most Catholics then and since when in an answer to these critics he stated: "There is no reason why we, more than others, should make protestation of our loyalty. . . . Our record for patriotism is without blot or stain, and it is not necessary for us to hold the flag in our hands when we walk the streets [or] to wave it when we speak. . . ."[14]

One of the distinguishing features of American life in the twentieth century has been the national passion for organization, especially along economic and social lines. To this trend the Catholics were no exception, and with older groups like the German Catholic Central Verein, begun in 1855, leading the way the movement was greatly accelerated in the early years of this century. In 1901, representatives of several of these

Catholic lay groups came together to form the American Federation of Catholic Societies with a view to co-ordinating their activities and gaining strength through their united efforts. The A.F. of C.S. grew rapidly, and by 1912 it claimed about three million members through its twenty-four affiliated Catholic societies of a nation-wide character. But after that time a decline set in, and although the federation had done a good deal to arouse the social consciousness of American Catholics, it did not become the permanent stimulus desired by the founders.

With the coming of the war in 1917, the Church, like all other institutions of the country, was confronted with a new situation. If the widely scattered manpower and resources of the Church were to be marshaled efficiently, something more would be required than diffused patriotism and undirected good will from the numerous Catholic societies and individuals. Such an end could be attained only through an efficient centralized control of the disparate Catholic groups. In the case of the A.F. of C.S. such a control had been lacking. Various units of the federation had enjoyed the co-operation of individual clergymen, notably of the federation's chief episcopal sponsor, James A. McFaul, Bishop of Trenton, but the A.F. of C.S. had never enlisted the broad support of the clergy in general, and to the end it had remained largely a lay enterprise. Nor had there been any national clearing house for general Catholic affairs among the churchmen themselves. The only approximation to such, the annual meeting of the archbishops of the country which had been a feature of the life of the American Church since 1890, was entirely inadequate in the present circumstances.

All of this was well known to a priest of singular vision and breadth of mind, and it was the initiative of Father John J. Burke, C.S.P., editor of the *Catholic World* and founder in the first days of the war of the Chaplains' Aid Association in New York, that brought forth a remedy. With the approval of the hierarchy, Burke called a meeting for August 11–12, 1917, at the Catholic University of America in Washington. Under his chairmanship 115 delegates of 68 dioceses and 27 national Catholic societies on that occasion founded the National Catholic War Council. The work of the council was divided among numerous committees of priests and laymen operating under an administrative committee of bishops. During the next year and a half the council functioned as a highly effective medium in almost every phase of Catholic participation in the war effort, from providing material assistance to chaplains serving with the troops to acting as an official agency designated by President Wilson to promote the war-loan drives.

Impressed by the admitted success of the National Catholic War Council, Peter J. Muldoon, Bishop of Rockford, and other members of the episcopal committee became convinced that some form of permanent organization should be continued as a peacetime co-ordinating agency for Catholic affairs when the war came to an end. Muldoon and his colleagues won Cardinal Gibbons to their idea, and at the first general meeting of the hierarchy held in September, 1919, which drew 92 of the 101 American bishops of the time, they voted by an overwhelming majority to establish such an organization. It was at first called the National Catholic Welfare Council and had an administrative committee of five prelates who were in direct charge and answerable to the general hierarchy for its activities.

At the meeting of September, 1919, one or two prelates, including Charles E. McDonnell, Bishop of Brooklyn, had objected to the proposed N.C.W.C. on the grounds that it would be an invasion of the jurisdiction which they exercised in their own dioceses. Eventually these bishops carried their objections to the Holy See, where certain officials of the Roman Curia, principally Gaetano Cardinal De Lai, Secretary of the Consistorial Congregation, were won over to opposition against the N.C.W.C. as an organization that might give rise to a "national" church in the United States. The opposition succeeded, in turn, in convincing Pope Benedict XV to withdraw the tentative approval he had given to the idea in April, 1919, and shortly before his death on January 22, 1922, the pope had a decree drawn up dissolving the organization. When his successor, Pius XI, came on the scene a few weeks later, finding this decree as a piece of unfinished business, he signed it and issued it on February 25.

News of this action naturally brought alarm to the sponsors of the N.C.W.C. The administrative committee held an emergency meeting in Cleveland where they framed a firm but respectful protest against the decree and asked that it be withheld from publication until they could be heard from. Meanwhile the committee decided to delegate one of their number, Joseph Schrembs, Bishop of Cleveland, to present their side of the case. Schrembs hurried to Rome and after a series of prolonged conferences with De Lai and other curial officials he cabled on June 23: "Fight is won. Keep program Bishops' meeting September. Official notice will be cabled next week. Hard struggle. Complete victory. At farewell audience Pope blesses Bishops and Welfare Council. Sail Olympic Aug. 2nd."[15] Through the energetic action of Schrembs and his colleagues, therefore, a new decree was issued on July 2, 1922, which restored the original plan; and the only change brought about by this contretemps was that at the annual meeting of the hierarchy in September, 1923, the word "conference" was substituted for "council" in the title of the organization as less likely to give rise to misunderstanding in ecclesiastical circles, "council" having a definite connotation in canon law. The opposition had originated in this country, but the promptness and energy with which its sponsors acted saved the N.C.W.C., and in the sequel the fears which some bishops had entertained concerning the curtailment of their diocesan authority were in no way borne out. The N.C.W.C. was, and still remains under its new name, the United States Catholic Conference, purely advisory to the hierarchy and is in no sense mandatory. It is true that through its Administrative Board it has become the highest authoritative body within the American Church, and through that medium pronouncements are made in the name of the entire hierarchy after being submitted to the assembled prelates in their annual meeting. But the canonical authority of the bishops in their dioceses still remains intact and has not been overridden in any vital particular by the decisions of the Administrative Board.

Thus, in brief, the N.C.W.C. came into being, an organization which operates eight major departments divided into various bureaus and sections which embrace almost every important area of Catholic interest and policy.[16] So far have the Roman doubts of a generation ago been dissipated that since World War II the N.C.W.C. has been cited by the Holy See as a model which the hierarchies of other countries might well follow, even if it has been less successful in removing the doubts of certain non-Catholic Americans about the sinister purposes which allegedly lie behind its manifold activities. Actually the N.C.W.C. exercised no more sinister influence than the National

Council of Churches of Christ or any other similar body intent upon the interests of those whom it was founded to serve.

Among the original five departments of the N.C.W.C.—Education, Lay Activities, Press, Social Action, and Missions—the one that has probably impinged more than any other on the national consciousness is the Social Action Department, organized in February, 1920. Its first director was the distinguished moralist and economist, the late Monsignor John A. Ryan, who retained the post until his death in September, 1945. Ryan's influence was very strong in shaping the policies of the department on social questions and in counseling the bishops in their public pronouncements along these lines. He had a minor part in the industrial relations section of the pastoral letter of the hierarchy issued in September, 1919. More important was a pamphlet which appeared on February 12, 1919, with the title of *Social Reconstruction: A General Review of the Problems and Survey of Remedies*. This was entirely of Ryan's authorship and embodied a detailed set of principles and suggestions on such subjects as the need for minimum-wage legislation, unemployment, health, and old-age insurance for workers, age limit for child labor, legal enforcement of the right of labor to organize, and the need for a public housing program and for a national employment service. These matters are today so commonplace in American life that it is difficult to comprehend the reaction this document aroused when it was first published. What gave it weight was the fact that the bishops of the Administrative Committee of the N.C.W.C. adopted Ryan's draft and made it their own over their official signatures. So radical was it thought by some that Stephen C. Mason, President of the National Association of Manufacturers, protested to Cardinal Gibbons and expressed his shock at reading proposals of this kind from a high Catholic source. Mason said:

It is pretty generally assumed that the Roman Catholic Church of the United States is, and always has been, unalterable in its antagonism to all forms of Socialism. It is our belief that a careful reading of this pamphlet will lead you to the conclusion we have reached, namely, that it involves what may prove to be a covert effort to disseminate partisan, pro-labor union, socialistic propaganda under the official insignia of the Roman Catholic Church in America.[17]

Written across the back of the letter in the hand of a secretary was the comment, "Not yet read article & so knows nothing of it except what he has heard." Nothing was done to suppress or to revise the bishops' statement, although as late as April, 1929, the report of the Joint Legislative Committee Investigating Seditious Activities of New York State referred to it as the work of "a certain group in the Catholic Church with leanings toward Socialism."[18] On the occasion of the death of Archbishop Schrembs in November, 1945, John T. McNicholas, O.P., Archbishop of Cincinnati, adverted in his funeral sermon to Schrembs having been one of the four bishops who had signed the publication of 1919, and he remarked that of the twelve major proposals incorporated into the pamphlet all but one, namely, that of giving labor a share in management, had since been enacted into law.[19] This so-called "Bishops' Program of Social Reconstruction" is, therefore, a key document in the history of the social philosophy followed by the American Church in the present century, and the fact that eleven of its twelve proposals have become law since 1919 attests the progressive character of Catholic leadership in this field, although by no means were Catholics in general conspicuous by the manner in which they carried out the directives of their leaders in this regard. What was called socialism by the president of the N.A.M. and the Lusk Committee of New York is now more or less universally recognized by Americans as nothing more than the principles of justice and common sense applied to the changing industrial pattern of the twentieth century.

The Church has not fostered socialism in the United States any more than it has done so elsewhere. In the American Federation of Labor, for example, where Catholics have from the outset been numerous—and increasingly prominent in recent years in the AFL-CIO—the philosophy of trade unionism has always been hostile to socialism, and no one has demonstrated a direct Catholic influence to the contrary.[20] It can be taken for granted that even a minimum of Catholic training on the part of these labor leaders would tend to make them opponents of the socialist movement. The same Catholic attitude toward doctrinaire socialism is operating in groups like the Association of Catholic Trade Unionists, founded in New York in 1937 under the leadership of Father John P. Monaghan, and among the "labor priests" who counsel union men in their relations with management and with their fellow workers. As for Marxian communism among the American laboring class, the Church's opposition has been even stronger. No American needs to be told now—regardless of what some may have thought a generation ago—of the danger of communism in any phase of national life. It is a menace which the Church recognized and denounced far in advance of almost everyone else. In the encyclical *Quanta cura* of December 8, 1864, Pope Pius IX exposed the fallacies of communism less than three months after Karl Marx had launched the First International at a meeting in London on September 28 of that year.

That the Church should be especially sensitive to Communist infiltration of labor unions should occasion no surprise when one recalls the unions' exceedingly large Catholic membership. Here is an area where the Church refuses to accept the dictum that this is a secular affair and none of its business. It is very much its business, whether in the Archdiocese of Bologna where for years Giacomo Cardinal Lecaro led a vigorous campaign against the Communists of that highly industrialized region of northern Italy, in the Archdiocese of Córdoba where Archbishop Firmin E. Lafitte was under fire in 1954 from General Perón's brand of totalitarianism because of his defense of the Argentinian workmen's interests, or in the Diocese of Peoria where on January 6, 1955, the members of the Farm Equipment-United Electrical Workers of the International Harvester Company's Farmall Works at Rock Island voted two to one to disaffiliate from that union and join the CIO's United Auto Workers after having been warned by their clergy that the FE-UE was Communist dominated. The CIO had expelled the FE-UE in 1949 for precisely the same reason which the Catholic clergy gave out from their pulpits.

Another social issue in which the Church in the United States has taken a forward stand is that of racial equality. In the previous chapter the reasons why the Church failed to gain a large Negro following after the Civil War were summarized. It has ever been a fundamental doctrine of Catholic theology that all men are equal in the sight of God, and that they are, therefore, entitled to be treated with the dignity that befits one who has been made in God's image. But the Church has likewise always shown a deep respect for local custom, and for that reason there was no radical Catholic departure from the general American pattern of segregation while the laws and national sentiment remained so strongly opposed. When the first signs of a break appeared, however, the bishops lost no time, and in the sequel the Church has often been out in front of national developments, in fact, often far in front of its own reluctant laity in this respect. For example, the Catholic University of America which had a colored graduate as early as 1896 reopened its doors to Negroes in 1936, being the first white university of the federal district to do so. Since then, most of the other Catholic colleges and universities of the country have done the same. Moreover, in September, 1947, Archbishop Joseph E. Ritter of St. Louis declared an end to segregation in the schools of his archdiocese seven years in 'advance of the Supreme Court's ruling of May, 1954. In June, 1953, Vincent S. Waters, Bishop of Raleigh—in defiance of strong opposition from both Catholics and non-Catholics in North Carolina—threw open the churches, schools, and hospitals of his diocese to those of every race. When the first steps taken to implement the decision of the Supreme Court occasioned a week of protest and general uneasiness in the national capital, the Catholic schools of the city passed through the disturbance without incident, having begun, at the instance of Archbishop Patrick A. O'Boyle, the integration of white and colored students in their classrooms in the fall of 1948. The Church often has anticipated the most enlightened public sentiment on matters of this kind.

That brings us to the status of Catholics in relation to other Americans in national leadership. Historians are extremely wary, and rightly so, of the scientific value of studies based on the polling and classification of a few thousand names that may in turn lead to facile generalizations about groups involving millions of persons. Yet a careful examination of numerous studies by reputable authors, ranging in time from that of William S. Ament in *School and Society*, September, 1927, to the

Maturing Catholicism in the United States

lengthy volume of Robert H. Knapp and Joseph J. Greenbaum, *The Younger American Scholar: His Collegiate Origins*, 1953, is of some value. Allowing for errors and discrepancies which may have crept into these publications and for the possibility of faulty judgments and unwarranted generalizations from the evidence at hand, one still may conclude that American Catholics since the turn of the century have exercised nowhere near the leadership and influence or attained the national prominence that proportionately might have been expected of them.[21] In this connection one is reminded of an English Catholic writer's remark when he stated that anyone interested in the history of English Catholicism in the nineteenth century was faced with two bewildering facts. "On the one hand," he said, "there is the enormous growth of the Church, and on the other its almost complete lack of influence. At the end of the century the Church is as much or more the Church of a minority than it was in the 1850's."[22] *Mutatis mutandis*—the same thing can be said of the Church in the United States during those years, and with even more cogency for the last half-century.

What is the explanation? In part it is due to the fact that up to recent years the principal energies of the Church have been expended on hundreds of thousands of immigrants. As D. W. Brogan, writing in 1941, said: "Not until this generation has the Church been given time (with the cessation of mass immigration), to take breath and take stock. One result of this preoccupation with the immigrants has been that the Catholic Church in America has counted for astonishingly little in the formation of the American intellectual climate."[23] A second reason is that we all live, unfortunately, in an environment strongly non-intellectual, and even anti-intellectual. Philip Blair Rice lamented that fact in the *Kenyon Review* in the summer of 1954, and it has been the theme of similar laments in an increasing number of articles since published in learned journals and scholarly reviews.[24]

In most of the anti-intellectual trends of our day American Catholics have taken their full share, even to adulterating what was once a solid program of studies for the enrichment of the human mind by the introduction into the curricula of their colleges and universities of what, to the minds of many, are pedagogical gimmicks that are gradually robbing Americans of the opportunity to become truly educated men. In April, 1937, Robert M. Hutchins, then President of the University of Chicago, gave a memorable address before the National Catholic Educational Association in which he forcefully reminded the Catholic educators of their obligation as heirs to preserve the enduring values which the Church had bequeathed to them in what he called "the longest intellectual tradition of any institution in the contemporary world."[25] Moreover, he added that it was likewise their duty to shun the influences which were producing what he termed "well-tubbed young Americans." It would be gratifying to record that a marked improvement had been noted among Catholic institutions in the intervening years, but there would seem to be little evidence to indicate that Hutchins' strictures wrought any serious change, for the "tubbing" process receives about the same emphasis in the more than 300 Catholic colleges and universities of the land as it does elsewhere.

A third factor which enters the picture is the discrimination against Catholics to keep them out of posts of leadership, regardless of their merits. In November, 1928, that fact was made evident for all the world to see when Alfred E. Smith was defeated after a presidential campaign in which, as Oscar Handlin says, "The violent propaganda . . . created an image of Catholicism as a menace because of its strangeness, its alliance with corrupt machine politics, its encouragement of intemperance and hostility to prohibition, and its internationalism."[26] It made little difference that Smith's record during four terms as Governor of New York was irreproachable. Nor in all likelihood would it have made any difference in 1933 when his sensible and courageous stand of five years before on prohibition was accepted by the American people in the repeal of the Eighteenth Amendment. To be sure, the discrimination that exists in certain high circles of business, politics, and education is not practiced with the blatancy that marked the campaign of 1928; it is far more subtle and is often not easily detected. But that it exists is a fact. Knowledge of this situation is widespread among educated Catholics, and it tends not only to heighten their sensitivity but also to frustrate many an American man and woman of the Catholic faith who might otherwise aspire to a higher role in his or her professional group. Discrimination of this kind is the quiet expression of what Professor Arthur M. Schlesinger, Sr., once characterized when he told the writer, "I regard the prejudice against your Church as the deepest bias in the history of the American people."

In politics, for example, Catholics have often risen to prominence on the municipal level, even though, in the case of some, it has not always been to their credit. But exceedingly few Catholics have achieved high policy-making positions on a national level; the chairmanship of the Democratic National Committee and the office of postmaster-general in the president's cabinet are not in the same category as, let us say, the secretary of state. Between 1789 and 1955, there have been only fourteen Catholics in cabinet posts, and ten of those received their appointments after 1933. In the same span of years only six Catholics have sat on the bench of the Supreme Court of the United States, although twice the chief justiceship was held by Catholics through lengthy periods of time. In 1955, there were ten Catholics in the United States Senate and seventy-two in the national House of Representatives, but in the Ninetieth Congress (January, 1967) they were the largest single religious group, with fourteen senators and ninety-four members of the House. In business, perhaps, Catholics have been most successful; several recent studies seem to indicate that their position in business leadership is now fairly representative and that Catholics have in general moved up the economic ladder at a rate that has occasioned some surprise on the part of investigators.[27]

The causes for anti-Catholic bias, when added to the lack of an intellectual tradition both Catholic and American, help to explain the failure of Catholics to make more of a mark in national life. It is a situation which constitutes the most serious weakness in contemporary American Catholicism; but it is likewise a situation which makes absurd the argument of certain critics of the Church to the effect that growing Catholic strength is a peril to the future of the Republic. As a matter of fact, Catholics have made relatively little progress in attaining posts of commanding leadership and influence.

In the realm of criticism of things Catholic there are few subjects of more perennial interest than the problem of Church and State, about which so much has been heard since World War II. It is now over eighty years since Viscount Bryce noted in his famous book *The American Commonwealth* that half the wars of Europe and half the internal troubles of European states had arisen from theological differences, or from the rival claims of Church and State. "This whole vast chapter

of debate and strife," said Bryce, "has remained virtually un-
opened in the United States."[28] Were the learned ambassador
to have lingered on the American scene, he would have had to
revise his judgment. In fact, the chapter is not only long since
opened, but it has become one of the most controversial topics of contemporary debate and domestic strife. Insofar as the
question relates to Catholics, from the end of the A.P.A., about
1905, it was not again a major concern until the revived Ku
Klux Klan of the 1920's forced it upon the attention of everyone. Today the Klan may seem to many Americans a weird
nightmare sprung from the brain of a group of fanatics who
might better be forgotten. But it was these same fanatics who
fanned the flames that set the country on fire with a religious
hatred that left an indelible scar on the minds of thousands of
Americans as an aftermath of the campaign of 1928. Having
proven triumphantly in that year that no Catholic could be
president of the United States, the agitators quieted down until
President Roosevelt in December, 1939, appointed Myron C.
Taylor as his personal representative at the Holy See. Even
then the discussion was in good measure limited to this alleged
violation of the principle of separation of Church and State,
and as the country edged closer to active participation in
World War II less was heard of the matter. Religious prejudice in the United States abated in wartime, but after the end
of the fighting in western Europe and the Far East in the late
summer of 1945 the question took on a broader aspect. It has
been with us ever since.[29]

Historically speaking, the problem of Church and State in
the United States has not revolved around the rigid principle
that some secular and liberal dogmatists of our day would have
us believe. The researches of men like Evarts B. Greene and

the three volumes of Canon Stokes published in 1950 demonstrated that the separation of Church and State has never
been complete.[30] As another writer said, "The actual relations
depend more on the shifting of sympathies than on precise legal
theory."[31] An indication of those shiftings of sympathies can
be found in the decisions of the Supreme Court over a quarter
century in such cases as the Oregon School Law of 1925 and
McCullom v. *Board of Education* of 1948.

It is true that differences exist between Catholics and a large
segment of non-Catholic Americans on questions like divorce,
birth control, euthansasia, abortion, and artificial insemination,
and many of these differences may, indeed, remain. In other
matters, too, such as censorship of the films and magazines, and
demands for public financial aid to religious schools, the viewpoint of Catholics is at variance with that of many of their
fellow citizens. Moreover, at times some Catholics do give unnecessary offense by public campaigning for things only re-
motely concerned with the moral code. But what is important
to keep in mind is that for the most part Catholics hold their
views from deep religious conviction based on their adherence
to divine and natural law or to the moral code which they
believe it is necessary to practice for the spiritual welfare of
themselves and their children. For Catholics to do less would
be, in a number of these questions, for them to cease to be
Catholics. As for the effects on American government and
society which follow from Catholics advocating their principles, Commager, in his survey of the years since 1880, stated
it this way: "Whatever conclusions might be drawn from a
scrutiny of Catholic doctrine, the fact was that Catholicism
had flourished as a major religion for three quarters of a century without raising serious difficulties except in the imagina-

tions of men and that democratic institutions seemed as sound when the church numbered twenty-four million members as they had been when it counted its communicants by the hundred thousand."[32]

And yet in the minds of many people in this country the Church is guilty of a cardinal sin—it does not conform to the general American religious pattern. In a thoughtful discussion of the various religions practiced in the United States, Daniel J. Boorstin summarized their principal characteristics as threefold: (1) they are "instrumental" in the sense that they recommend themselves for the services which they perform, not for the truths which they teach; (2) closely related to the first point, they are "personal" in that they emphasize what religion can do for the individual; (3) there exists a peculiarly American phenomenon termed "non-denominationalism," which Boorstin illustrated by a statement of President Eisenhower when the latter was interrogated by a reporter at the time he assumed the presidency of Columbia University.[33] Asked if he were a religious man, he replied: "I am the most intensely religious man I know. Nobody goes through six years of war without faith. That doesn't mean that I adhere to any sect. A democracy cannot exist without a religious base. I believe in democracy."[34]

No Catholic theologian wishes to minimize the undoubted attraction which religion has for a man who desires to benefit from the services which it can perform for his spiritual and social uplift; but where he differs with those who hold this view is in the primary emphasis which he places on the dogmatic truths which the Church teaches. According to Catholic theology, it is in these truths, stemming from divine revelation and tradition, that the source of man's ultimate happiness lies, and no transitory benefit to individual persons may be permitted to replace them. As for the tendency to create a least common denominator in American religious life, to foster a point of view where the truths of religion become irrelevant after the fashion of William James, and to evolve a generalized religion which, to use Boorstin's phrase, "is itself virtually without dogma,"[35] here Catholics are and must always remain nonconformists. But this inability to conform to the national religious ethos entails no necessary conflict with the country's institutions, least of all with the tenets of democracy as its political philosophy. On the contrary, the history of the American Church proves that Catholicism can, and does—as de Tocqueville predicted over a century ago—flourish under democratic auspices to the complete satisfaction of its members. Conformity of the type which some Americans have mistakenly advocated in religious matters is not healthy for the general community any more than conformity in political shades of opinion is healthy for democracy. Lord Acton spoke on that point nearly a century ago: "It is bad to be oppressed by a minority, but it is worse to be oppressed by a majority. For there is a reserve of latent power in the masses which, if it is called into play, the minority can seldom resist. But from the absolute will of an entire people there is no appeal, no redemption, no refuge but treason."[36] In this sense, then, Catholicism is nonconformist and will continue to be so. As Boorstin suggested, however, that very fact gives it a valuable role to play in American culture, for while it accepts the political premises of the community without question, it can still judge those premises by a standard outside the community's history.[37]

Serious damage is done by imputing base motives to Catholics for their opinions and actions just as Catholics do damage by imputing similar motives to those outside their Church—and viewing every move by Catholics as an attempt to seize power and convert the American Republic to the image which their critics have created in their minds of a country like Franco's Spain. It is said that Catholics want to convert the whole of the American people to their Church. Of course they do! And one would think very little of any American Episcopalian or Lutheran whose devotion to the truth of his religious faith was not deep enough to give him hope that his church might one day gain the allegiance of all Americans. But this goal on the part of the Church implies no unfair or dishonorable methods to win other Americans to its faith. As a matter of fact, there is not a Catholic priest in the land who would even so much as receive an adherent of one of the Protestant churches into the Catholic fold until he was fully convinced that the prospective convert had been free of all duress and scruple in changing his religious belief.

As has been said, the very real differences between Catholics and their countrymen in no sense need imply a war to the death, for the fundamental principle of separation of Church and State has always been accepted by the American hierarchy from the time of Archbishop Carroll to our own day. Some years ago in a close study of this question, the results of which were published in *Harper's Magazine*, I did not find a single instance where an American Catholic bishop had given expression, either publicly or privately, to a view at variance with the statement of the chairman of the Administrative Board of the National Catholic Welfare Conference when in January, 1948, he said:

No group in America is seeking union of church and state; and least of all are Catholics. We deny absolutely and without any qualification that the Catholic Bishops of the United States are seeking a union of church and state by any endeavors whatsoever, either proximate or remote. If tomorrow Catholics constituted a majority of our country, they would not seek a union of church and state. They would then, as now, uphold the Constitution and all its Amendments, recognizing the moral obligation imposed on all Catholics to observe and defend the Constitution and its Amendments.[38]

There is not a bishop in the American Church today who would not wholeheartedly subscribe to what Cardinal Manning told Gladstone in 1875: "If Catholics were in power to-morrow in England, not a penal law would be proposed, not the shadow of a constraint put upon the faith of any man. We would that all men fully believed the truth; but a forced faith is a hypocrisy hateful to God and man."[39]

What, then, is the future of the Church-State controversy that in recent years has embittered Americans of differing religious beliefs? That depends entirely upon the temper in which it is discussed. If it be in the measured terms of the Protestant, Charles C. Marshall, whose serious volume on the question followed the 1928 presidential campaign,[40] or of the Jewish writer, Will Herberg, whose thoughtful and constructive books and articles have done much in recent years to dissipate misunderstanding,[41] or the Catholic publications and lectures of the late John Courtney Murray, S.J.,[42] then there is genuine hope for gain and clarification on both sides and for a calm, judicious, beneficial approach to the problem. But if the matter is left in the hands of those deep in prejudice, we can anticipate nothing better than an increase of the spirit that has divided men on this question during past decades. As one foreign critic has said of us, we Americans unfortunately have never learned to discuss delicate issues of this nature other than at the top of our voices. A case in point is the near hysteria that seized so many at the appointment of Mr. Taylor by President Roosevelt and the nomination by President Truman in October, 1951, of General Mark Clark as ambassador to Vatican City. In that connection a story told by a distinguished Episcopalian rector in Washington some years ago is pertinent. He spoke of having attended a luncheon with a number of leading Protestant clergymen of the national capital where a visiting Anglican bishop was the guest of honor. The Taylor appointment came up for discussion and all the Americans, except the Episcopalian rector, were opposed to it. Meanwhile the British bishop had sat in silence. Finally one of the Americans asked his opinion, and the Anglican divine, recalling his own country's appointment of a minister to the Vatican in 1914, replied, "Why in England we have had a regular representative since World War I. We think it works very well, and we do not regard it as a religious issue at all."[43]

The story illustrates a failing that is all too common among Americans, namely, allowing their emotions and prejudices to override their reason. A Catholic may be indifferent to the appointment of Taylor and Clark as touching his religious faith; as an American citizen he should regret it if bias were permitted to stand in the way of what the officials of his government believed to be in the nation's best interests. Even so advanced an anticlerical philosophical liberal as Max Salvadori recognized the importance of the Church in what all free men admit is the major crisis of our time. In 1951 he wrote:

Separation between church and state is a basic tenet of Liberalism. But today Catholicism is possibly the greatest force checking the spread of Communism in the Western world. . . . On the borders of the Communist empire, what holds Western Germans, Italians and Filipinos against Communism is not so much love for liberty and for democracy, or even independence, as the Catholic Church. Necessity dictates co-operation between the American nation and the Catholic and other churches.[44]

If Americans wish to oppose communism, it is scarcely the part of wisdom to continue attacks upon a Church which at the end of 1954 counted 186 of its bishops among those exiled, imprisoned, or deprived of their sees—to say nothing of thousands of priests, religious, and laity—by the tyranny which holds so much of eastern Europe and the continent of Asia in its grip. Nor is there very much sense in the persistently negative attitude of those whose ideology was aptly described in the remark, "Catholic-baiting is the anti-Semitism of the liberals."[45]

A further point that would greatly improve relations between Catholics and Protestants in the United States would be a cessation to the practice of blaming American Catholics for what others may disapprove in the policies of the Spanish government and the Spanish hierarchy. In this respect Catholics might with equally bad logic hold American Protestants, especially those of Calvinistic beliefs, responsible for the racial policies pursued by the government of Dr. Malan and his successors in South Africa. Again, if the actions of private groups of Catholics somewhere in the United States at times annoy non-Catholics, it is just as silly to hold the Church responsible for everything they do or say as it would be for Catholics to place the blame on all American Protestants for the strange antics of certain snake-charming Protestant sects in the hills of Tennessee. If, too, Catholics are to be constantly challenged because of their spiritual allegiance to the Holy See, they might logically raise the question of the double allegiance implied for many American Jews in the proposal announced in 1954 by Chief Rabbi Isaac Halevy Herzog of Israel to establish an

Orthodox Jewish counterpart of the Vatican in Jerusalem.[46] Nowhere has anyone detected a disposition among Americans of the Catholic faith to inaugurate a campaign along the comparative lines mentioned, nor would such a thing be in any way conducive to the national welfare. It would be helpful if critics of the Church were to cease holding American Catholics accountable for matters over which they have no control. Similarly, it would be desirable if some Catholics were to set a higher evaluation on good community relations and confine their efforts to areas where disagreement is a matter of necessity dictated by the teaching of the Church. In such cases if their defense of the Catholic position were conducted with more regard for the ancient patristic maxim, *In necessariis, unitas; in dubiis, libertas; in omnibus, caritas*, it would be a gain for all concerned.

What, therefore, is to be done to remedy this situation which for several decades has been seriously distracting the American people? By way of conclusion I should like to submit the following simple answer. Catholics have been in America for four centuries, and their history reveals the maximum of loyalty and service to every fundamental ideal and principle upon which the Republic was founded and has endured. There are now nearly fifty million Americans whose religious faith and theological beliefs are—and will remain—those of the universal Church of Rome. American Catholics are here to stay, and those who seem to make something of a career out of criticism of this largest of American religious groups might as well reconcile themselves to that fact. When I think of what is to be done about this matter, there comes to mind a question that I once heard addressed to a friend of mine about the problem in Chicago at a time of severe racial tension. "What are you going to do about the Negroes in Chicago?" he was asked. He replied without a moment's hesitation, "Learn to live with them." It was an answer based on charity, wisdom, and common sense with which no conscientious and thoughtful citizen would care to differ. It is obvious that Protestants, Catholics, Jews, and men of no religious faith are here and will remain, and that they will, therefore, have to go on living together. The welfare and future strength of the Republic demand that this fact be recognized by Americans of every religious faith and that they act accordingly. To do less were to abdicate the responsibility which citizenship imposes upon us all.

V

The Changing Church
1956–68

"In a higher world it is otherwise, but here below to live is to change, and to be perfect is to have changed often." Writers on religious subjects are fond of quoting John Henry Newman, but it is doubtful if during the present decade any statement of his has been more frequently quoted than this arresting sentence from Newman's famous *Essay on the Development of Christian Doctrine* published late in 1845.[1] It is symbolic, perhaps, of the growing ascendancy of the great cardinal's thought over the minds of religious thinkers, an ascendancy that has been markedly advanced during and since Vatican Council II. Every age, to be sure, is an age of change, and that is as true in the ecclesiastical order as it is in the civil order. But in the Catholic Church's history of nearly two thousand years one must go back to the third decade of the sixteenth century, when the movement begun by Martin Luther started to spread, to find a parallel to the revolutionary transformation that has taken place since the election in October, 1958, of Pope John XXIII. The change is seen and experienced in every aspect of Catholic life: in the Church's approach to the world, in the style and manner of her apostolate to those outside her fold as well as to her own members, in the attitude of those members to the Church itself, and this on virtually every level and in every rank of ecclesiastical and clerical authority—among diocesan priests or those of religious congregations and among members of active or contemplative orders—as well as in the varied social classes of men and women who constitute the Church's lay membership.

What has been true of the worldwide Catholic Church has been equally true of the Church in the United States, for scarcely any old and familiar feature or pattern of the religious life of American Catholics has remained untouched by the ferment of the past ten years. And the adaptation to the new order in the Church has at times been made more difficult for some by reason of the drastic changes that have taken place simultaneously in the secular aspects of American life. Nor in this instance has there been—as was the case ever since the formal organization of the American Church in 1790—the comforting knowledge that the Catholic community was growing rapidly in numbers and consequently in strength. On the contrary, the rate of growth has noticeably declined in recent years; in 1964 it was 1.7 per cent as compared to 2.4 per cent in the previous year. Growth by natural increase has fallen off by reason of the Church's pronouncedly urban character as well as the increasing prevalence of the practice of birth control among Catholics. Also, since the early 1950's the number of converts to the faith has been declining, with 1967 having only 110,717 converts, the lowest figure since 1953. Moreover, what was once an almost too plentiful channel of growth, namely, immigration, is no longer a major source of supply. The latest immigration law, which went into effect on July 1, 1968, dropped

The Changing Church

the national origins quota system and limited the over-all total admitted to 170,000, on the principle of equality for all nations, with the exception of those of the Western Hemisphere. And the entrance of thousands of Puerto Ricans and Mexicans has presented an added anxiety rather than a solution to the Church's problems.

Allowing that the total of 47,468,333 Catholics reported by the *Official Catholic Directory* as of January 1, 1968, is known to be considerably below the true figure, which is closer to and, perhaps, even in excess of 50,000,000, the prospect is still not a bright one. The perennial problem of leakage which has been with the Church from her founding has taken a severe toll on Catholic membership in the United States. For example, whereas the Catholic population figures from 1951 through 1961 revealed that for those ten years the infant baptisms and adult converts contributed 13,798,833 new Catholics, the increase reported in the *Official Catholic Directory* for the same decade was only 12,451,650. Allowing for inaccurate reporting by some pastors eager to hold down their parochial census figures because of diocesan assessments and to keep the parish from being broken up, the discrepancy of 1,347,183 was still due in the main to lapses from the faith. That the all-pervading secularization of national life has caused an inevitable corrosion of religious values affecting Catholics as well as all other Americans is generally admitted. And to that external circumstance there has been added a serious loss to the Church's membership. Like their coreligionists in other countries, Catholics in the United States have experienced the mounting stress and strain that have accompanied changes in the liturgy and in other features of their religious life sanctioned by Vatican Council II.

The result has been widespread disillusion and discontent

with their Church on the part of many Catholics, either because their bishops and clergy have failed to implement these changes fully, or, among those of a highly conservative mind, because the changes were introduced at all. While defections from the faith have normally been more numerous on the left than on the right, there is good reason for believing that this situation has been the occasion for losses on both ends of the spectrum and that very likely the future will add to those who have already taken their departure. Moreover, an additional factor of growing significance is the number of Catholics who have joined one or another of the Orthodox or Protestant churches. Granted that Will Oursler's methods of computing their number were successfully challenged when his figures were published in the *Christian Herald* in April, 1954, it can no longer be denied that Catholics changed their religious affiliation on an increasing scale during the decade or more before 1961. Thus, by 1961, the question of declining numbers became more acute and complicated and the burden of responsibility heavier for those whose duty it was to chart the Church's course through the years immediately ahead.

We have previously discussed how the Church developed in the United States as overwhelmingly urban in character. The heavy urban predominance is emphasized by the fact that, of the 3,080 counties in the United States, there were 671 without a single resident Catholic priest at the end of 1967. True, since 1960 there has been a net gain of 52 counties in this regard, but by late 1967 roughly 40,000,000 Americans were not within practical reach of a Catholic priest or community. While no more need be said here about this matter, the radical changes in the socioeconomic patterns of urban life since 1956 and their effects on the Church do call for discussion. The first real strength of the Catholics in this country was born in the American cities where the immigrants of the last century settled in great numbers. It was a strength centered largely in the so-called national parishes within whose confines first the Irish and the Germans and later the Poles and the Italians—to name only the largest of the Catholic immigrant groups—created enclaves where their respective languages, social customs, and original cultures were cultivated to the extent possible in a foreign land. To be sure, these national parishes were set apart from the general American population, who often looked with a critical eye on the immigrants' parochial schools where German, Hungarian, or Polish was the prevailing language of instruction, on the social clubs and other centers of entertainment maintained for their own people, on their foreign language newspapers and magazines,[2] and on their parish church where the sermons, hymns, and as much of the liturgy as was allowed were heard in the same strange tongues.

The hostile eye of Americans notwithstanding, the first generation immigrants held tenaciously to their Old World ways, convinced that, if they lost their language and all that was associated with it, they would lose their faith. One may question the validity of their reasoning, but one can scarcely question the fact that the national parish, while undoubtedly the creator of awkward situations at times embarrassing and annoying to the Church's leaders, was the most powerful single agency for the substantial fidelity of hundreds of thousands of these immigrants to the religion of their ancestors. But if the first generation of these ethnic groups clung to their respective ghettos, their children were much less content to do so, and their grandchildren broke entirely with the Old World framework and sought—with striking success—to enter the mainstream of American life.

One of the clearest indications of this success is the swelling number of Catholic families whose income has enabled them to become full-fledged members of the affluent society of the late twentieth century. And with the new affluence these families, like their Protestant, Jewish, and non-religious counterparts, have long since quit the scene of their grandparents' original settlement, indeed, even that of their parents, and are among the inhabitants of suburbia. Meanwhile the Church in the inner city, deprived of the poor immigrant classes she once knew, has found herself with half-empty houses of worship and with parochial schools and other parish facilities that cannot be maintained on a sound financial basis for lack of patronage. The time has passed when Arthur M. Schlesinger, writing of the late nineteenth century, could contrast the Catholic Church favorably with the relative failure of the Protestant churches to hold the urban poor, and to say of the former that it "reared its edifices where humanity was densest, and thronged its pews three or four times each Sunday with worshipers whose hands and clothing plainly betrayed their humble station."[3] Those who have replaced the Catholic ethnic groups who once "thronged the pews" are mostly Negroes and Protestant whites of the poorer classes. Obviously, the Puerto Ricans and Mexicans are an exception, but aside from cities like New York and Chicago for the former and Los Angeles and San Antonio for the latter, the Puerto Ricans and the Mexicans have never migrated to the cities in the same proportion as the Negroes.

It is precisely here that the Church's failure to make a serious approach to the Negroes in the last century and the early decades of this century showed to the greatest disadvantage. Yet if a recent Negro writer is correct, Catholicism still retains a strong attraction for his people. Remarking the difficulty in ascertaining Catholic influence among the Negroes because of the comparatively few of that race who had become converts to the faith, this writer said, "What is clear is that there is an unprecedented movement of Negroes toward Catholicism."[4] This movement would have been strengthened considerably if a change had been allowed in the canonical regulations governing the Sacrament of Matrimony, which has been the major stumbling block to the Negro's entrance to the Church. All too frequently the Negro seeking to become a Catholic has been prevented from doing so by reason of a previous marriage, and canon law leaves no room for his having had no intention to contract a binding union in the first instance. If a change in the law concerning the binding character of the first marriage could be brought about, plus the Negroes' generally favorable attitude toward the Church and the enlivened Catholic apostolate to men of that race since World War II, there would be reason to anticipate that the figure of early 1968 of 808,332 Catholics among the more than 22,000,000 blacks in the United States would be noticeably increased. In that connection, the American hierarchy's pastoral letter dated January 21, 1968, gives eloquent witness of a realistic approach to the critics of the late 1960's in elaborating on the social implications of the Church's teaching that a vocation to Catholic life is also "a vocation of service to every member of the human family."[5] The bishops maintained:

This concern is not accidental to the devout life. . . . It is the faith at work, the faith alive in the works without which faith is dead. It is a concern active in us when fellow men are denied human or civil rights, when there are riots in our streets, when death and devastation are rained on other men's cities, when men hunger and thirst in other lands or in our own.[6]

And that the hierarchy was then under no illusion that the Catholic community of this country had fully lived up to these high ideals is also evident. Quoting a critic of the Church in another country and another generation who said, "It is not your encyclicals which we despise; what we despise is the neglect with which you yourselves treat them!" the bishops concluded, "there is no point in pretending that it cannot be applied with equal force and fury against us in America in our decade."[7]

An additional obstacle to the proper execution of the Church's commitment in the inner city is the outmoded character of the traditional parish structure. The large and expensive parochial facilities that for many years admirably served the closed society of the teeming immigrant population are quite unsuited to the open and "swinging" social groups that have inherited these neighborhoods; nor in all likelihood would the latter have the income to sustain them even if they were practicing members of the Church. If the mass emigration of Protestant churches from the city in the first half of the present century could be described by Harvey Cox as "a shamefully documented fact," more recent decades have found Catholics following the same pattern, even if proportionately they may have remained behind longer and in greater numbers than the Protestants. Meanwhile, aside from an isolated instance here and there, such as the team of young priests who went into Chicago's inner city with the sanction of the late Cardinal Meyer, a widespread reluctance of many in ecclesiastical authority to permit change and experimentation has hampered the

Church's response to the new situation. In that sense what Cox says of the Protestant churches applies as well to the Catholic Church; he maintained that what was needed in the blighted areas "are not incursions of rescue bands from outside, but a basic redistribution of power so that there is no longer any need for condescension. But this is asking for a sacrifice on the part of suburban churches that very few are willing to make."[8]

It is not the historian's place to usurp the function of the sociologist in accumulating and analyzing the data on contemporary society. Yet when he writes about the Church in that society, it is his business to record the discernible trends and, when the evidence warrants, to speak of the causes that lie behind those trends. In view of the radically changed conditions of urban society of which we have been speaking, therefore, it is hardly too venturesome to suggest that the days of the typical inner city parish whose pastor received his appointment by reason of seniority in ordination should be regarded as numbered if the Church is to fulfill her true purpose among men. Far more in tune with the realities of the present moment would be small Christian communities headed not by "a pastor and his assistants," but by several young priests assisted by apostolic laymen and laywomen whose energy and zeal are not frustrated by the immobility of older churchmen. They should, needless to say, have a personal attraction for this type of apostolate and be willing to spend and be spent in the exceedingly difficult mission of regaining even a small percentage of the thousands of unchurched Americans who inhabit the human jungles that constitute the heart of every large city in the land. Nor does the American Church lack priests, religious, and laity who are prepared to make this sacrifice. They are men and women who, imbued with the spirit of Vatican Council II, feel keenly about this matter and they are restive at the slowness of pace with which the conciliar reforms are being put into practice in some dioceses. In other words, they are people eager that the words of the council's "Pastoral Constitution on the Church in the Modern World" should be taken literally:

. . . when circumstances of time and place create the need, she (the Church) can and indeed should initiate activities on behalf of all men. This is particularly true of activities designed for the needy, such as the works of mercy and similar undertakings.[9]

In fact, it would not be an exaggeration to say that no small amount of the tension within Catholic ranks revolves around the question of how and when the Church should meet her obligations to men generally—not just to Catholics—in the inner recesses of the great cities of the United States.

If proof were needed that Catholics have been sharply divided on what pertains to a remedy for the ills of the inner city, that proof was forthcoming when efforts were made to introduce a policy of open housing in heavily Catholic neighborhoods in a number of large urban centers. The strange spectacle in the summer of 1966 of Catholic people hurling rocks and stones at priests and nuns who accompanied the marches into Cicero and Berwyn, suburbs of Chicago with notably large Catholic populations of Slavic background, were only more openly ugly and ominous than the earlier stubborn resistance offered by those of predominantly Irish extraction to Negro families on Chicago's south side. The year 1967 will probably stand out in this record for the opposition shown by Milwaukee's south side Catholics of Polish ancestry to the open housing marches led over a period of months by Father James E. Groppi of Saint Boniface Parish. In the same year the race riots in Detroit, Newark, and other cities touched the Church directly and sharpened the focus of her responsibility in this delicate and sensitive aspect of American life.

Yet among American Catholics strong champions of social justice have not been lacking, as was manifested in the spring of 1965 when approximately four hundred priests, including James P. Shannon, Auxiliary Bishop of Saint Paul–Minneapolis, together with scores of brothers, sisters, and members of the laity, marched in the historic gatherings at Selma, Alabama, even if it was made unmistakably clear at the time that Thomas J. Toolen, Bishop of Mobile-Birmingham, regarded their presence as an unwarranted interference in the affairs of his diocese. And thus the controversy has continued in the Catholic community with articulate supporters on both sides as, for example, in the Archdiocese of Chicago, where in the spring of 1967 a group organized itself under the name of Concerned Parents in opposition to a series of religion textbooks called *Word and Worship* which were used in the archdiocesan elementary schools. These Catholic parents found one of the series offensive because it cited Dr. Martin Luther King as an example of Christian bravery, while others professed shock at reading expressions like "Jesus our Brother" since, according to their view, Christ was divine and, therefore, it was irreverent to call Him "our Brother." Still others took umbrage at the textbooks for stating that a Christian should endeavor to live his life after "the mind and heart of Christ"; the members of Concerned Parents were not impressed when told the phrase was taken from Saint Paul.

The principal anxiety over the *Word and Worship* series seemed to center in the books' teaching that all men are equal, and by implication that Negroes are entitled to as much respect as whites. In the circumstances it was not surprising that Monsignor George G. Higgins should have made known his surprise and chagrin in a syndicated article entitled, "What Have We Taught Our People?"[10] Obviously, the Church's teaching on social justice as contained in papal encyclicals from Leo XIII's *Rerum novarum* of 1891 to Paul VI's *Progressio populorum of* 1967 had not influenced these Catholics, nor had the American hierarchy's pronouncements on the evils of racism, such as their pastoral letter of November, 1958, found acceptance. Doubtless it was this sort of thing that was uppermost in the mind of Robert E. Tracy, Bishop of Baton Rouge, when on October 24, 1963, he suggested to the fathers of Vatican Council II, "in the name of the bishops of the United States of North America," that the council place "clearer emphasis on the equality of everyone in the Church with no distinction on account of race." He mentioned the repeated efforts of the American hierarchy to inculcate a correct attitude on matters of social justice, and he added, "Now, if the Council issues a solemn and concrete affirmation on the equality of all races, it will greatly help the bishops to teach their people more effectively."[11]

Race prejudice, however, is a very stubborn thing and it has survived among American Catholics in spite of innumerable exhortations from their bishops and clergy to observe Christ's law of universal love of all men. Moreover, the historic bias against the Negro that characterized so many of the Irish during the period of their dominance of the Church in this country has not been a monopoly of that particular group. For as the second and third generations of all the varied Catholic immigrant strains have moved into the middle class, their attitude on this subject seems to have hardened and to have revealed no appreciable differences along nationalist lines. It may have been considerations of this kind that prompted the Cardinal Archbishop of Washington to tell his people in a pastoral letter of July 28, 1967, in the wake of the summer's race riots:

We must be willing to acknowledge our own responsibility for perpetuating a system which sooner or later, as the recent riots have tragically demonstrated, was inevitably bound to erupt in violence.

We must honestly recognize and admit that we have not done many of the things that we should have been doing and have too often done things which we ought not have been doing in the field of social justice.

Our efforts to eliminate segregated slum housing have been feeble. Our support of desperately needed programs of job training and job opportunities for unemployed Negroes in our ghettos has been far less than adequate. . . . Our welfare programs have too often been paternalistic, demeaning, and inadequate and have weakened family life.

All the foregoing was more than confirmed for the nation at large in the Kerner Report, one of the major conclusions of which stated, "White racism is essentially responsible for the explosive mixture which has been accumulating in our cities since the end of World War II."[12]

Perhaps even more generally divisive than the race issue—for all Catholics are not confronted by that problem—have been the liturgical changes which were adumbrated in the pontificate of Pope Pius XII but which received thorough and effective treatment only in Vatican Council II. During October and November, 1962, the council heard 328 oral interventions on the liturgical schema of which 18 were delivered by bishops from the United States. The opposing sides among the Americans were clearly set forth by the Archbishops of Los Angeles and Atlanta. On October 23 Cardinal James Francis McIntyre stated that the instruction of the Congregation of Rites of September, 1958, had made it evident that the primary attention in assisting at Mass should be directed toward "the contemplation of the mystery of the Eucharist." In his opinion the discussion about active participation of the laity was, therefore, receiving "more consideration than needed," and he added, "Furthermore, active participation is frequently a distraction."[13] Eight days later Archbishop Paul J. Hallinan presented the contrary position when, he said, he spoke "for many bishops (although not for all) of the United States" in expressing the hope for "the more vital, conscious and fruitful participation of our people in the Mass."[14] Variations of opinion between those of the cardinal and the archbishop were voiced during the debates by other Americans, but when on November 14, the decisive test came and 2,162 bishops voted in favor of the schema to only 46 in opposition, it was evident that the position taken by those of the mind of Cardinal McIntyre was not that of the majority. The wide publicity given to these debates prepared the religious world, therefore, for Paul VI's formal promulgation on December 3, 1963, of the "Constitution on the Sacred Liturgy" at the close of the council's second session.

In the time since the liturgical constitution went into effect few branches of the Church, unless it be that of the Netherlands, have been under more tension because of the language and form of public worship than the American branch. A wide variety of practice has obtained in the United States from diocese to diocese, even from parish to parish within the same diocese. A number of bishops and pastors have been slow to implement changes such as the use of the vernacular in place of Latin, the offering of Mass with the priest facing the people, the use of guitars and wind instruments to accompany the new, and sometimes Protestant, hymns during the so-called folk

The Changing Church

Masses, the joining of the congregation in making the responses to the priest as well as in the singing of hymns throughout the service, Masses in private homes, and the stronger position given to the Scriptures in the liturgy generally, to say nothing of a para-liturgical service such as Bible vigils. As might have been anticipated, enthusiasts for the innovations have been found principally among the younger clergy and the more youthful laity, but Catholics' differences over the liturgy are by no means to be explained solely by their age.

In the final analysis the state of the liturgy in a given diocese or parish has normally been a reflection of the mind of the respective ecclesiastical authority. That is the reason why liturgical affairs in the Archdiocese of Los Angeles have remained largely static while those, for example, in the Diocese of Oklahoma City–Tulsa have shown an open and warm reception to change. That the pace of change in the American Church has in many instances been far too slow for some is patently true, and in consequence there have slowly developed here and there throughout the country groups who have taken matters into their own hands and introduced sufficiently radical alterations in the liturgy to warrant mention of an "underground Church." Granted that some of the innovations have been clearly in contravention of the laws governing the liturgy, and on occasion in violation of the reverence and good taste that should surround the Church's official acts of worship, it seems evident that there would have been less provocation on this score if the request of the late Archbishop Hallinan, chairman of the hierarchy's Committee on the Liturgical Apostolate, for creative experimentation had been heeded. Alluding to the widespread discontent among many Catholics, both clergy and laity, the Archbishop of Atlanta remarked that if the Church's leaders would but listen to this unrest, "no matter how untrained the voices are, they will catch some authentic sounds." Given the fact that the present strain in that regard may well become a still greater threat to Catholic unity if allowed to go unremedied, it is difficult to see how the validity of the archbishop's eloquent plea for imaginative leadership on this vital matter could be denied:

Those who guide the new liturgy should live with those caught up in today's grossness. They must talk with them, share with them, and even suffer with them. When a young man has cause to rejoice, the liturgist should know how to collaborate with him in composing a new hymn or a fresh prayer. And because the pastor and bishop are leaders for the Lord, each should take the lead in opening up new channels for the Lord's children. Structuring Catholic life is his role; sadly at times, so is correction and reproof. Today perhaps, the most urgent of his tasks is to stimulate and help. He should stand, not in a shady corner, but in the midst of his people. There he serves by love and compassion, but also by pointing the way.[15]

If some Americans may have been tardy in this regard, such cannot be said for all their coreligionists. To mention only four, Archbishop Hallinan did not only give enlightened guidance to the Catholics of his own country: he carried his keen and imaginative mind into the counsels of the Universal Church where he was the sole American member of the Consilium for the Execution of the Constitution on the Sacred Liturgy instituted in February, 1964, by Pope Paul, as well as a representative of the United States on the international committee for the vernacular in the liturgy of all the English-speaking countries. Father Godfrey Diekmann, O.S.B., worthy successor to the pioneer promoter of liturgical reform at Saint John's Abbey, Virgil Michel, O.S.B., also served the worldwide Church as a *peritus* of Vatican Council II while carrying on Michel's

The Changing Church

traditions as editor of *Worship* and lecturer on liturgical subjects both here and abroad. Another man to whom much is owed for the liturgical advances made in the American Church is Father Frederick R. McManus of the Catholic University of America, who served two terms as president of the Liturgical Conference and who was named director in 1965 of the hierarchy's Committee on the Liturgical Apostolate. Finally, the widespread and intelligent interest of many of the laity in the Church's liturgical life during most of these critical years was symbolized by the able leadership of John B. Mannion, who until 1967 was Executive Secretary of the Liturgical Conference.

At the opposite end of the spectrum there has been the postconciliar development known as the Catholic Traditionalist Movement founded by Father Gommar A. De Pauw, formerly of the faculty of Mount Saint Mary's Seminary in Emmitsburg, Maryland. Precisely how many members the movement has had, it is impossible to say, but the published aims of its chief spokesman leave no doubt that they would not only return if they could to a Latin liturgy, but that they would also abolish most of the changes introduced into the Church's public worship since Vatican Council II. The objectives and methods of the Catholic Traditionalist Movement have at times been obscured by its leader's jurisdictional differences with his ecclesiastical superior, Cardinal Lawrence Shehan of Baltimore, and thus we must await the judgment of a future historian of the American Church concerning how far Father De Pauw's influence extended and how many disciples with a deep commitment the Catholic Traditionalist Movement drew to its standard.

Closely allied to the changes in the liturgy have been the

changed attitudes of American Catholics generally toward those of other religious faiths, in other words, in their acceptance of the ideas that brought about the ecumenical movement among all branches of the Christian family. As in the field of biblical studies, so in ecumenism Protestants have been quite in advance of Catholics. By way of illustrating the new mentality of Catholics on this subject I have more than once told lecture audiences that, in my early teens in the small village in northern Illinois where I was born and raised, one of my jobs on Sunday morning, either before or after I went to Mass, was to drive my devout Methodist paternal grandmother to her church. And as I recall it, my mother, who was born in the same village of Irish Catholic parents, would caution me, "Take your grandmother to church, but do not go beyond the door." We have now arrived at a time when cardinals and archbishops not only go beyond the door; they even ascend the pulpits of Protestant churches and receive a respectful hearing as they invoke the Word of God.

Americans are a notoriously mobile people, and in few aspects of their twentieth-century life have they demonstrated this mobility more clearly than in what pertained to so-called Protestant America. As Winthrop S. Hudson says, "in 1900 few would have disputed the contention that the United States was a Protestant nation," but a half-century later the situation had changed so drastically that the educated public did not think it strange when Arnold S. Nash gave to his introductory chapter to the symposium, *Protestant Thought in the Twentieth Century* the title "America at the End of the Protestant Era."[16] It was more than the end of an era; it was the end of over three centuries of Protestant dominance in English-speaking America. There replaced it what Will Herberg termed

The Changing Church

"a three-religion country" where Judaism, Protestantism, and Catholicism all paid homage in their own fashion to the central theme of the cultural-religious pluralism that bound them together in what was known as the American Way of Life.[17]

Through that same half-century the psychological enclosure that surrounded the Catholics remained practically unshaken. It is now difficult to believe that hardly more than twenty years ago priests like Edward V. Cardinal, C.S.V., John A. O'Brien, and others were still encountering occasional stiff resistance from diocesan chanceries when they sought permission to appear before interfaith gatherings with a minister and a rabbi. What, one may ask, caused men's attitudes to change so radically and so suddenly? Stories of the fraternization of the German Protestants and Catholics in the Nazi and Communist prison camps had something to do with it among Americans who had longed for years to draw closer to their separated brethren, and after the organization in 1948 of the World Council of Churches its programs likewise proved beneficial. Nor should the deepening realization by religious minds of various Christian communions that all churches are imperiled by the spreading secularization of life, with its attendant destruction of moral values, be omitted. More important, perhaps, than all these, for ideas must necessarily find articulation in persons to be effective, was the deep impression made on religious-minded Americans by the bold and imaginative speaking and writing of Protestant leaders like Eugene Carson Blake, and the extraordinary influence in both Catholic and Protestant circles of Pope John XXIII, who made Christian reunion one of the key objectives of his brief pontificate and whose death in June, 1963, was the occasion of the kind of universal grief that inspired a Protestant poet to write:

American Catholicism

No sentry need be posted,
No watchman set to guard
The tomb that is a hundred million hearts.[18]

Like most important ideas, that of Christian reunion evolved almost mysteriously. As Newman said, writing about how an idea takes possession of the popular mind:

At first men will not fully realize what it is that moves them and will express and explain themselves inadequately. There will be a general agitation of thought, and an action of mind upon mind. There will be a time of confusion, when conceptions and misconceptions are in conflict, and it is uncertain whether anything is to come of the idea at all, or which view of it is to get the start of the others.[19]

Those lines are a fair description of how the concept of ecumenism spread among American Catholics through the new opening to their Protestant, Orthodox, and Jewish brethren. The concept had a somewhat unsettling effect on a number of conservative members of the Church, although in this instance the opponents were probably a smaller minority than on any other issue dividing the faithful during these years. Thousands of Catholics had been waiting for a long time for a signal from their Church that they might fraternize more closely with other Americans, and the ecumenical thrust thus carried overtones of social acceptance as well as a broadened Christian brotherhood for many members of the Church of Rome in this country.

In any case, once the ice had been broken and the Vatican Council's "Decree on Ecumenism" had been promulgated in November, 1964, the thaw expanded with considerable speed. Credit for opening the American Church so that Catholics might see their fellow citizens of other faiths, and the latter might look into the Catholic enclosure, is due in no small measure to the enlightenment afforded by several publications, for example, the essays of the seven writers edited in 1959 by Philip Scharper in *American Catholics: A Protestant-Jewish View*, and the charter, so to speak, of the movement in this country, *An American Dialogue: A Protestant Looks at Catholicism and a Catholic Looks at Protestantism* by Robert McAfee Brown and Gustave Weigel, S.J., which came out the following year. The latter work gives helpful guidelines, beginning with Professor Brown's perceptive observation that "the first thing Protestants and Catholics must do is learn to talk to one another."[20] There follow his six "ground rules for dialogue," and, in turn, Father Weigel's candid and kindly scrutiny of Protestantism in the United States.

With something still lingering of the benign heritage willed to Baltimore in these matters by Cardinal Gibbons at his death in 1921, his third successor, Lawrence J. Shehan, set up an Archdiocesan Commission for Christian Unity on January 3, 1962, the first in the United States and, in fact, along with the Archdiocese of Paris which acted the same day, the first in the Catholic world. Moreover, the first official pronouncement of the present Cardinal Shehan upon his succession to the Archdiocese of Baltimore on December 8, 1961, was a pastoral letter on ecumenism. Thus was the premier see of the United States a pioneer in ecumenical concern. Action on a national scale was taken in November, 1964, when the National Conference of Catholic Bishops (so called after November, 1966) established the Committee for Ecumenical and Interreligious Affairs with Monsignor William A. Baum as its first director and with four special secretariats to treat of Catholic relations to Christian unity, the Jews, non-Christian religions, and non-believers. The changed atmosphere has been evident in a number of other ways, such as the series of discussions between Catholics and

Lutherans on the Eucharist, as well as the participation of Americans in international groups like the Catholic-Methodist conversations held in Italy late in 1967. And on a more public level the trend has been indicated by the more frequent appearance of Catholics in Protestant pulpits and vice versa, the participation of Catholics in acts of worship with Protestants and Orthodox clergymen, and even their occasional joint officiating at mixed marriages. Moreover, not only the Catholic community but Americans generally have become increasingly aware of the new spirit of friendliness among Christians with the televising of highly publicized Catholic religious services, such as the funeral of Cardinal Spellman in Saint Patrick's Cathedral on December 7, 1967, and the consecration of Bishop Mark J. Hurley in Saint Ignatius Church, San Francisco, on January 4, 1968. Thousands have thus been able to see the places of honor now accorded in Catholic sanctuaries to representatives of the Orthodox and Protestant Churches. Meanwhile the less spectacular but essential work of discussion of doctrinal differences has proceeded at a more measured pace.

One of the notable effects that followed from Catholics' active participation in the ecumenical dialogue was to make them much more acceptable to other Americans. Nearly a half-century ago George Santayana, writing of the faith of the Catholics of the United States in relation to their fellow citizens, said, "It confronts the boastful natural man, such as the American is, with a thousand denials and menaces," and he then added:

Everything in American life is at the antipodes to such a system. Yet the American Catholic is entirely at peace. His tone in everything, even in religion, is cheerfully American. It is wonderful how silently, amicably, and happily he lives in a community whose spirit is profoundly hostile to that of his religion.[21]

The Changing Church

Allowing for the change in American thinking on these matters since Santayana wrote in 1920, and for the oversimplification that his lines suggest, more than a grain of truth still remains in the judgment. While the Catholic was not then, and is not now—any more than any other American—"entirely at peace," it would be difficult to deny that in the main he has prospered in politics, in business, in the professions, and, more recently, in the "best" society in spite of a religious faith that at so many points has been at odds with his environment. The explanation for his feeling more at home, in addition to the barriers lowered by the ecumenical movement, is, of course, in part due to the fact that the Catholic has conformed more closely to the social philosophy in which he moves, for example, in the practice of birth control. For certainly it would be quite unreal to fancy that American society in general has drawn nearer to the Church and to her doctrinal beliefs and moral values.

In many ways, the measure of a man's acceptance by society is his ability to offer himself for public office and to receive the endorsement of his fellow citizens at the polls. Success in business or commerce, in the professions of medicine and law, as well as in the more creative walks of life like the theater, architecture, and the fine arts is, indeed, a mark of acceptance of a kind, as it is also a tribute to a man's intellectual ability, professional skill, originality, imagination, and powers of administration. A large number of Catholics have achieved distinction in these varied professions from the early national period until the present,[22] but their success does not to the same degree reflect their fellow Americans' acceptance as does a victory at the polls.

Perhaps it was something of this kind that Archbishop John Ireland had in mind when less than three weeks before the presidential election of November 3, 1908, he told a large audience at the Hotel Jefferson in Saint Louis:

I urge on all Catholics to make yourselves fit for the highest offices in the country, according to your number. There are now 17,000,000 Catholics in this country, and they are not represented in its great offices as they should be. I have heard the statement that there will never be a Catholic President, this is all nonsense. When the right man is presented the United States will choose him and not discriminate because of his religion.[23]

At that time this must have sounded like a wildly optimistic assertion coming from the country's most politically active Catholic prelate, and even twenty years later the sequel to the campaign of Alfred E. Smith would seem to have confirmed Ireland's judgment as faulty. A generation after Smith's defeat, however, the prediction of the Archbishop of Saint Paul became a reality, and with it the entire Catholic community of the United States marked a major milestone in their history.

As Senator John F. Kennedy of Massachusetts moved cautiously toward the Democratic presidential candidacy in the late 1950's his political astuteness told him that his Catholic faith would be the main obstacle to be overcome. But, among the candidate's assets that helped to sustain him, assets that had been lacking to Governor Smith thirty years before, were a splendid education and a special knowledge of American history. Kennedy was a man of marked sophistication, and a recent writer could rightly say of him:

He did not regard every voter who doubted the desirability of a Catholic in the White House as a bigot. As he told Unitarian Ted Sorensen, he would have to answer all reasonable as well as unreasonable questions. He could not afford to be defensive or silent to questions which seemed unfair or even insulting. This approach was far different from that of Al Smith, who could not understand anti-Catholic attacks as having any reasonable basis at all. Kennedy understood their historical roots.[24]

The Changing Church

During the campaign the Democratic candidate had numerous and delicate confrontations because of his religion, but none so portentous for his future as that which occurred on the evening of September 12, 1960, when he appeared before the Greater Houston Ministerial Association in Houston, Texas. Given the circumstances, Kennedy not only made a masterful speech but met questions from the floor in a forthright and open way that left his audience more than satisfied. It was not an exaggeration, therefore, for Theodore H. White to state, "When he had finished, he had not only closed Round One of his election campaign—he had for the first time more fully and explicitly than any other thinker of his faith defined the personal doctrine of a modern Catholic in democratic society."[25]

Five years later the entire issue of one's individual religious commitment and one's stand on relations of Church and State were to be infinitely easier for a Catholic candidate for office to meet, because of the "Declaration on Religious Freedom" promulgated by Pope Paul VI on December 7, 1965. But in 1960 it was an entirely different matter, for the non-Catholic American could, and did, with telling effect press the traditional teaching of Catholic theologians on the union of Church and State and logically raise the question how a Catholic in the White House could reconcile this teaching with his country's Constitution and the tradition that had evolved since the nation's birth. True, John F. Kennedy was an immensely attractive candidate on many counts, but, as the wisest political analysts sensed from the outset, his religious faith constituted a major barrier in the path to victory. That victory on November 8, 1960, real though it was, was won only by a very narrow margin of the popular vote. Early in the following summer there appeared a serious analysis of the election returns by four political scientists at the University of Michigan. Among what they called the "short-term forces" in the election was that of religion, about which they said, "There is every reason to believe that these preliminary estimates under-estimate the importance of religion in the 1960 vote and, in particular, under-estimate the magnitude of the anti-Catholic vote."[26] The authors were confident that no short-term force had moved so large a fraction of the 1960 electorate as had the issue of a Catholic candidate. "This was the major cause," they said, "of the net departure of the vote totals from the division which the comparative underlying strength of the two parties in 1960 would have led us to expect."[27]

Regardless of the slender plurality of votes, Kennedy's election marked a singular triumph. The choice for the first time of a Catholic for President was the kind of event after which issues closely related to it would never again be the same. Professor Fuchs describes well the election's deeper significance:

Because he was a Catholic, representing the one sectarian religion thought to be at odds with the culture-religion of Americanism, Kennedy, as a culture-hero, helped to broaden the basis of consensus in American life by encouraging the forces of encounter within American Catholicism, and by opening the minds of non-Catholics to new opportunities for human communication, learning and growth in dialogue with Catholics.[28]

Even at this date the ultimate significance of John Kennedy's election and tragically brief tenure of the presidency has yet to be fully weighed. It would be difficult, however, to deny the extraordinary effects of his public career, as it would be to refute what Fuchs wrote in his evaluation of its widespread influence. "Before his death," he said, "and perhaps even prior to his election, he was to do more to blunt the ancient mutual hatred of Catholics and non-Catholics than any American had ever done."[29] Yet it would be folly for an American Catholic seeking public office to entertain the idea that he would no longer be challenged about his religious views. That was made unmistakably clear early in 1968 when the organ of the Protestants and Other Americans for Separation of Church and State (POAU) listed the leading presidential candidates, mentioned the Catholic Church's traditional stand on such controversial subjects as public support of private schools and dissemination of birth control information, and contended that Senators Eugene J. McCarthy and Robert F. Kennedy had not to their knowledge made clear their position on these questions. To the POAU the two senators had failed to match "the unequivocal stand taken some years earlier by the latter's brother," whereupon they concluded, "If there is any 'religious problem' in the coming political campaign, it lies with these men and they alone can resolve it."[30] The lurking suspicion of the waning POAU, however, should not be taken as typical of American Protestantism.

John F. Kennedy's election to the presidency was, of course, only the most spectacular gain made by a Catholic in American politics. Politics had long been a field in which Catholics were well represented on national, state, and local levels. In fact, in some large municipalities they had been for years the dominant element in political life. The status of Catholics in American politics was reflected in the rather steady increase of their number in Congress. When, for example, the Eighty-ninth Congress convened in January, 1965, it was found that for the first time Catholics constituted the largest religious group, with 94 members of the House of Representatives and 14 senators, the total of 108 being fourteen above the Methodists, who had 94 members in that session.[31] The Ninety-first Congress that opened in January, 1969, had 111 Catholics with the next largest religious group being the Methodists, who numbered 90.

Closely related to the nation's political life is what has been referred to as the "civil religion" of the United States, a concept that has generally meant more to politicians of all religious groups—whether in Congress or in state legislatures or in county and city governments—than to their millions of constituents (for whom, nonetheless, it means much). For in addition to the allegiance that men pay to their respective churches and synagogues most citizens of the Republic, including the Catholics, accept the vague quasi-cult that binds all together in recognition of the moral imperatives contained in what might be called the nation's creed, especially as these imperatives relate to the rest of the world. True this "civil religion" has often been employed by rascals and mountebanks for selfish purposes, just as it has given birth on occasion to expressions of national self-righteousness that men of other lands find highly irritating. Yet the almost universal respect paid to what has been described as possessing "its own prophets and its own martyrs, its own sacred events and sacred places, its own solemn rituals and symbols,"[32] has been in general a kind of religion over and above that practiced by individual Protestants, Jews, and Catholics.

Nor have Catholics been laggard in this regard. On the contrary, until recent years their insecurity about their acceptance in the body politic because of their near-immigrant status induced an eagerness to "belong." This motive, plus a sincerity of conviction on the part of most, made them more vocal on these themes than may always have been justified. A fair-sized volume might be compiled containing the expressions of approval of one or another aspect of this national "cult," all the

The Changing Church

way from Archbishop John Carroll, founder of the American hierarchy, through John Hughes, Archbishop of New York, who, though he was probably the strongest ultramontanist (Rome oriented) in the history of the Church of the United States, found no problem in reconciling the two views. That harmony was suggested in a letter he addressed to the Society for the Propagation of the Faith at Lyons in which he said, "We deplore in the conditions of Catholic Europe, the absence of that liberty of the Church, which we enjoy in this Protestant republic, and we shall not allow this blessing to be interfered with by any influence except that wh. it is our pride to proclaim and our glory to submit to, in the successor of St. Peter, the supreme pastor of the Universal Church."[33]

Cardinal Gibbons and Archbishop Ireland were in this same tradition of high patriotism, but its most eloquent exponent was probably the late Cardinal Spellman, who while on a visit to Vietnam in Christmas Week of 1965 countered critics of American policy there by repeating Stephen Decatur's toast of 1815, "Our country! In her intercourse with foreign nations may she always be in the right; but our country, right or wrong."[34] This school of thought has encountered a rising tide of criticism from all Americans in the 1960's, and again the new-found power that comes from numbers and wealth, the increased psychological security which this power induces, and the growing sophistication of the laity, has accounted for notable breaks with tradition in Catholic ranks. It can be seen in the editorial policies of *Commonweal* and the *National Catholic Reporter* on American involvement in Vietnam, to say nothing of the personal stands taken by public figures like Senators McCarthy and Kennedy. Among the most publicized cases of draft card burners and loud protesters against the

American presence in Vietnam, has been a growing number
of Catholics who feel that the official voices of their Church
have been far too mild in their denunciation of the bombing
and the consequent cruelty and suffering inflicted on civilians
in Vietnam. Nor is this type of Catholic in the least impressed
by the traditional arguments used against the spread of Communism, for to them, as to Peter Steinfels, "To raise opposition
to Communism to an absolute in whose name all can be done
is to offer blood sacrifice before a false god."[35] For the first
time in the history of the American Church, therefore, the
conflict in Vietnam has found a sizable and articulate group
of members in open opposition to the government's prosecu-
tion of a war. It is but another indication of the independence
of spirit vis-à-vis the bishops that marks the Catholics of this
generation. In other words, they make up their own minds on
issues of this kind whereas their grandparents would have
docilely waited for the clue from their bishops and priests. It
is a natural sequel to the greatly improved education and
sophistication of lay members of the Church. In fact, in this
case the bishops' national pastoral letter of November, 1968,
adopted an advanced position on conscientious objection to a
particular war and to the need for a change in the draft law.

When the historian of contemporary Catholicism in the
United States turns from politics to education he is quick to
realize that he has entered upon a far more complicated terrain.
Allowing for the period of uncertainty through which it is
passing, the world's largest private school system is still a for-
midable structure. As of January 1, 1968, there were 10,757
elementary schools with 4,165,504 students and 2,275 secondary schools with a total enrollment of 1,089,272, entirely apart
from the seminaries and institutions of higher learning. The

problems involved in operating this far-flung educational empire have always been serious, but during the 1960's they have become enormously more complex, and in some areas virtually insoluble. With the steady decline of vocations to the priesthood and to the religious life—the total number of sisters alone in this country dropped by 4,750 during 1966—the principal source of the Church's teaching personnel has been gravely threatened. And whereas the priests and religious—to whom in many instances the most meager salaries have been paid—decreased, the lay teachers in the Catholic schools, have increased 190 per cent over the ten years between 1956 and 1966, while during the same decade the religious serving as teachers increased only 14.3 per cent. It takes little imagination to picture what this change in personnel has meant to diocesan and parochial budgets in the way of rising costs to pay the more than 90,000 lay teachers the kind of salaries that befit their personal dignity, their training, and their needs.

Yet it is not simply a matter of dollars and cents that causes anxiety to those associated with the Church's schools. The reasons for the "agonizing reappraisal" that has characterized these schools during the 1960's are numerous and varied. A central point is a new chapter in the periodic controversy over federal aid to private schools, with some Catholics, such as the late Cardinal Spellman, taking the position that the Church's schools would be forced out of existence if they did not get government assistance. Few matters of public policy have separated Catholics from their fellow citizens more markedly than their differences over private schools. The often sharp and bitter debate has led, in turn, to a more searching comparison between the public and the parochial schools, and a growing number of Catholics—especially the more affluent who live in suburban areas and who are, perhaps, more closely touched by the general secularization of the national mind—have come to believe that the public schools would afford their children a superior education because of their better equipment, the smaller size of the classes, and the more complete training of the teachers. This belief has been accompanied by a conviction that the expanded and improved programs of the Confraternity of Christian Doctrine would serve their children's religious interests and thus the latter would suffer no serious deprivation by attending the public schools. When these reasons are given greater force by the inability of parishes to finance new schools or additions to existing schools, one can understand the dropping enrollment in the elementary schools of the Church and the slowing down of growth in the Catholic high school population.

The changing attitude of Catholics on this subject was highlighted in 1964 with the publication of Mary Perkins Ryan's volume, *Are Parochial Schools the Answer?* Mrs. Ryan's book caused a stir in Catholic educational circles. Although she had not explicitly called for the elimination of Catholic schools as some of her critics contended, numerous champions of the traditional parochial school system spoke in defense of the system. As the decade wore on, a further factor appeared in the minds of an increasing number of Catholics who participated in this debate. Granted that there were available adequately trained personnel and money to operate the parochial schools, these Catholics felt that the problem was more fundamental, and they asked themselves such questions as these: Should the schools' resources be diverted into a ghettoized educational system? Would this not make the Church ingrown rather than outgoing at a time when the spirit of Vatican Council II seemed to have encouraged the latter? Should not the assets formerly expended on parochial schools be directed rather to other areas which would help to make the Church more relevant to the secular community as a whole—for example, to a social involvement that would assist in healing the wounds of that community? Should not the Church's resources, both personnel and money, be employed with a broader Christian motivation to extend Catholics' efforts to the world in which they live, rather than simply to take care of the educational needs of Catholic children in a way that often duplicated existing facilities and opportunities available to all American children? Catholics thinking along these lines saw the Church's school system as too self-centered to allow a fulfillment of the basic obligation of love, that is, to be outgoing in its service to others as a Christian conscience should demand. Such, then, have been the questions asked not only by many of the Catholic laity but also by a growing number of young pastors and the younger clergy and religious generally.

Yet the private religious schools have not been without benefit of serious studies demonstrating from empirical evidence not only that a good number of the schools have more than maintained a high general average of intellectual achievement but that some of them are, indeed, superior to their public school counterparts. Scholarly investigators like Andrew M. Greeley and Peter H. Rossi,[36] to cite but one example, found after a two-year study that these facts were true, and they likewise found no data to support the position that Catholic schools were "divisive." By the same token, however, they concluded that the religious education imparted to three-fourths of the students had little or no practical effect on the latter's adult lives, except in the case of those reared in homes that set a high premium on religious values. Reports such as the Greeley-Rossi study, followed within a few weeks in the early autumn of 1966 by the four-year investigation of the Church's elementary and secondary schools conducted at the University of Notre Dame on a grant from the Carnegie Corporation,[37] opened a new chapter in the heated debate over parochial versus public schools for Catholic students. Nor has this debate shown any signs of abating with the appearance of new factors such as increasing demands for experimentation, especially on the elementary school level, demands that many bishops, pastors, superintendents, and school principals have not been willing to meet. Two additional considerations, beyond the rising costs of maintaining these schools, have served to deepen the crisis facing Catholic schools in the late 1960's. First, there is the tumult into which many of them were plunged by efforts of their administrators—often furiously opposed by parents of the students—to involve the schools in integrating the races. Second, there is the inevitably disturbing effect produced in many classrooms by the grave anxiety over personal identity which has overtaken so many of the teachers belonging to religious congregations. The desire for a more varied and less structured apostolate of the Immaculate Heart of Mary Sisters is a case in point; the proposed program brought conflict with Cardinal McIntyre and inevitably involved the twenty-eight elementary schools and seven high schools in the Archdiocese of Los Angeles where these sisters were teaching.

With a view to assessing the Catholic schools' condition and, if possible, to making recommendations for their future, a week-long symposium was held in Washington in November, 1967, under the auspices of the National Catholic Educational Association. The prolonged discussions of some 120 experts from all sections of the country revealed a wide variety of views, and when the symposium's statement, drawn up by an editorial committee of thirteen of the participants, was issued over three months later, several who had been present dissociated themselves from it. The latter felt either that the statement did not reflect the urgency of the situation or that it gave undue prominence to higher education and not sufficient emphasis to the diocesan superintendents of schools. Although on the whole the report leaned toward the preservation of the traditional system of Catholic schools, its authors stated, "We recognize the existence of a wide range of options in Christian education. We urge openness in weighing choices among them."[38] Such an attitude would seem the dictate of common sense at a time when the Church is faced with so many imponderables in regard to her schools. A certain amount of centralization within each diocese is, of course, necessary in order to operate a diocesan-wide school system efficiently. But such centralization should allow for such things as interparochial planning wherein the voices of the Catholic community could play a more decisive role than they have in the past. One of the most effective ways for those voices to be heard has been in the parochial and diocesan school boards, which, as some have foreseen, will in time be supplemented by interparochial boards. In the matter of hearing the voices of the Catholic community no American diocese had so clear and direct a mandate concerning its schools as that given to officials of the Archdiocese of Vancouver in June, 1965, when at the instance of Archbishop Martin M. Johnson a referendum of the Catholic people was held on what policy should be adopted regarding the future of the archdiocesan schools. The result was that 26,057, or 90 per cent of those voting, pledged support to an expanded school system to be controlled by laymen, while 2,997 were registered in opposition to these proposals. At the end of the same summer Archbishop Johnson gave his approval for the election of a twelve-man archdiocesan school board, all laymen, to whom control of the system was transferred.

In the United States there has been a limited number of experiments on the local or diocesan level. To cite two examples, there was the plan inaugurated in September, 1964, in the Archdiocese of Cincinnati which eliminated the first grade in all its parochial schools with results that a year later were regarded as both favorable and unfavorable.[39] Second, in the Diocese of Saint Cloud, the Board of Education, prompted by the shortage of religious teachers and the rising school costs, appointed a committee of educators and community representatives to evaluate the program of the schools. Following the acceptance of the committee's report by the board, the recommendations were presented in open meetings to the pastors and parents. One of the recommendations adopted was to eliminate the seventh and eighth grades in those communities where the Catholic educational program was regarded as inferior to that of the public schools and where the religious instruction of the students could be absorbed by the Confraternity of Christian Doctrine or by a released-time program. Exceptions were permitted in those communities where parents and pastors agreed to hire additional qualified lay teachers, but in the final reckoning 75 per cent of the grade schools of the diocese discontinued the seventh and eighth grades.

In all that pertains to parochial schools, those dioceses that have given over more and more control of the schools to diocesan and parochial boards composed of laymen have shown a far more realistic approach than have those where policy decisions have been made exclusively by bishops, pastors, and clerical or religious school administrators. A predominantly lay school board—or a board of mixed clergy, religious, and laity—is a much more faithful reflection of the spirit of Vatican Council II, of the democratic process in which Americans have been reared, and of a valid sampling of the Catholic community likely to win generous support for the schools than is the purely clerical or religious management that dominated the parochial school system from its beginning. Normally, the laity are more competent in matters relating to finance and administration than are most of the clergy, and they likewise are often as well or better informed in educational policies and trends. It would be difficult, indeed, to think of a more appropriate area for the genuine implementation of the recent ecumenical council's "Decree on the Apostolate of the Laity" than that of the Church's schools. The council fathers stated:

Bishops, pastors of parishes, and other priests of both branches of the clergy should keep in mind that the right and duty to exercise the apostolate is common to all the faithful, both clergy and laity, and that the laity also have their own proper roles in building up the Church.[40]

Whether the Catholic school boards are to be composed of laymen or of clergy, however, has become for some a secondary consideration in view of spiraling school costs and of a serious threat posed early in 1968 to the educational assistance that children in private schools had been receiving from the federal government since the passage of the Elementary and Secondary School Act of 1965. In 1961 the late President Kennedy stated unequivocally that aid to church-related schools was clearly unconstitutional and, therefore, that the question admitted of no debate. In spite of Kennedy's strong stand, debate continued, but an announcement by President Johnson in January, 1965, that the government would extend educational services to all children in educationally deprived areas, regardless of what kind of school they attended, foreshadowed a change in policy. In the course of that year Congress passed the measure mentioned above (Public Law 89-10) with a carefully devised formula which provided monetary aid to local public educational agencies that served areas inhabited by a large number of low-income families; all children in these areas, whether in public or non-public schools, were to be eligible for the services provided. The emphasis here was on the child, not on the private school as an institution; the school was not to be the recipient of funds but rather the child was to be the recipient of the services. These services included school library resources and the loan of books, provision of printed and published instructional materials, grants for supplementary educational centers to serve children in both public and private schools, and grants for research and training in the field of education to be administered by colleges, universities, and other public and private agencies.

Analyzing this law shortly after its enactment, Francis T. Hurley, Assistant General Secretary of what was soon to be renamed the United States Catholic Conference, maintained that the question was not what immediate benefits would accrue to the parochial schools. "Rather," he inquired, "is there a disposition in the school systems of the country to make a new cooperative venture in education work?" And Monsignor Hurley concluded, "If one will grant that the national temper of harmony that helped produce PL 89-10 is merely a reflection of the harmony that prevails locally, the answer is affirmative."[41] It was true that there had been a change of mind on this controversial matter on the part of many Americans over that of a decade or two before. As time went on, Catholics found themselves less and less isolated from other Americans in their belief that government assistance to children in private schools was not a violation of the principle of separation of Church and State. Among others, Milton Himmelfarb wrote in the summer of 1966:

Catholics, therefore, have a real grievance. To remove the grievance would be just. It would also be statesmanlike, and would help to improve the education of a significant part of the American population. People are coming to see that. In the past few years the public-opinion polls have shown a steady rise in the proportion of respondents favoring governmental aid, until now there are more for it than against it.[42]

While there had, indeed, been a noticeable swing of public opinion in the direction indicated by Himmelfarb, the "national temper of harmony," of which Monsignor Hurley spoke in regard to the passage of PL 89-10, had not been universally reflected on the local level. And in 1967 this law received a serious challenge in New York concerning textbooks loaned by the state to private school children. Thus in January, 1968, the stage was set for another of the numerous encounters between the contending sides on this issue; the Supreme Court of the United States agreed to rule on the constitutionality of New York's textbook law. True, the case involved only textbooks, but its implications went quite beyond that single matter. It also had a special relevance for New York, where a heated election campaign had been fought some months before over the adoption of a new state constitution that omitted the so-called Blaine Amendment of 1894 forbidding public financial aid to private schools. The defeat in November, 1967, of the proposed

constitution by over 2,000,000 votes was, perhaps too simplisti-
cally, interpreted as due in part to the omission of the Blaine
Amendment—the fear of added taxes was also a factor. When,
therefore, the state senate attempted to bring New York law
into harmony with PL 89-10, the *New York Times* contended
editorially that the senate should await the Supreme Court's
decision and that, by moving ahead, it had shown "a reckless
willingness to abandon the protection provided by the State
Constitution for the last 74 years without even knowing what
it was accepting in its place."[43] Groups that consistently opposed public aid to private schools could be depended upon to
align themselves on the side of the *New York Times*. For that
reason with the broad implications of the case that the Supreme
Court agreed to hear in the early days of 1968, *America*'s editorial comment was not without point. "It is no exaggeration,"
declared the Jesuit weekly, "to say that a very important part
of the future of American education hangs decisively in the
balance."[44] A reprieve, so to speak, was gained on June 10,
1968, when the Supreme Court declared the New York law
constitutional on the score that the loaned textbooks benefited
students, not parochial schools, and thus it did not constitute
state support of religion.

If the Church's elementary and secondary schools may be said
to have been in a state of great uncertainty, what is one to say
of conditions over the past twelve years in her institutions of
higher learning? First, insofar as the academic goals of these
institutions are concerned, there has taken place a general tight-
ening of standards, a serious and genuine effort to achieve
excellence, and a far greater degree of emphasis on quality
education than was true a decade and a half ago. In the autumn
of 1955, when the present writer published a strong indictment

of Catholic colleges and universities for their failure to emphasize these goals and to achieve any real distinction, Bishop John J. Wright stated that the study, "provoked a reaction that is in itself irrefutable evidence of how well timed and accurate are his contentions."[45] While the writer received at that time a great deal of support,[46] it should not be forgotten that there was also vigorous dissent in Catholic circles, especially among some members of the hierarchy, such as Cardinal Spellman, who felt a grave disservice had been done to the Church by an openly critical appraisal of this kind.

In that respect the Catholics of the United States have traveled far since 1955. Books and articles by those of her own faith have criticized the Church's commitment in higher education to the point that such criticism has become practically the order of the day, and except for a few discordant voices, it has won general acceptance. The reason is simple. In their new maturity most Catholics find themselves as convinced as other Americans that if there is to be improvement, their colleges and universities must undergo constant and close scrutiny of their academic performance. In the autumn of 1962 Dennis W. Brogan, emeritus professor of political science of the University of Cambridge, put the matter succinctly at the end of a lecture in Washington, D.C. The present writer asked upon what evidence he based his assertion that there had been noticeable improvement in higher education in the United States. "Americans used to wish to have their sons and daughters go to college," said Brogan; "now they wish to have them go to a good college." At that time the answer was about as representative of the changing attitudes of the parents of Catholic college students as it was of the parents of students of other and of no religious faith. As a recent report of the Danforth

Commission said, "The Roman Catholic Church is becoming an American middle-class church, and this is finding expression in Catholic institutions."[47]

The Catholic colleges and universities of the 1960's have been dealing, therefore, with a more sophisticated clientele than they had known in previous generations. Nor are these institutions any longer operating on the simple philosophy that inspired their founding and guided their development from the opening in 1791 of the future Georgetown University down almost to the present decade. That philosophy was unwittingly summarized by Canon Josef Salzbacher of Saint Stephen's Cathedral, Vienna, on a visit to this country in 1842. Noticing the desire of many Catholic youths for higher education to prepare them for the professions, he remarked, ". . . it has long been the ambition of the bishops to erect such higher institutions of learning and to supervise them in order that these young men, who otherwise would attend the public state schools, might not go astray."[48] In other words, the Church's leaders of that time, and for a long time thereafter, looked upon Catholic colleges and universities for the most part as citadels within which students' religious faith would be protected against the hazards encountered on secular campuses instead of regarding these institutions as "houses of the intellect."

If by 1960 Catholics had cultivated a desire for "good" colleges for their sons and daughters, and in so doing had furnished a further strong motivation to administrators and faculties of Catholic institutions for the academic excellence and high quality instruction that had been lacking, other factors had meanwhile moved to the center of the stage of Catholic higher education and now demanded the attention of the audience. For the more than 300 Catholic colleges and universities

The Changing Church

of the United States with their combined enrollments of approximately 450,000 students, two insistent and as yet unsolved problems remain in what may be called the American Church's post-conciliar age; and those two problems have left lingering doubts in some minds that these institutions can ever achieve their professed goals. One is the almost frightening rise in the costs of operating a private institution of learning, a problem that haunts roughly two-thirds of the nation's colleges and universities. The other is a problem which, if not entirely unique to Catholic institutions, has at least a special relevance for them, namely, the delicate matter of reconciling academic freedom with religious teaching as represented in the magisterium of the Church. The latter has become especially acute since the Catholic world moved into the period that has witnessed on all sides the broad effects of the "Declaration on Religious Freedom" of Vatican Council II. For as the late John Courtney Murray, S.J., wisely remarked shortly after the promulgation of that document in December, 1965: "The conciliar affirmation of the principle of freedom was narrowly limited—in the text. But the text itself was flung into a pool whose shores are wide as the universal Church. The ripples will run far."[49] In no sector of the multiple and varied activities of the Church has the running of these "ripples" been experienced with more meaning for the present and more significance for the future than in the colleges and universities operating either directly or indirectly under her auspices.

When the president of Yale University, which then had an endowment of approximately $450,000,000, candidly stated in the spring of 1967 that Yale "has never had a more difficult financial prospect," there was no dissent to his further comment that "a serious strain on resources for Yale is a crisis for other places."[50] For every Catholic college and university of significant quality and size it is, indeed, a crisis, and one of the first magnitude, allowing even for the contributed services of numerous members of religious congregations whose vows of poverty do not permit them to accept a salary. Not one of the Catholic institutions has financial resources within sight of Yale's, to say nothing of the billion-dollar endowment of Harvard. Among the Catholics the largest endowment is that of the University of Notre Dame, which in June, 1967, was estimated at $52,711,564 for a student body of 7,425, only 1,248 under that of Yale's 8,673 students. The combined ten highest endowments of the Catholic universities amounted to not much more than the endowment of Princeton University. The Catholic University of America, the only so-called national Catholic university in the United States, supported by all the dioceses, had an endowment of $7,200,000 for about 6,600 students. This institution's financial resources have always been inadequate, in spite of the fact that it has been owned and operated since its opening in 1889 by the hierarchy of the United States, and that since 1903 it has been the recipient of an annual collection amounting in recent years to about $2,000,000 taken up among the laity in all the dioceses of the country. What has aggravated the financial problems of the Catholic University of America is that of all the Catholic universities in this country it has consistently maintained the most ambitious program of graduate studies and has the highest percentage of graduate students, features that add to operating costs substantially more than do course offerings and students on other than graduate levels.

The financial crisis in American private colleges and universities has frequently been described and needs no restatement here. To mention only three examples, *Time*'s article of late June, 1967, featuring President Kingman Brewster, Jr., of Yale, was followed three months later by a sobering survey in *America* that treated the special relevance of this problem for Catholic institutions of higher learning, and then in October of the same year Duncan Norton-Taylor supplied confirming evidence for the readers of *Fortune* in an article whose title told its own tale, "Private Colleges—a Question of Survival."[51] When it is recalled that the percentage of lay faculty members over priests and religious has risen steadily in Catholic schools to the point where it is between 75 and 95 per cent of the faculties of the largest and the best of these institutions, and that these are only "the best" because they compete as keenly as their secular counterparts for first-class professors, it is understandable why Neil G. McCluskey's remark that "the situation is moving from grim to desperate,"[52] could be applied with special force to Catholic higher education.

Granted with Father McCluskey that there have been hopeful signs—hitherto unknown—of collaboration and co-operation among the Catholic institutions during recent years; granted, too, that he skillfully summarized the principal causes for the present plight of the Catholic colleges and universities, I trust I may be pardoned if I reply, "We have been here before." In September, 1955, these same causes were set forth in considerable detail in an essay entitled, "American Catholics and the Intellectual Life," and, using as a parallel the formation that year of the Council of the Western European Union which had come into being out of fear of Communism, the essay said:

The Catholic institutions of higher learning in this country may soon face an equally grave threat to their survival. It will not be the peril of communist occupation that will bring them together to counsel for their mutual welfare, but it may well be a thing that Americans understand much better, namely, the peril of financial bankruptcy . . . in my judgment the danger of insolvency, and that alone, will put an end to the senseless duplication of effort and the wasteful proliferation that have robbed Catholic graduate schools of the hope of superior achievement.[53]

What this essay said about Catholic graduate schools was in a certain sense confirmed in 1966 by Allan M. Cartter's detailed study revealing that, among the 106 institutions covered, the over-all ratings of the graduate programs of 7 Catholic universities scarcely rose above the level of mediocrity.[54] Moreover, the detrimental effects of proliferation and all that it implied were also applicable in 1955—as they still are—to undergraduate and professional training under Catholic auspices. Yet the collaboration between these institutions over the interval of thirteen years has been trivial in comparison with what the situation demanded. Nor has the "Declaration on Christian Education" of Vatican Council II made any noticeable difference by its advice:

At the diocesan, national, and international level, the spirit of cooperation grows daily more urgent and effective. Since this same spirit is most necessary in educational work, every effort should be made to see that suitable coordination is fostered between various Catholic schools, and that between these schools and others that kind of collaboration develops which the well-being of the whole human family demands.[55]

Although the prospect of financial bankruptcy is more imminent by far for more colleges in 1969 than it was in 1955, one still looks almost in vain for really radical steps such as the move in 1968 of Marymount College, joined by Saint Joseph College of Orange, California, to the campus of Loyola University of Los Angeles. Consolidating educational resources in this fashion—and little short of this—would save many Catholic institutions, and at the same time assure a high quality of education. For a few the pressure had already become too great by 1968, and experienced educators anticipated that others would follow Duchesne College in Omaha, which announced early in the year that it would close in the following summer.

During the post-conciliar period a new development in Catholic circles has been the converting of boards of trustees from priests and religious to boards composed predominantly of laymen. From every point of view this is a step forward. It is in the spirit of Vatican Council II's emphasis on the need for enhancing the laity's role in the Church; it brings into the councils of the Catholic colleges and universities numerous dedicated business and professional men of great competence in financial affairs; and it serves also to involve both Catholic and non-Catholic laymen in the life of educational institutions that are thereby able to render better service to the entire community of which they formed a part.

This action has been taken in different ways. For example, at Webster College the Sisters of Loretto, who founded the institution in 1915, have stepped aside entirely from legal control, and at the University of Notre Dame and Saint Louis University, the Holy Cross Fathers and Jesuit Fathers, respectively, have become a minority among the newly appointed lay trustees. Various motives are suggested by these changes, not the least of which is the hope that, by bringing the laymen into a majority among the trustees, the laymen's controlling voice will offer greater assurance that these colleges and universities will continue to benefit from the substantial assistance they have been receiving in one form or another from government grants. But when the United States Supreme Court declined in November, 1966, to take cognizance of two school aid appeals against the decision of the Maryland Court of Appeals that had declared the legislature's grants to three religiously affiliated colleges unconstitutional because of their sectarian character, the prospect of assistance from government was called into serious question. Without such aid it would be virtually impossible for many Catholic colleges and universities to continue to exist. The time ahead may, therefore, prove that if this source of help is denied, the sole hope for Catholic higher education will lie in the drastic cutting back of its commitment, the closing of a number of institutions, and the much closer collaboration or even merging of others. Grim as it might seem in anticipation, it is an eventuality that could bring its blessing as well as its blight if it will insure a superior quality of education in those institutions that manage to survive.

Another problem that has become increasingly vexatious for Catholic institutions results from the stronger emphasis on freedom within the American academic community generally, both for faculty members and for students. The historians of academic freedom in the United States have noted that the restrictive atmosphere of the old colleges and universities established after the Civil War was due chiefly to the "religious commitments and sectarian aspirations" of these institutions. For this reason, said Hofstadter and Metzger, religious leaders figured "in an exceptionally prominent way among the opponents of intellectual freedom"[56] down almost to the present century. If relatively few Catholic names are found among these religious leaders, it is because of the well-nigh universal docile acceptance in Catholic circles not only of the teachings of the Church but also of the authoritarian regimes that governed the Church's colleges. To question an article of Catholic belief or to challenge a ruling by a president or a dean in a Catholic institution was almost unthinkable.

Some years before Vatican Council II, however, a more critical spirit and a greater eagerness for the democratic process began to pervade the leading Catholic centers of learning. With the new thinking engendered by the ecumenical council, and with the accelerated movement for freedom of thought and action on most of the nation's campuses, there ensued in Catholic circles a notable change in mood. It would have been altogether strange had such a change not taken place, for Catholics are as much the heirs of the American tradition as anyone else. Furthermore, the new mood was encouraged by the "Pastoral Constitution on the Church in the Modern World" promulgated in December, 1965, at the end of Vatican Council II; speaking of the enhanced role of the educated laymen, it stated:

In order that such persons may fulfill their proper function, let it be recognized that all the faithful, clerical and lay, possess a lawful freedom of inquiry and of thought, and the freedom to express their minds humbly and courageously about those matters in which they enjoy competence.[57]

One of the first places where the conflict between the proponents of a broader and more genuine freedom for faculty and students and a highly conservative administration broke into the open was the Catholic University of America. In February, 1963, *The Tower*, the students' weekly newspaper, made it known that the administration of the university had banned four distinguished theologians as possible choices for a series of student-sponsored lectures. The reason given by the administration was that since these four men—Godfrey Diekmann, O.S.B., Hans Küng, John Courtney Murray, S.J., and

Gustave Weigel, S.J.—all represented the progressive school of thought, and since the institution belonged to the entire hierarchy of the United States, the university should not show partiality to any single aspect of theological thought while the ecumenical council was still debating certain controverted issues on which the four theologians were thought to hold a single point of view. The fact that in banning the representatives of this point of view an advantage was implicitly given to the opposing side in a way that jeopardized the neutrality which the administration was desirous of safeguarding, seems to have been overlooked by the rector of the university and his associates. The matter was not pressed further by the students, but the widespread publicity attending the controversy made it something of a *cause célèbre* both here and abroad, and three years later one critic stated that this case "marked not only a new high point in the intransigence of the conservatives but also a turning point in the history of freedom in the Catholic Church in America."[58]

During the 1960's there has been a series of eruptions on Catholic campuses over the freedom to which faculty and students felt entitled, either against the confining tendencies of academic administrators or against ecclesiastical authorities who invoke their right to act as the voice of the Church's magisterium. The most notorious case of the former was the summary dismissal by the administration of Saint John's University, Jamaica, New York, in December, 1965, of thirty-three professors—two terminations were later withdrawn—an action that was regarded as so reprehensible by the American Association of University Professors that in passing censure on Saint John's in April, 1966, it stated:

The Changing Church

Owing to the extraordinary seriousness of the violation of academic freedom and tenure by St. John's University, the Fifty-second Annual Meeting of the Association approved an action of Committee A which states that, although "we do not recommend imposing an absolute obligation upon our members to decline appointments, we do feel that in the case of St. John's University it would be inappropriate for our members to accept appointments at St. John's University."[59]

Other institutions where less serious feuds arose over differences between administration and faculty were the College of Saint Thomas, Duquesne University, and the San Diego College for Women.

Nowhere has the issue of academic freedom versus ecclesiastical authority been more sharply joined than at the University of Dayton. There a dispute among certain members of the departments of philosophy and theology led to the charge of heresy against some of the professors. The controversy occasioned the appointment of a committee of investigation by the local ordinary, Karl J. Alter, Archbishop of Cincinnati, as well as a later committee by the university's president, Raymond J. Roesch, S.M. After months of investigating, the latter group's report of September, 1967, seemed to bring a quietus as far as the general public was aware. This committee maintained that the Church's teaching authority had only an "indirect" control over what was taught in a Catholic university. A university of this kind, they said, "cannot accept any direct relationship to the magisterium in academic matters," since, they contended, this was confined to Catholic faculty members' status as individual Catholics and did not relate to their role as university instructors. "To say otherwise," the committee concluded, "is to make the university an organ of the official teaching Church."[60] Also in an area that touched closely on the teaching

213

of the Church was the case of the dismissal of an instructor in classics from Saint Mary's College, Winona, in May, 1967, because he had married a girl from the neighboring College of Saint Teresa in a civil ceremony, both being Catholics.

A constructive development from these controversies is the serious discussion initiated by the entire issue of academic freedom in the Catholic framework. A good sample of this widespread concern in Catholic circles was the symposium held at the University of Notre Dame in April, 1966, on the general theme, "Academic Freedom and the Catholic University." The eight papers ranged over a broad spectrum of topics including the question of one's personal commitment, student freedom, the freedom of the priest-scholar, and the knotty question of "The University and the Church." In the mind of Philip Gleason, who treated the subject from a historical point of view, academic freedom was then "the most crucial problem facing Catholic higher education." It was one that Catholic universities should approach fearlessly, since, he said, it went to the very heart of the problem of faith and knowledge "at a time when their own theological, philosophical, pedagogical, and general intellectual positions are in greater uncertainty than at any previous period in the history of American Catholic higher education."[61] John E. Walsh, C.S.C., maintained that it was a very serious mistake to speak of the Catholic university "as part of the teaching function of the Roman Catholic Church or even its teaching apostolate." To Father Walsh the university was one of the manifestations "—perhaps the highest formal, explicit, and systematic manifestation—of the Church *learning*."[62] In other words, the university was no part of what the theologians called the *Ecclesia docens*, and if that point were universally accepted, much of the ground for dispute between the two would be eliminated. Speaking of the problems encountered by priest-scholars in relation to censorship of their writings, John L. McKenzie, S.J., stated that he would submit for consideration the thesis, "that the principle of censorship is basically irrational and immoral." The immorality of the action, according to Father McKenzie, lay in applying what he described as "crude power to resolve problems which of their nature demand close and methodical scholarly examination." The learned Scripture scholar then went on to say:

Censorship settles scholarly differences of opinion by a moral bludgeon. And censorship is totally unnecessary, because scholarship is equipped to do better what censorship pretends to do; and that is to protect the reading public from irresponsible publication.[63]

These excerpts from the Notre Dame symposium of 1966 are one illustration of the candid and open criticism that Catholic scholars have currently been applying to this delicate matter.[64] It has been a problem for other religiously affiliated colleges and universities as well as for those of the Catholic Church, and it was of sufficient concern to educators generally that in 1965 the American Association of University Professors appointed a Special Committee on Academic Freedom in Church-Related Institutions, which over a period of two years worked out a statement elaborating on the AAUP's 1940 "Statement of Principles on Academic Freedom and Tenure" with the church-related college especially in mind. The committee made six general recommendations aimed to safeguard the individual professor's rights and at the same time to guarantee the institution's special character as affiliated with a church and its creed.[65]

The year 1967 proved to be especially memorable in Catholic higher educational circles for the mounting emphasis on academic freedom. Saint John's and Dayton continued to draw attention, but the controversial issues that had involved these universities were quite overshadowed in April by the sudden and unexplained refusal of the Board of Trustees of the Catholic University of America to renew the contract of Father Charles E. Curran, assistant professor of moral theology. News of the board's action at its Chicago meeting set off a spontaneous reaction on the campus during which the faculty of the School of Theology unanimously reaffirmed their confidence in Father Curran, noted that no charges had been brought against their colleague, and stated, in the words of Walter J. Schmitz, S.S., the dean, that "the academic freedom and the security of every professor of this University is jeopardized." In the circumstances, said Father Schmitz, "we can not and will not function until Father Curran is reinstated."[66] He concluded by inviting the other schools of the university to join the theologians' protest, an appeal that met with an immediate and overwhelming response from most of the other faculties, except that of the School of Education. Almost within a matter of hours the institution came to a standstill by a virtually total boycott of classes until such time as Father Curran would be restored to his post.

What made the action of the administration and the trustees all the more open to criticism was the fact that the faculty of the School of Theology had by a unanimous vote the previous November recommended Father Curran for promotion to the rank of associate professor, and the academic senate had unanimously approved this recommendation at its meeting on March 21, a meeting at which the top administrators in attendance raised no objection. The reason for the punitive measure against Father Curran was never clearly stated, although it had been rumored that it had resulted from his teaching on birth control, a rumor that was stoutly denied by the university's chancellor, Archbishop Patrick A. O'Boyle. In any case, the trustees' procedure at Chicago, to which Paul J. Hallinan, Archbishop of Atlanta, had alone entered a negative vote, met with such instant, vigorous, and sustained opposition from both faculty and students that after a week of boycott the trustees capitulated completely and the chancellor announced that Father Curran had been reinstated and his promotion approved.

The boycott of classes during a week's time made academic history for the Catholic universities as well as for others, a fact that was indelibly impressed on the American public by the extraordinary publicity given to the case. Every academic institution has its hazards, and the Catholic University of America is no exception. In both the Curran case and that of the banned theologians in 1963 informed persons realized that the progress of the university in these and other matters was hampered in no small measure by the prime weakness from which the institution suffered and which lay at the bottom of many of its difficulties. That weakness stemmed from what might be described as "excessive ecclesiasticism" which periodically showed in various forms, especially in the use of the university as a steppingstone for careers in the Church and, second, in the interference from time to time in its academic affairs of high ecclesiastics whose knowledge and understanding of what a university was about left much to be desired.

In contrast to such a lack of understanding, one of the most balanced presentations of the case for a Catholic university in today's world—quite at variance with the dictum of George Bernard Shaw that "a Catholic university is a contradiction in terms"—was that of Theodore M. Hesburgh, C.S.C., president of the University of Notre Dame. The occasion was the university's 125th anniversary commemorated on December 9, 1967, when Father Hesburgh urbanely countered educators like Jacqueline Grennan, president of Webster College, Rosemary Lauer of Saint John's College, Annapolis, and other contemporary Catholics who subscribed more or less to the Shaw thesis. In doing so he was at pains to give due recognition to the special complexities of the problem, while also making a stirring defense of freedom within the Catholic university. And he stated a principle which it would behoove all churchmen connected in any way with a university to make their own:

> The university is not the kind of place that one can or should try to rule by authority external to the university. The best and only traditional authority in the university is intellectual competence: this is the coin of the realm.[67]

Less than two months before the Hesburgh address the freedom of the Catholic university received eloquent expression from the Pacific Coast. A highly vocal right-wing element of the alumni of the University of Santa Clara sought to have the program of the university's newly founded Center for the Study of Contemporary Values canceled because it included a Marxian theoretician and several controversial figures, such as the Protestant Episcopal Bishop James A. Pike. "Antiseptically pure of ideas themselves," said Patrick A. Donohoe, S.J., Santa Clara's president at the time, "they cannot distinguish between dialogue and espousal." He went on to say that the Catholic university had to grow up, and he then added, "So do Catholic alumni and friends of the University. The formal work of the institution is not to prepare monks and nuns, but citizens of the world—and the world is made up of a vast spectrum of ideas ranging from Mao to Robert Welch."[68] Catholic educational circles had rarely if ever heard a stouter defense of academic freedom from a highly placed administrator.

Obviously, the complicated problems associated with academic freedom and its ramifications are not unique to Catholic colleges and universities; tensions of one kind or another on this score have plagued all institutions of learning, public or private, as they always will in any community of scholars and students, whether the institution that draws them together is affiliated with a particular church or not. The religiously oriented institution must sail between Scylla and Charybdis in these matters, but there is no intrinsic reason why it cannot complete a safe voyage without betraying either its religious heritage or its academic integrity. The formula of Pattillo and Mackenzie for what they termed the "free Christian college" (or "free Jewish college," as the case may be), would here seem to merit consideration. Such a school, said these authors, "stands unapologetically for religion and liberal education, but it relies on example, persuasive presentation of ideas, and a climate of conviction, rather than on conformity, to accomplish its ends."[69]

The open and honest manner in which academic policy has been conducted during the 1960's by a growing number of Catholic institutions—like Saint Louis University, to cite but one example, where in December, 1966, the administration was not afraid to have students hear Roger Garaudy, a leading French Marxian theoretician—gives reason to believe that an era such as Catholic colleges and universities have never known might well be at hand. One reason for optimism is the strong contrast of the 1960's with the widespread suppression of freedom of thought and expression that characterized Catholic circles in the

1950's. In the latter decade the tone had to some extent been set
by the cautionary and warning words of Pius XII's encyclical,
Humani generis, of August 12, 1950. In the years that followed,
prominent Catholic scholars both in Europe and in the Americas—for example, the late John Courtney Murray, S.J.—were
frustrated and discouraged by the fact that repeated admoni-
tions from ecclesiastical authorities had made openness and
freedom conspicuous by their absence. The spirit of the 1950's
was given striking expression on June 3, 1961, when Egidio
Vagnozzi, at the time Apostolic Delegate to the United States,
delivered a baccalaureate sermon at Marquette University. Alluding to the dangers facing Catholic intellectuals from what
he described as "the modern, massive opposition of secularism
and naturalism," he made clear that it was not the attitude of
the secularist intellectuals and their errors that was on his
mind. "I am concerned," said the delegate, "with the uneasiness and preoccupations of some Catholic intellectuals."[70] Ap-
parently the archbishop had serious misgivings about the soundness of faith of some of the latter. In any case, one can readily
understand the effect on the Catholic academic community of
this country on hearing the highest ranking representative of
the Holy See in the United States say:

> The complaint has been voiced more than once that in high ec-
> clesiastical circles the intellectual is often underestimated and also
> mistrusted. The question is whether we are confronted with true
> and genuine intellectuals, who are inspired by a sincere love of truth,
> humbly disposed to submit to God's Revelation and the authority
> of His Church, or whether we are confronted with intellectuals
> who believe, first of all, in the absolute supremacy and unlimited
> freedom of human reason, a reason which has shown itself so often
> fallacious and subject to error.[71]

Less than a year and a half later, Vatican Council II opened
at Rome, and there ultimately emerged a far different attitude

toward intellectuals both within and without the Church than that expressed by Archbishop Vagnozzi. The change was manifest on the closing day of the council, December 8, 1965, when one of the final addresses was directed to "men of thought and science." Its principal author, Cardinal Paul-Émile Léger, then Archbishop of Montreal, asked what the bishops' efforts had amounted to over the council's four years if it was not "a more attentive search for and deepening of the message of truth." For that reason, said the cardinal, "our paths could not fail to cross," and he then added: "Your road is ours: Your paths are never foreign to ours. We are the friends of your vocation as searchers, companions in your fatigues, admirers of your successes, and, if necessary, consolers in your discouragement and your failures."[72]

This eloquent affirmation lent emphasis to the distance that official Catholic thinking had traveled in a few brief years, and it lent supporting evidence to the emergence of a new era for Catholic institutions of higher learning. Only the future would tell what the ultimate reality would be, but there was reason to believe that it might not be as grim for these schools as one writer maintained when he said the idea of the Church conducting an institution identifiable as a "Catholic university" would "one day seem as anachronistic as the papal states."[73] This prediction may in time prove to have been a sound one, but since prophecy is not the historian's function, he can only state that the Catholic university and college have outlived a childhood and youth marked by all too frequent subjection to the whims of local bishops or religious superiors. And now the best of these institutions—and it is only with the best that the future need concern itself—have come of age, and one of the most unmistakable signs of adulthood is their forthright facing up to the intricacies of translating into reality their own freedom as centers of research and teaching within the American Catholic framework.

The late 1960's, it is true, have witnessed an increasing number of devoted and loyal Catholics who ask if, perhaps, the adulthood of Catholic higher education has not arrived too late. Needless to say, the general malaise that has overtaken American society in regard to traditional moral values, political norms, and social customs has made itself felt among Catholic college and university students as among those in other institutions. As the fathers of Vatican Council II noted of the changing attitudes that have frequently called accepted values into question, "This is especially true of young people, who have grown impatient on more than one occasion, and indeed become rebels in their distress."[74] True, the change has come about in consequence of myriad alterations in men's thinking on the basic moral code of Christianity and their adoption in its place of a materialist and hedonistic philosophy.

To the causes for the rebellion of the world's youth against the values of their elders, American youth added their particular anguish at the loss of President Kennedy, who for many of their numbers was a hero. In asking, "What is at the bottom of so much of the young people's dissent, contempt, disrespect, cynicism, disobedience and violence?" Donald McDonald was not alone in believing that it could be traced in no small measure to Kennedy's assassination, and to what he described as "the subsequent behavior of Mr. Kennedy's successor, Lyndon Johnson, and his government."[75] To borrow one of youth's current expressions, it was unquestionably true that Kennedy "turned them on," and it was just as true that Johnson "turned them off." In the young president they saw an openness, an honesty, and an idealism to which they gave enthusiastic response, whereas in what followed him, especially as it related to the war in Vietnam, with its cruelty and suffering among civilians and its repeated revelations of concealment of the truth by high American officials, youth's pride in and affection for their country have been shattered. What makes the situation worse is that so few factors in the current domestic life of the Republic offer any corrective to cynicism or display any untarnished ideals on which the young can anchor a firm hope.

That this universal disillusionment has made wide inroads into Catholic institutions is beyond dispute. During its development their nearly 450,000 students, to say nothing of nearly three times that number of their coreligionists in the secular colleges and universities, have not only questioned the traditional answers furnished by the Church's spokesmen on matters of lesser importance in doctrine and morals; the more advanced have likewise questioned essential truths of the Catholic creed, such as the Trinity, the divinity of Christ, the infallibility of the pope, and the right of the Church's magisterium to speak authoritatively to them and for them on subjects like birth control and premarital sex relations. Should one doubt the nature of youth's alienation in these matters, one has only to listen to what they are saying. Granted that what is written or said is not always representative of all American Catholic youth, samples such as the *Commonweal's* symposium, "The Cool Generation and the Church,"[76] and the summary of student attitudes toward death that appeared a few months later,[77] contained enough that is typical to illustrate the revolution in thought that has taken place among Catholic youth on religious matters.

American Catholicism

Whenever one considers the students in the Church's schools in the United States—on the elementary, secondary, or college and university level—it is natural to associate them with the religious orders and congregations, for it was the religious who either brought the majority of these schools into existence, or who staffed them through most of their history. Just as every segment of the Church has experienced radical changes, so the religious congregations have passed through a profound alteration in the "renewal" inspired by the ecumenical council. The council's "Decree on the Appropriate Renewal of the Religious Life," states that "all communities should participate in the life of the Church," and it goes on to say that "according to its individual character, each should make its own and foster in every possible way the enterprises and objectives of the Church."[78] Quoting that directive, Father Illtud Evans, O.P., the learned Welshman who served as American correspondent for *The Tablet* of London during an extended visit to the United States, remarked that the religious should, indeed, "provide the clearest evidence of what renewal means, and be prepared to pay the price of it." In this country at least, according to Father Evans, there can be no doubt "that change has become the order, if not the disorder, of the day among religious men and women alike."[79]

In this transformation no religious community has escaped the disturbing effects that accompanied the movement among the 120 or more orders and congregations of men that late in 1967 numbered 22,350 priests, the 29 congregations of brothers that had 12,261 members, and the more than 460 congregations of sisters who at that time had a total membership of 176,341. It is impossible to treat all these groups, but a word should be said about the Cistercians or Trappists, the best known of the contemplative orders, and what is said of them can *mutatis mutandis* be said of the other contemplative communities of both men and women. In an interview given in April, 1961, the late Gabriel Sortais, O.C.S.O., Abbot General of the Cistercians, had words of praise for the Americans as contemplatives and stated that they were on a par with their European counterparts. At that time the Americans numbered approximately 1,200 monks in twelve monasteries, or more than one-fourth of the order's world membership.[80] Less than seven years later, however, they found themselves in the midst of a crisis the effects of which one writer summarized thus: "Along with a sharp decline in those entering and a sharper increase in those leaving, the Trappist establishment has seen three groups of monks break away recently to found diocesan monasteries in Minnesota, Illinois and New Hampshire."[81]

The causes for this startling change differ, of course, from monastery to monastery and from monk to monk, but there seems to be agreement that one of the underlying reasons for the unrest—in addition to the general restiveness prevalent throughout the Catholic community of the United States—was the Cistercians' failure in the years after World War II to be more discriminating about the numerous GI's and others who presented themselves for admittance. Whatever the causes may have been, by 1968 it was evident that the high promise of the early 1960's had faded and that the monks would have to re-think their vocation as contemplatives in the context of the new developments. In reply to a journalist's account of their difficulties, their most famous American member, the late Thomas Merton (Father Louis), maintained that monastic renewal depended entirely on a recovery of what he called, "the true sense of the monastic charism." And to Father Louis that charism was one of freedom, "involving the freedom not to count in the world and not to get visible results in it. Above all the monastic charism is a freedom from set routine official tasks, a freedom from the treadmill of putting out a superfluous religious magazine, of preaching retreats that are driving nuns stark mad, of bullying married couples."[82]

If Father Louis' words may have left some outsiders more puzzled than enlightened, they are probably understood by a majority of the members of the active priests' orders and congregations, even if the latter do not all agree with him. For in these communities one of the most pressing problems is that of adaptation or of changing the aims or emphasis of their particular apostolate to meet the needs of both the contemporary world and the Church. In their search for a "renewal" that would leave their traditional rule basically intact, these congregations have shown an especially keen interest in the problems of the poor in a manner that augurs well for the Church's presence in economically and culturally deprived areas of the United States, both rural and urban, as well as in the far more drastic programs needed in countries in Latin America, the Middle East, and Southeast Asia. It was these problems that were preoccupying the 5,369 Americans who in January, 1967, were serving Latin America, a figure that included 2,441 diocesan clergy and religious priests and brothers, 2,567 sisters, and 361 lay volunteers.

It was to be expected that in the course of this movement involving the more than 200,000 religious of the American Church there should occasionally appear an aberration striking at a vital aspect of these congregations. The suggestion in August, 1967, of a Jesuit that there might be a "third way," one by which religious men with a vow of chastity could adopt with one of the opposite sex a medium approach between celibacy and married life, was quickly condemned by Pedro Arrupe, S.J., General of the Society of Jesus.[83] Unfortunately, in the wide-scale reporting of a sensational item of this kind the deep and genuine renewal that the Jesuits launched in their general congregation of 1965–66, and since that time have sought to implement in their individual provinces, was obscured in the public mind. Other religious communities of men have acted similarly as, for example, the Brothers of the Christian Schools, whose broad and up-to-date directives issued late in 1967 were intended as a charter for renewal among their nearly 18,000 members throughout the world, of whom over 2,400 are in the eight provinces of the United States.

One of the most heartening features of the new spirit stirring among the religious orders of men whose principal apostolate is teaching is the trend toward serious collaboration with one another in the education of their members, such as those represented at Saint Meinrad Seminary in Indiana, at Saint Louis University, and the combined efforts of different congregations in the immediate neighborhoods of the University of California, Berkeley, and of the University of Chicago, with their rich resources in libraries, science laboratories, and other facilities. Every step of this kind is an advance toward the elimination of more of the all too numerous small and inadequate seminaries and scholasticates of religious men which numbered 437 in this country at the end of 1967. Here the Americans might well take a page from the book of their Canadian counterparts whose Seminary of Saint Augustine near Quebec opened in 1966 with fifteen orders and congregations participating in the joint undertaking, while on an adjacent campus five congregations of teaching brothers combined for a similar purpose.

American Catholicism

Official sanction for comparatively sweeping changes along the lines of proximity to university centers and a combined educational commitment for the spiritual and intellectual formation of the clergy was given by Cardinal Gabriel Garrone, Prefect of the Congregation for Christian Education, in a set of guidelines issued in June, 1968. These were intended to update Pope Pius XI's apostolic constitution, *Deus Scientiarum Dominus*, of 1931 for pontifical universities and faculties of theology and to bring the Roman Curia into line with some of the world's most progressive developments in seminary education.[84]

If it is important that the religious orders rethink their educational goals in terms of the revolutionary movements of a new age, *a fortiori* it is imperative that the diocesan clergy, whose principal commitment is to the lay people in the parishes, do likewise. Especially is this true in a period when certain signs seemed to indicate that the prophetic vision of John Henry Newman expressed nearly a century ago might find its fulfillment. Preaching at the dedication of Saint Bernard's Seminary for the Diocese of Birmingham in England, Newman said:

> The special peril of the time before us is the spread of that plague of infidelity, that the Apostles and our Lord Himself have predicted as the worst calamity of the last times of the Church. And at least a shadow, a typical image of the last time is coming over the world. I do not mean to presume to say that this is the last time, but that it has had the evil prerogative of being like that more terrible season, when it is said that the elect themselves will be in danger of falling away.[85]

If Newman felt justified in speaking in those terms in October, 1873, the status of Christianity in the 1960's would suggest more than "at least a shadow" for a time when, as a recent critic has said, "The unresolved questions of the Fifties became the inheritance of the succeeding decade," and the de-mythologizing of the Christian creed has progressed at such a pace that the same writer could add with plausibility, "There were three indications of the ascendancy of secularism: Faith no longer required an actual theological object; Christianity no longer gave culture any special tone; syncretism made Christianity superfluous."[86]

In the face of a situation of this kind, with the interpretation of which most discerning observers would not seriously quarrel, it need hardly be emphasized that the monastic discipline of the seminary, the static scholasticism that so long dominated its curriculum, the authoritarian teaching methods, and the general tone of the Council of Trent that has permeated virtually every seminary in the Catholic world since the days of the great French architects of the Church's seminary system like Father Jean Jacques Olier (d. 1657) and Saint Vincent de Paul (d. 1660) would all have to undergo radical changes.[87] Otherwise bishops might as well abandon the hope of attracting any of the superior minds among the young men of the 1960's for the diocesan priesthood. The falling seminary enrollments, the dropouts, and, indeed, the defection of a good number of recently ordained priests—phenomena familiar to Protestant and Orthodox circles as well—have been too widespread to call for restatement here. In fact, in the late 1960's a number of Catholic seminaries have witnessed a condition bordering on open rebellion of students who feel that the pace of reform is too slow or that they have been denied a meaningful role in working out the necessary changes. In this regard the cases of the major seminaries of the archdioceses of Boston and Philadelphia are better known because they have received more widespread publicity. True, at the end of 1967 there was still a total of 22,232 candidates for the diocesan priesthood studying in the 124 diocesan seminaries and in seminaries conducted by religious orders. But it was no secret that their numbers were declining so rapidly that if the trend was not reversed, the Church in the United States would be confronted with the same critical shortage of priests that for years has haunted other parts of the Catholic world such as Latin America.

That a sufficient number of responsible churchmen have recognized the proportions of the crisis to take steps to remedy matters, is evident in a number of American dioceses. Most of the programs for reform, as was to be expected, have taken as their starting point the "Decree on Priestly Formation" of Vatican Council II promulgated by Paul VI on October 28, 1965. In the response that he was invited to make to this decree Warren A. Quanbeck, professor of systematic theology in the Lutheran Theological Seminary of Saint Paul and one of the leading Protestant observers at the council, noted with approval the emphasis on the Word of God as the "foundation and center of the theological curriculum," the stress on adaptation to local conditions, and the statement concerning the need for bringing the ecumenical viewpoint into priestly training. It was the decree's insistence on a historical approach to dogmatic theology, however, that Quanbeck found particularly encouraging. "The Council's will to relate to the contemporary world," he said, "will be set forward more by taking this seriously than by anything else which could be mentioned." On the negative side the same writer had some misgiving about the decree's repeated assertion concerning the perennial nature of the thought of Saint Thomas Aquinas; he remarked that virtually nothing was said about one of the most important tools of theological education, the library;[88] and he would have appreciated a more ample treatment of the seminary faculty.

The Changing Church

A start was made, however, with the council's decree, and the American hierarchy gave the subject serious consideration in 1966 when it appointed from its own membership the Bishops' Committee on Priestly Formation, which was assisted by a number of specialists in seminary education. The committee's investigation and analysis of conditions obtaining in the Church's seminaries in every region of the country, and the preparation of reports based on authenticated data and containing recommendations for improvement of the seminary's training program in all its varied aspects, offered hope that concerted action would assist in eliminating weaknesses and introducing up-to-date pedagogical methods. Those American Catholic seminaries that survived the test would thus be brought into line with the academic standards of the American Association of Theological Schools with which the Catholic institutions had begun to affiliate, while at the same time conforming to the regulations of the Congregation for Christian Education and seeking to heighten the spiritual content and tone that would enrich the personal lives of the Church's future priests.

"American religious women were thirty or forty years ahead of their sisters in Europe. Despite the similarity in their garb, they did not seem to belong to the same species at all—almost as if some mutation of feminine religious life had taken place during the Atlantic crossing."[89] Such was the way in which a foreign visitor, Robert Bosc, S.J., of the Catholic Institute of Paris, saw the American sisters in March, 1966. That many of the 175,000 or more religious women of the Church of the United States had taken tremendous strides toward putting themselves *au courant* with the world in which they lived and worked, was well known to those who observed them at all closely. While it is impossible to date this movement precisely, the founding in 1954 of the Sister Formation Conference with a view to advancing the sisters' spiritual and professional training, marked an important milestone. Two years later this organization became an auxiliary of the Conference of Major Superiors of Women Religious, and in 1959 Marillac College was dedicated at Normandy, Missouri, an institution sponsored by the Daughters of Charity of Saint Vincent de Paul as a joint undertaking with a number of other religious communities to carry out the objectives of the conference. Since that date similar institutions have opened in other parts of the country, notably the Religious Educators Foundation established by the Sisters of Notre Dame de Namur of Trinity College in Washington, D.C., which finished its first academic year in June, 1967, having given financial assistance to fifty-five junior sisters from the co-operating religious communities.

From the time when Blessed Elizabeth Seton founded her Sisters of Charity in July, 1809, until the present the sisters of the Catholic Church have occupied a special place in the minds not only of the Catholic clergy and laity but in the esteem and affection of many non-Catholic Americans as well. That regard has been earned through memorable services such as nursing the wounded and the prisoners during the Civil War and in local calamities like the smallpox epidemic that broke out in San Francisco in March, 1868, and raged for over a year. In salutation to community service of this kind many Americans not of the Catholic faith would have agreed with the editor of the *Cleveland Herald* in January, 1878, who, declaring it would be difficult to find "a more earnest Protestant than the writer," maintained that "no more devoted, self-sacrificing faithful women who spend their lives in charity and doing good

can be found than the Sisters or nuns of the Catholic Church.
. . . the sisterhoods have, as a class, deserved and received the
honor and respect of mankind."[90] It is partly due to that honor
and respect, along with a certain mystique about the sisters,
often the result of a mingled awe and curiosity, that their
efforts at renewal of their respective congregations have gained
such widespread notice. *Newsweek*'s cover story for Christmas,
1967, "The Nun: Going Modern," is only one example of this
interest."[91] And when the Immaculate Heart Sisters of Los
Angeles encountered the opposition of Cardinal McIntyre because of the changes voted in their general chapter, changes
which he declared undermined their character as a congregation of religious women, and when they prepared to remove
themselves at the cardinal's request from the schools in which
they were teaching in the Archdiocese of Los Angeles, the
controversy was a prime news item for much of the communications media, with the sisters generally receiving a more favorable press than the cardinal.[92]

Absorbing as these matters are for those sisters immediately
involved, they are but a small part of this dramatic development in Catholic life that promises to affect the Church and
her mission in this country for years to come. That the turmoil
in which most religious communities of women find themselves
in the late 1960's is taking its toll of their membership is undeniable. Not only did the total number of sisters drop by
4,750 between the end of 1965 and the end of 1966, but vocations to the sisterhoods fell off drastically. Something of this
nature was inevitable in so radical a series of changes as these
communities experienced. The breaking up into smaller units,
experimentation within already established community groups,
living without a designated superior, the advent of new forms

of the apostolate, the changes in garb, the innovations in community spiritual exercises—these and a score of other changes all play a part in what has become for many of an older generation wedded to traditional ways an "agonizing reappraisal." On the other hand, the changes have been greeted with joy and fresh hope by younger women whose decision to remain or to leave the convents often hinges on the likelihood that these changes or reforms will be introduced and maintained. In the community of the Glenmary Sisters of Cincinnati an agreement was ultimately reached for a parting of the ways, one group entering a new kind of lay institute and the other remaining essentially as it had been, although modified by less radical changes. Still other congregations, like the Sisters of Charity of the Blessed Virgin Mary centered in Dubuque, Iowa, launched long-range self-studies to scrutinize every aspect of their lives with outsiders called in as advisers.

Behind it all, and fundamental to an understanding of the phenomenon, were the excessive surveillance of sisters' lives warranted in the community rules of a bygone era and the failure of some bishops and pastors to appreciate in a practical way the sisters' services in the schools, to say nothing of their failure to understand that teaching sisters might wish to serve the Church in other capacities. There is likewise a pervading desire to be a "person" recognized for her individual worth as a sister, rather than merely a member of a community, together with a desire to make herself relevant to her moment in time, to relate more closely to outsiders, especially to the poor and the dispossessed. A central thread running through much of the sisters' unrest had its origin in their wish to vary their congregations' commitments so that the classroom would not be the sole channel through which sisters might exercise their zeal,

The Changing Church

but rather a commitment that would extend to the slums, the public forum, the secular campus, or to a hundred and one other aspects of American life where they could be witnesses to Christ. It is a wish that, as has been mentioned, has brought uneasiness to some bishops, pastors, and school administrators lest the religious women's already declining numbers be further depleted, thus necessitating the hiring of yet more lay teachers to whom higher salaries will have to be paid.

As the 1960's draw to a close no one can predict with any precision what the outcome will be, except that it appears morally certain that the role of the religious women in the American Church will be vastly different from what it was in the past, and that it will be much more varied than in the years before Vatican Council II. A further observation for which there is solid evidence is that the changing sisterhoods imply an altered status also for other aspects of Catholic life in this country not only for schools but also for hospitals, orphanages, homes for the aged, and the numerous other institutions staffed by sisters. The question of secularization of these institutions in the matter of legal ownership is but one straw in the wind that heralds a new era in their history.

The sisters' future is, then, all important both for themselves and for the Church. But in trying to gauge what that future might hold, we should not forget their history, for they are no exception to Pierre Teilhard de Chardin's statement that "everything is the sum of the past and . . . nothing is comprehensible except through its history."[93] In this sense knowledge of the history of the Church's religious women offers a steadying influence not found elsewhere. For example, Angela Merici (d. 1540) surprised her generation by founding in 1535 the Ursuline Sisters with no fixed garb, no vows, no community life, and no concession to the customary enclosure, thus establishing the Church's first community of women for the education of young girls. And nearly a century later Mary Ward (d. 1646) struggled heroically for twenty years or more to establish her Institute of Mary against the harsh condemnation of high churchmen scandalized because her sisters, too, were uncloistered and without any distinctive habit. Neither lived to win ecclesiastical approbation for her sisters; yet both began what ultimately succeeded in giving to the Church viable religious congregations. And in breaking with precedent they played a not unimportant part in helping to usher the Church out of the Middle Ages and into the modern age. In the final analysis, then, the turbulence among the religious women of the 1960's might in time be seen to have assisted in providing what Father Illtud Evans called "the clearest evidence of what renewal means," because in the crucible of this turbulence they were found to have been, "prepared to pay the price of it."[94]

The 1960's will always be remembered by the Catholics of the United States, and by their coreligionists in other countries, as the decade of Vatican Council II, from which came so much of the inspiration and impetus for what has been described in the preceding pages. Numerically speaking, the 246 American bishops who attended all or part of the council were a striking contrast to their 49 predecessors who had gone to Rome in 1869 for Vatican Council I. Had the reserve they showed during the first and second sessions (1962–63)—when some referred to them as the "Church of Silence"—continued to the end, they would have resembled their predecessors in their relative taciturnity. But when the third session opened in 1964, the bishops seemed to have found themselves, and thereafter their interventions became more frequent. From the very outset, however, the voice of the United States was heard in the 61 bishops and *periti* from this country who served on the various preparatory commissions, whereas in Vatican Council I only a single American, Father James A. Corcoran, held a position of this kind.

An ecumenical council of the Catholic Church is a rare occurrence. Vatican Council I was the first such gathering since the Council of Trent, 306 years before, and 92 more years were to pass before Vatican Council II. It was a unique opportunity for an American bishop—as it was for a bishop from any country—to mingle daily with the 2,400 or more bishops assembled from virtually every corner of the globe. He could broaden his horizons, gain the acquaintance of the Church's leading theologians who were in attendance as *periti,* and through this experience share directly and in a significant way in the *aggiornamento* launched by Pope John. While undoubtedly there were genuine gains for the American representatives because of their extended stay in the Eternal City between October, 1962, and December, 1965, their conciliar interventions, as well as their post-conciliar pronouncements and programs, with a few notable exceptions demonstrated little of a truly original and innovative nature.

It would have been all but unthinkable, for example, for an American to have taken the initiative of Cardinal Josef Frings, Archbishop of Cologne, and Cardinal Achille Liénart, Bishop of Lille, when on October 13, 1962, the first working day of the council, they challenged the Roman Curia's selection of personnel to compose the conciliar committees without previous consultation with the bishops. The action of Frings and Liénart won a quick adjournment of the day's business so that the various hierarchies might discuss the matter, exchange views, and make their voices heard on who should be appointed to these all-important committees. Insofar as the Americans were concerned, the independent thinking—always expressed in terms fundamentally respectful of the Holy See's authority —that had characterized many bishops' dealings with Rome in the late nineteenth century had long since disappeared. In the ecclesiastical climate that replaced it in the United States, for an American to speak an opinion at variance with that of powerful curial churchmen was regarded as tantamount to disloyalty to the pope himself. Peter Nichols, the astute correspondent who after 1957 served *The Times* of London on Vatican affairs, stated that, curiously enough, it was not so much the Italians in the Roman Curia but the non-Italians who became the most curial-minded. It was due, he thought, to the fact that the latter felt less at home there, and for that reason they subconsciously made a greater effort to conform. In any case, he added a remark that was not without bearing on the attitude of a large number of bishops from the United States who attended the council: "By far the worst are the Americans, who lose character and gain fussiness at an alarming rate in Rome's ecclesiastical circles, becoming far more tiresome to deal with than the Italians."[95]

The principal interests of the American prelates at Vatican Council II could in part be gauged by the frequency with which they submitted either written or spoken interventions. Judging by this criterion, of the sixteen major subjects on which the council produced final documents the following six drew most attention from the Americans: the two "Dogmatic Constitutions" dealing with the Church and with the liturgy, the "Pastoral Constitution on the Church in the Modern World," the "Decree on Ecumenism" and the "Decree on the

Bishop's Pastoral Office in the Church," and the "Declaration on Religious Freedom." That some spoke frequently was illustrated by the fact that of the 341 texts delivered to the editor of the American interventions, 131 came from Cardinal Spellman.[96] On occasion a single bishop spoke for others among his colleagues, as for example, on October 31, 1962, when Archbishop Hallinan made an eloquent appeal for the liturgy in the vernacular and declared that he spoke "for many bishops (although not for all) of the United States.[97] In the same manner, as we have seen, a year later, on October 24, 1963, Bishop Tracy, speaking "in the name of the bishops of the United States," sought a statement from the council on the equality of all races in the Church.[98]

Obviously, it is not possible here to tell the full story of American participation in Vatican Council II. There is one topic, however, that merits special mention because of the Americans' signal contribution to it and the leading role they played in its final enactment, namely, religious freedom. They brought to the discussion the experience of over 170 years of separation of Church and State and while making due allowance for the American Church's undoubted flaws, the number and the prosperity of the institutions and the flourishing religious life of most of the approximately 50,000,000 Catholics in the United States—all of which had happened under a government that had espoused the principle of religious freedom from its establishment—were facts that spoke eloquently for this principle. Not only were thirteen interventions from the United States heard in the council on this subject—four in the name of "many" or "almost all" the bishops of this country— but the draft schema itself was in the main the work of an American, the late John Courtney Murray, S.J.

Nor was there a dissent from any of the American delegation about the desirability of a conciliar pronouncement on religious freedom. All agreed with Cardinal Richard Cushing, Archbishop of Boston, who on September 15, 1965, stated that not only was the doctrine of man's right of freedom in religious matters based on Catholic teaching but "the promulgation of this teaching over the entire world is today a pastoral necessity of the first order."[99] In the early and formative stages of the schema, however, the battle was closely drawn in the preparatory commission, and the tenacity and determination with which the opponents pursued their objective was manifest when, on the eve of the day that a vote was scheduled in the council, they succeeded in winning a postponement by the steering committee. It was recognized at once that the council had reached something of a crisis, but the matter was quickly resolved the following morning, September 21, 1965, when Pope Paul VI interposed to say there would be a vote; before the council adjourned that day, 1,997 bishops had voted in favor of the schema as against 224 opposed. From that time until the document was formally promulgated by the pontiff on December 7, it was merely a matter of making certain minor emendations and of polishing the final text. In the "Declaration on Religious Freedom," then, the Americans made their most significant contribution to Vatican Council II.[100]

It is easy enough for the historian to chronicle the principal happenings of an ecumenical council; it is quite another matter for him to assess its influence on the Church in the years that immediately followed. We have already quoted Father Murray to the effect that, "the conciliar affirmation of the principle of freedom was narrowly limited—in the text," but, he added, "the text itself was flung into a pool whose shores are wide as the universal Church. The ripples will run far."[101] In the years since the close of Vatican Council II the American Catholics have been witness to the fact that the "ripples [have] run far" in their Church, and even now it is too soon to say how far those ripples will carry and how deep and enduring a change they will make in the lives of the Church's members. For over and above the council's sixteen major conciliar enactments, the Church of the United States, like that of the rest of the world, has found it necessary to adjust and to adapt to a new mood, a new style, often an entirely new school of thought. Here again the Church is, to be sure, influenced by the age with its strong emphasis on individual freedom, on a personalist philosophy, on an openness of approach, on honesty of expression. These constitute part of the *Zeitgeist* of the present age, and the Church has never been totally unaffected by the spirit that dominated any period of her long history.

Nor is the American Church a stranger to these new currents of thought and action of the present, for they have engrossed the attention and captivated the imagination of numerous members of her own household. Like their fellow countrymen generally, the American Catholics have not been noted for many original contributions to philosophy and theology, and the judgment of George H. Tavard, A.A., is, therefore, not unfair. In treating the advances made in theology by the Germans and other European Catholics, he remarked, "The United States lagged behind, in spite of the valuable but very specialized productions of the Franciscan Institute and the distinguished contributions of *Theological Studies*."[102] But because Americans have not been in the fore of speculative thought, it does not follow that they have been insensitive to the stagnation of the Church's progress owing to the static patterns of thinking that lingered from the Council of Trent and the spirit of Vatican Council I. And they have been made aware of it in a practical way because some among them have been victimized, for their critical and open-minded views, by the same spirit, a spirit described by Yves Congar, O.P., when he said, "The regime of strong authority which has prevailed in the Church since the middle of the sixteenth century is responsible for that attitude which resents all criticism as proceeding from a spirit of opposition bordering on a dubious orthodoxy."[103]

Consequently, the council's suggestions for new structures within the Church to bring about a broader measure of representative opinion in policy decisions met with an enthusiastic response from the majority of priests and laymen and, indeed, from a number of bishops in the United States. One of the earliest changes effected was a reorganization of the National Catholic Welfare Conference into the United States Catholic Conference, the Washington secretariat of the National Conference of Catholic Bishops, which took place in November, 1966. The setting up of new boards and commissions proceeded at a varying pace on all levels—national, diocesan, and parochial. Thus by December, 1967, there were 106 diocesan school boards and 2,100 parish school boards with 88 per cent of the former including laymen and 63 per cent of these boards having jurisdiction, although subject to the approval of the bishop, while 6 per cent had both jurisdiction and autonomous authority. Still another of the new post-conciliar structures is illustrated by the Sisters' Council inaugurated in October, 1967, by Lawrence B. Casey, Bishop of Paterson, for the women religious of his diocese.

With the passing of time, both the clergy and the laity have grown more insistent in their demands to be heard in the policy-making counsels of the Church, with the result that in dioceses ruled by highly conservative bishops who were either loath to share their authority, or whose vision was clouded by a certain paranoia at the prospect of runaway priests and laymen carrying the Church into schism, there has been strain and tension. For example, in their espousal of the parish council, one of the new structures that emerged in the post-conciliar period, few have been as forthright as Bernard J. Flanagan, Bishop of Worcester. In February, 1968, in calling for the establishment of these councils in all 129 parishes of his diocese, he told the more than 700 lay participants in a seminar on the subject, "The pastor must not look upon himself as a ruler holding dominative authority, but as a servant of his people. . . . We, bishop and pastors, are to serve your needs; our service must be to let you exercise your freedom as sons of God."[104] At that time the parish councils were still in their formative stage, with the composition of laity, religious, and clergy varying from parish to parish.

Another post-conciliar development that probably has given the greatest promise of all for the future of the American Church is the organization of priests under different names and auspices, such as senates of priests, associations of priests, and priests' councils. The first of these, the senate of priests, had specific authorization from the Holy See in a *motu proprio* issued by Paul VI on August 6, 1966, and by the end of that year forty-five senates were operating in American dioceses. Among the earlier jurisdictions to take action was the Archdiocese of San Francisco, where after approximately a year's detailed study and preparation the senate was formally inaugurated in May, 1967; it consisted of twenty-four priests who had been elected by their fellow priests, and at the time had the only full-time secretary in the country, Raymond G. Decker. From the outset Father Decker not only played a leading role in San Francisco's senate, but when 340 priests of the United States, representing 114 of the 154 dioceses of the country, met on February 12–13, 1968, in a suburb of Chicago to organize on a national scale, he read one of the major papers, and the following May was elected treasurer of the national organization. According to Father Decker, the principal distinction between the two different types or groups of priests was that the "association" was an organization within a diocese created among the priests themselves for the purpose of furthering "a genuine spirit of priestly fraternity, and based on this spirit, to develop a mutual appreciation of and desire for professionalism." The "senate," on the other hand, was "a representative body of the presbytery which forms a part of the official policy making structure of a diocese by being officially an advisory body to the bishop in expressing the consensus of thought and opinion of the presbytery."[105] The meeting in February, 1968, was preparatory to the formal organization that emerged as the National Federation of Priests' Councils when delegates from 117 of the 156 dioceses of the United States met the following May; the 117 dioceses represented over 40,000, or more than two-thirds, of the nearly 60,000 American priests.

In any case, it was a matter of prime importance that the priests of the American Church should be organized in one form or another if remedial steps were to be taken to overcome the widespread disaffection in their ranks. Throughout her history the Church of the United States has known the disgruntled priest, the priest who for one reason or another no longer felt able or disposed to bear the burden and who departed the ministry, and the priest who, though like all other men experienced his moments of depression, was substantially happy and content in his vocation to the end of his life. But at no time in that history has the Church witnessed so pervading a spirit of unrest as in the years after Vatican Council II. The phenomenon was not, to be sure, a monopoly of the 59,803 men who composed the American priesthood at the close of 1967, for it was present throughout the entire Catholic world. The causes were many and varied, and among them was a feeling that although the ecumenical council had addressed itself to the problems of the bishops and the laity, it had not confronted the problems of the priest in the same realistic way. Added to this was the mounting tension in many places between the older and younger priests, the different concept of the apostolate that divided the two age groups, as well as the widening gap between them on the subject of ecclesiastical authority in general and their mutual relationships in this matter in particular. An increasing number of priests likewise felt that optional celibacy should be introduced into the Latin Rite as had been the practice for centuries among the priests of the Eastern rites subject to the Church of Rome.

In all that pertains to priests, their relations with their bishops are, needless to say, of paramount importance. Unquestionably, a few of the younger clergy have on occasion been guilty of grave infractions of the Church's disciplinary regulations and in a number of these cases serious damage and scandal have resulted from their recalcitrant ways and have been highly publicized by the communications media. On the other hand, the unhappy situation has also been aggravated by certain bishops and elder clergy who have stubbornly adhered to rules and regulations badly in need of being either abolished or modernized. The assignment to inner city pastorates of priests too old and insensitive to change is a case in point. It was with a view to seeking a remedy for the malaise that had overtaken so many American priests that the hierarchy instituted at their meeting in November, 1967, a new group to study these problems. This body, called the Committee for the Life and Ministry of Priests and consisting of seven bishops and eight priests, held its initial meeting on December 16 of that year, took cognizance of the unrest, and stated in a news release that its work was "a response to a crisis growing out of the expanding and changing role of the clergy in the world today."[106]

This committee was to address itself not only to the question of celibacy among the diocesan clergy but also to another question that drew major attention at the national priests' meeting at Des Plaines in February, 1968. On that occasion Father Decker raised the question of the growing demand by many of the clergy for a voice in the nomination of bishops; if this became an actuality, it could, he said, "conceivably contribute more effectively in the choosing of bishops more pastorally minded than curial and canonically oriented."[107] When one considers how much the welfare of the Church depends on the caliber of the bishops chosen to govern her dioceses, as well as on the necessity for close co-operation, harmony, and mutual respect between bishops and their priests and the laity, it is understandable that the priests, and the laity also—in response to the general spirit of democratization that has been one of the slowly emerging characteristics of Catholic life since Vatican Council II—should have asked for a share in the nomination of priests for the espiscopal office.

As the historian of contemporary Catholicism in the United States attempts to survey the problems that beset the priests of the 1960's he not only quickly realizes how vast and deep a subject it has become, but he also grows painfully aware of how inadequate is a brief treatment such as that presented here. For example, nothing has been said of the National Association for Pastoral Renewal, an independent group embracing priests from all sections of the country whose main preoccupation, were one to judge by the notices in the press, has centered on optional celibacy. Among other matters not treated here are pioneering groups such as the Association of Chicago Priests organized in October, 1966, and the numerous brushes between individual bishops and priests over issues involving the limits of ecclesiastical authority, the extent and degree of ecumenical activities, and the priests' demands for liturgical experimentation which when refused gave rise in certain instances to the so-called underground Church. Tensions and open conflict there certainly have been in the Catholic clerical body, facts freely admitted by the five priest participants in symposia such as that on "The Troubled Priest."[108]

But it is also true that exaggerated and irresponsible reports of clerical differences have circulated widely owing to careless reporting and to the desire of some of those in the communications media to satisfy the craving of a portion of their readers and viewers for sensation. And reporting of this type is much less excusable when it emanates from supposedly responsible and learned theologians like Edward Schillebeeckx, O.P., of the Catholic University of Nijmegen in the Netherlands, who after a two-month tour of the United States gave an interview to the Dutch national Catholic daily, *De Tijd*, on January 20, 1968. Here Father Schillebeeckx was said to have characterized the state of the American Church as "alarming" and more likely to lead to schism than the Church of his own country, stated that of the 265 bishops he could find only 12 who could be considered "open and progressive," and, in the most extreme statement of the interview, predicted that in the following three years 10,000 priests would defect from their ministries in the United States.[109] No well-informed American Catholic would deny that there have been numerous defections from the priesthood during the 1960's, by far the largest number, indeed, that the Church has ever experienced here; nor would the same Catholic deny that there is the prospect of many more priests leaving before the trend is reversed. Yet, obviously, Father Schillebeeckx possessed no more reliable data on these and other questions that beset the Church at the time than did the American Catholics themselves, to say nothing of the patently uninformed guesses that interlarded his remarks in *De Tijd*. The true nature of the Schillebeeckx interview was properly assessed by another non-American Dominican with a far longer residence in the United States than that of his Dutch confrère. Father Illtud Evans made it clear that he wished to dissociate himself from what he termed Schillebeeckx' "mischievous and unfounded views," while deploring that "under the guise of theological eminence" the latter had seen fit to castigate "virtually the whole American hierarchy" and to give off statements that were as "unprovable in fact as they are destructive in intention."[110]

Again no perceptive and honest Catholic in this country would disguise the fact that some American bishops' leadership has often left much to be desired, and that a good number of the bishops might without injustice be placed in the same category as many of their European colleagues whom Peter Nichols described "as back in the rearguard again and the faithful unfortunates who missed the years of formative debate in Rome are looking patiently over their shoulders at their trailing hierarchies in the hope that they might be seen moving again, with every dignity of course but at the head of their pastoral flocks instead of behind them."[111] But cognizance should also be taken of the American bishops who have made serious efforts to implement the directives of Vatican Council II, such as Cardinal Shehan, Archbishops Hallinan and John F. Dearden, and Bishops Charles A. Buswell of Pueblo, Victor J. Reed of Oklahoma City–Tulsa, and Lawrence B. Casey of Paterson, to name only half a dozen. Nor would an informed Catholic make any effort to conceal the widely known fact that marked differences in opinion exist in the Catholic community, a fact conspicuously displayed by the dialogue of the six prominent Catholics published under the title "Issues That Divide the Church" by the *National Catholic Reporter* in successive issues in the early spring of 1967 and later published in book form.[112] Once again, sophisticated Catholics of the late 1960's who believe sincerely in an open and honest Church have presented a viewpoint entirely different from that of their parents and grandparents on a wide spectrum of subjects relating to their religious faith, a viewpoint that is much more critical, for example, of the churchmen who act as spokesmen for that faith.

The same Catholics are far less impressed than their forebears by the old-style triumphalist ceremonies of high prelates. In the same category was the appointment in January, 1968, for the second time of an American, the late Cardinal Francis Brennan, to head one of the major departments of the central government of the Church as Prefect of the Congregation of the Sacraments. They would, to be sure, wish Cardinal Brennan every success and happiness in his new post, but they would be more inclined to rejoice in it as a sign of the further internationalization of the Roman Curia than they would as an honor paid to the Church of their own country. In fact, when in May, 1967, Pope Paul VI chose four Americans among the twenty-seven prelates added to the College of Cardinals, bringing the representation of the United States for the first time to nine, a widely prevailing feeling among Catholics was regret that the college should have been enlarged at all instead of allowing it gradually to die out. There was also on this occasion the expression of regret by some that the pontiff had made certain American choices for the red hat and omitted others. It was all part of the new mood, the new style, to which reference has previously been made, a mood and a style that gives little enthusiasm and response to ecclesiastical matters that would once have aroused hearty applause.

It is true that views of this new-style American Catholic have at times been interpreted as indicating a lack of faith. And that a real crisis of faith for a number of Catholics has ended in their leaving the Church is undeniable. This has been a fairly constant pattern following ecumenical councils. As Henry Edward Manning, Archbishop of Westminster, reminded Catholics shortly after Vatican Council I, eighty bishops left the Church in the year 325 following the Council of Nicaea and "carried multitudes with them," thirty bishops departed after the Council of Ephesus in 431 as followers of the Nestorian heresy, and, as a result of the Council of Chalcedon of 451, "the Monophysites separated themselves from Catholic unity."[113] Yet it would be false to judge the vast majority of the approximately 50,000,000 Catholics of this country by the relatively few who have departed from the faith, a fact that the novelist Morris L. West illustrated late in 1967. Having outlined his religious belief in a manner that would not have been understood by many Catholics a generation ago, West confessed,

The Changing Church

"This is our aggiornamento. This is for us, the renewal of the life of the Spirit—and there are strange mystical elements in it." But in his conclusion, where he opened his arms to embrace all men—Marxist, Jew, black, yellow, *et al.*—there was no hint of despair but rather one of hope: "We are men and women, granted the same gift of existence upon this spinning earth, condemned to the same suffering and the same death, given equally the promise that none of us will be left orphans."[114]

By no means all the reasons for the Church's losses are to be found within her own household. At the opening of the 1960's Henry J. Browne surveyed the American Catholic past and, with his customary acuteness, cited a major source of loss. Father Browne remarked that Catholics themselves would never claim to have had "a great effect on American culture or values," and he then added:

They know that they and their predecessors have to some extent carried their beliefs into education and industry and other avenues of life, even into the field of entertainment. But they have much more often conformed to values than changed them. Where those before them found a Protestant society, they find today a more secular one maintaining only the vaguest of religious standards.[115]

It is the conforming of many Catholics to the secular standards of their society that has accounted for their lapses from the religious faith of their ancestors. Precisely how many have been lost through succumbing to environmental influences, of course, is known only to the recording angel.

As the historian nears the end of this survey he thinks regretfully of subjects that deserve treatment but have failed to receive it because some kind of priority must be maintained among the myriad facets of American Catholicism. But at least several should be mentioned. For example, 9,303 Catholics from the United States were in the foreign mission fields of the Church on January 1, 1966, a figure that represented a real gain over that of a decade before. But when compared with the Church in small nations like the Netherlands that has but 2 per cent of the Catholics of the world and yet contributes 12 per cent of the Church's foreign missionaries, or of Ireland where 70 per cent of the priests and religious left their homeland for the missions, the number of American personnel is slight. In monetary assistance the American Catholics have done much better; they contributed approximately $16,000,000 to the Society for the Propagation of the Faith in the final year that Bishop Sheen served as national director (1966), to say nothing of the $159,925,508 collected by Catholic Relief Services from the Catholics of this country in the year ending September 30, 1964, for the relief of every type of suffering and deprivation throughout the world.

Another sector of Catholic life that has shown marked changes in the 1960's is reflected in the attitude toward censorship of the films by the National Catholic Office for Motion Pictures, which has been much more lenient in its judgment of the movies than was its predecessor; and the same attitude has prevailed in matters pertaining to the *imprimatur*, once demanded for a wide range of Catholic books or for books written by Catholics but now greatly relaxed. Mention should also be made of projects to remedy the Church's situation in the inner city, such as the survey initiated by Cardinal Shehan in Baltimore in 1965 and conducted under the direction of Father Robert G. Howes of the Catholic University of America and a trained staff over a period of two years; this survey resulted in the publication in 1967 of *Baltimore Urban Parish*

Study, a blueprint for action in fifty-two of the seventy parishes situated in the city of Baltimore. There have also been independent undertakings like that of Strycker's Bay Neighborhood Council in New York, the president of which was a priest, Henry J. Browne, former professor of history in Saint Joseph's Seminary, whose alertness to social questions reflects the tradition established by his teacher, the late Father John P. Monaghan, founder of the Association of Catholic Trade Unionists.

Father Robert Bosc, S.J., who visited the United States in 1966 and for some time studied the Catholics here at close range, thought the most characteristic traits of the American Church were generosity, seriousness and a desire for excellence." In the judgment of this foreign observer, American Catholics in the years ahead could not fail to bring to the worldwide Church what, as he said, "the great-souled St. Peter brought to the Apostolic College: a stimulating witness of ardor, enthusiasm and spontaneity."[116] If that prediction is to become a reality, the American Catholic community will have to give witness to something of the changes mentioned by Karl Rahner, S.J., when he wrote of the way in which the post-conciliar reforms were left in Catholics' hands as commissions which could be realistically fulfilled. The conditions for that fulfillment as summarized by the distinguished German theologian for all his coreligionists throughout the worldwide Church may serve here as a fitting conclusion addressed in particular to the Catholics of the United States. Said Father Rahner:

When the government of the bishops is service, humble, humbler than before; when the priests more selflessly and purely, whether with results or not, administer the word of God and the grace of the sacraments; when the laymen criticize less and cooperate more eagerly; when all take up the cross of their existence and carry it after Christ more patiently, and see the light of God in the darkness with brighter eyes of faith; when everyone recognizes himself as a sinner and yet redeemed by the grace of God; when everyone begins to love God more; when everyone tries a little bit more each day to replace the egotistic hardness of his heart with a little more active love of neighbor; when there are Christians who are influenced neither by the brutal bellowing uproar nor by the cowardly whispering of nationalistic or militaristic egotism; when a few Christian men and women in the openness of their living more clearly demand and more clearly say what is right and not what is merely expedient, then the Council will have achieved its goal, will have fulfilled its meaning. This goal disappears into the silent mystery of God, who alone knows our hearts and deeds. But the Church must have the courage to face the inevitability of her mission. Otherwise she would not be what she is and must become.[117]

Notes

1. Peter Guilday, *A History of the Councils of Baltimore, 1791–1884* (New York, 1932), p. 178.

2. Christopher Dawson, *Understanding Europe* (New York, 1952), p. 13.

CHAPTER I

1. Acton Papers (University of Cambridge Library, Add. 4902), G. E. Fasnacht to the writer, Oxford, August 20, 1954.

2. Herbert Eugene Bolton, "The Epic of Greater America," *American Historical Review*, XXXVIII (April, 1933), 448–74.

3. Samuel Eliot Morison, *Admiral of the Ocean Sea: A Life of Christopher Columbus* (Boston, 1942), I, 204. After quoting the original entry, Morison remarks: "So begins the most detailed, the most interesting and the most entrancing sea journal of any voyage in history."

4. Martin Fernández de Navarrete (ed.), *Collección de los viages y descubrimientos que hicieron por mar los Españoles* (Madrid, 1829), III, 156.

5. For an English translation of *Universalis ecclesiae* cf. J. Lloyd Mecham, *Church and State in Latin America*, rev. ed. (Chapel Hill, 1966), pp. 16–18.

6. Francis Augustus MacNutt, *Bartholomew de Las Casas* (New York, 1909), p. 429. The full text of *Sublimus Deus* of Paul III is given here in an English translation (pp. 426–31).

7. Herbert Eugene Bolton, "The Mission as a Frontier Institution in the Spanish American Colonies," *American Historical Review*, XXIII (October, 1917), 61.

8. Circular letter of Junípero Serra to the California missions, San Carlos, June 15, 1780, in possession of the Academy of American Franciscan History.

9. France V. Scholes, *Church and State in New Mexico, 1610–1650* (Albuquerque, 1937), p. 192. On this question cf. also John Francis Bannon, *History of the Americas* (New York, 1952), I, 367 ff.

10. Herbert Ingram Priestley, *The Coming of the White Man, 1492–1848* (New York, 1929), p. 1.

11. Mason Wade, *The French Canadians, 1760–1945* (Toronto, 1955), p. 39.

12. Jean de Brébeuf, S.J., "Instructions for the Fathers of Our Society Who Shall Be Sent to the Hurons," incorporated into the relation of Paul le Jeune, S.J., for 1637, ed. Reuben Gold Thwaites, *The Jesuit Relations and Allied Documents* (Cleveland, 1898), XIII, 123. For a recent treatment of the subject of these missions cf. John H. Kennedy, *Jesuit and Savage in New France* (New Haven, 1950).

13. Francis Parkman, *The Jesuits in North America in the Seventeenth Century* (Boston, 1910), II, 213–14.

14. The description of the ceremony is contained in the relation of Claude Dablon, S.J., for 1670–71 in Thwaites, *op. cit.*, LV, 111.

15. Francis Parkman, *La Salle and the Discovery of the Great West* (Boston, 1910), pp. 59–60. In regard to Parkman's use of the words "adoration" and "worship" to describe Marquette's devotion to the Mother of God, it ought to be stated that it is commonly understood among Catholics in English-speaking lands that these terms describe man's relationship to God alone. Traditionally, they have preferred to use "veneration" when speaking of their relationship to Mary. If non-Catholic writers would note this important distinction, some confusion might be avoided.

16. François Philibert Watrin, S.J., Paris, September 3, 1764, "Banishment of the Jesuits from Louisiana," in Thwaites, *op. cit.*, LXX, 281.

17. Charles and Mary Beard, *The Rise of American Civilization* (New York, 1931), I, 9.

18. D. W. Brogan, *The American Character* (New York, 1944), p. 12.

19. Louis B. Wright, *Religion and Empire: The Alliance between Piety and Commerce in English Expansion, 1558–1625* (Chapel Hill, 1943), p. 114.

20. Louis B. Wright, *Culture on the Moving Frontier* (Bloomington, 1955), p. 241. Not all would agree with the emphasis that Wright gives to British influences in American culture. For example, Russell Blankenship has said: "Next to the melting pot fallacy, the most common mistake in thinking of racial contributions to our culture is to believe that one race has contributed everything. . . . The theory that American thought is wholly of English origin collapses at the first critical touch" (*American Literature as an Expression of the National Mind* [New York, 1931], pp. 21–22).

21. Burke to Sir Hercules Langrishe, January 3, 1792, *The Works of the Right Honorable Edmund Burke* (7th ed.; Boston, 1881), IV, 305.

22. Charles M. Andrews, *The Colonial Period of American History* (New Haven, 1936). The Beards were less than just in saying: "From first to last the Maryland colony was viewed by the Baltimores as an economic venture . . ." (*op. cit.*, I, 60).

23. Francis Newton Thorpe (ed.), *The Federal and State Constitutions* (Washington, 1909), III, 1679.

24. Clayton Colman (ed.), *Narratives of Early Maryland, 1633–1684* (New York, 1910), p. 16.

25. Justin Winsor, *Narrative and Critical History of America* (Boston, 1884), III, 530. Williams gave religious liberties to Jews and Catholics as well as to Protestant Christians, although there is no record of a Catholic ever having been in Rhode Island during the colonial period. In Maryland the formal grant of religious toleration was restricted to Christians, and a Jew named Jacob Lumbrozo encountered initial difficulties when he appeared about 1658. These overcome, he settled down to a peaceful existence and was found serving on a jury in 1664 (cf. William T. Russell, *Maryland: The Land of Sanctuary* [Baltimore, 1907], pp. 271–74).

26. E. A. Dalrymple (ed.), *Narrative of a Voyage to Maryland by Father Andrew White, S.J.: An Account of the Colony of the Lord Baron of Baltimore* (Baltimore, 1874), p. 33.

27. Andrews, *op. cit.*, II, 291.

28. *Ibid.*, pp. 309–10.

29. William Hand Browne (ed.), *Archives of Maryland: Proceedings and Acts of the General Assembly of Maryland, January 1637/38–September 1664* (Baltimore, 1883), I, 264.

30. In March, 1642, Virginia had passed a law against Catholics and priests. In May, 1647, a more stringent measure was enacted in Massachusetts Bay.

31. Sanford H. Cobb, *The Rise of Religious Liberty in America* (New York, 1902), p. 451.

32. Neale to Charles Shireburn, S.J., April 25, 1741, in Thomas Hughes, S.J. (ed.), *History of the Society of Jesus in North America: Documents* (Cleveland, 1908), I, 342.

33. A recent scholarly account of the Acadian exiles is that of Lawrence Henry Gipson, *The Great War for the Empire: The Years of Defeat, 1754–1757* (New York, 1946), pp. 243–344.

34. Hunter to John Dennett, S.J., July 23, 1765, in Hughes, *op. cit.*, I, 335–38, 351–52.

35. For the period of Dutch rule cf. Frederick J. Zwierlein, *Religion in New Netherland* (Rochester, 1910).

36. Edward T. Corwin (ed.), *Ecclesiastical Records of the State of New York* (Albany, 1901), II, 864.

37. On the confused question of jurisdiction cf. Edwin H. Burton, *The Life and Times of Bishop Challoner, 1691–1781* (New York, 1909), II, 123–48.

38. Kate Mason Rowland, *The Life of Charles Carroll of Carrollton, 1737–1832, with His Correspondence and Public Papers* (New York, 1898), I, 285.

39. Jonathan Boucher, *A View of the Causes and Consequences of the American Revolution* (London, 1797), p. 242.

40. Worthington Chauncey Ford (ed.), *Journals of the Continental Congress, 1774–1789* (Washington, 1904), I, 88.

41. *Ibid.*, pp. 112–13.

42. John C. Fitzpatrick (ed.), *The Writings of George Washington* (Washington, 1931), IV, 65.

43. Quoted in Peter Guilday, *The Life and Times of John Carroll, Archbishop of Baltimore, 1735–1815* (New York, 1922), I, 97.

44. *An Address to the Roman Catholics of the United States of America, by a Catholic Clergyman* [John Carroll] (Annapolis, 1784), p. 115.

45. *American Catholic Historical Researches*, VII (October, 1890), 167, which reprints the brochure of J. P. Coghlan, *A Short Account of the Establishment of the New See of Baltimore, Maryland, and of Consecrating the Right Rev. Dr. John Carroll* (London, 1790).

46. Copy of Washington to the Catholics, March 12, 1790, Washington Papers (Library of Congress, Division of Manuscripts), 334.

CHAPTER II

1. Henry Adams, *History of the United States of America* (New York, 1891), I, 176.

2. Gerald Shaughnessy, S.M., *Has the Immigrant Kept the Faith?* (New York, 1925), p. 52. Shaughnessy estimated that in 1790 there were approximately 275,000 Americans of Catholic descent, and he concluded, therefore, that "the Church had suffered here a loss of 240,000 members or possible members by the year 1790." This is the best general work on Catholic population figures. For the colonial population cf. Evarts B. Greene and Virginia D. Harrington, *American Population before the Federal Census of 1790* (New York, 1932).

3. Quoted in Adams, *op. cit.*, I, 157.

4. Tracy to an unnamed correspondent, August 7, 1800, in Samuel Eliot Morison, *The Life and Letters of Harrison Gray Otis, Federalist, 1765–1848* (Boston, 1913), I, 107, n. 1. Morison added: "By 1798 the alliance between native democracy and the Irish vote, which has endured to this day, was already cemented. The apprehension of his party is reflected in a remark of Otis in a letter to his wife: 'If some means are not adopted to prevent the indiscriminate admission of wild Irishmen & others to the right of suffrage, there will soon be an end to liberty & property.' "

5. Cf. Joseph L. J. Kirlin, *Catholicity in Philadelphia* (Philadelphia, 1909), pp. 123–29, 151–59.

6. *Brooksiana; or, The Controversy between Senator Brooks and Archbishop Hughes, Growing Out of the Recently Enacted Church Property Bill* (New York, 1855), p. 5. Hughes's statement on the lay trustee system was made in the introduction which he wrote for this volume and which he dated July, 1853. Erastus Brooks, a Know-Nothing state senator at Albany, was one of the chief pro-

moters of the Putnam Bill, which passed the legislature in 1855 and which aimed at preventing Catholic clergymen from holding church property in their own names.

7. Martha L. Edwards, "Religious Forces in the United States, 1815–1830," *Mississippi Valley Historical Review*, V (March, 1919), 441–42. For two studies of trusteeism on a sectional basis cf. Robert F. McNamara, "Trusteeism in the Atlantic States, 1785–1863," *Catholic Historical Review*, XXX (July, 1944), 135–54, and Alfred G. Stritch, "Trusteeism in the Old Northwest, 1800–1850," *Catholic Historical Review*, XXX (July, 1944), 155–64.

8. Whitfield to Rosati, December 12, 1832, "Documents," *St. Louis Catholic Historical Review*, V (October, 1923), 244–25.

9. Shaughnessy, *op. cit.*, pp. 73, 117, 125, 134.

10. On the characteristics of the Catholic minority in the early national period cf. the studies of Thomas T. McAvoy, C.S.C., "The Catholic Minority in the United States, 1789–1821," *Historical Records and Studies*, XXXIX–XL (1952), 33–50, and "The Formation of the Catholic Minority in the United States, 1820–1860," *Review of Politics*, X (January, 1948), 13–34.

11. J. Hector St. John [Michel Guillaume St. Jean de Crèvecœur], *Letters from an American Farmer*, ed. Warren Barton Blake (New York, 1904), p. 43. Crèvecœur's book was first published in London in 1782.

12. *Ibid.*

13. Russell Blankenship, *American Literature as an Expression of the National Mind* (New York, 1931), p. 21.

14. J. Franklin Jameson, *The American Revolution Considered as a Social Movement* (Princeton, 1926), p. 74. This volume contained four lectures delivered by Jameson at Princeton University in November, 1925, with a view to broadening the base of study of the American Revolution beyond political and military history. Of the final lecture, entitled "Thought and Feeling," Frederick B. Tolles of Swarthmore College stated: "What Jameson did—and it was no trifling achievement—was to bring American church history within the purview of American historians—to take, as it were, the first steps toward giving this neglected orphan child a home and a standing within the family of historical disciplines" ("The American Revolution Considered as a Social Movement: A Re-evaluation," *American Historical Review*, LX [October, 1954], 10).

15. Adams, *op. cit.*, I, 93.

16. Luke 23:31.

17. John Gilmary Shea, *Memorial of the First Centenary of Georgetown College, D.C.* (New York, 1891), p. 12.

18. Carroll to Leonardo Cardinal Antonelli, April 23, 1792, in Peter Guilday, *The Life and Times of John Carroll, Archbishop of Baltimore, 1735–1815* (New York), II, 471.

19. Joseph W. Ruane, *The Beginnings of the Society of St. Sulpice in the United States, 1791–1829* (Washington, 1935), p. 189.

20. The literature on the history of American Catholic institutions of charity leaves much to be desired. For one of the best works cf. Daniel T. McColgan, *A Century of Charity: The First One Hundred Years of the Society of St. Vincent de Paul in the United States* (2 vols.; Milwaukee, 1951). For the theory motivating Catholics in these matters cf. C. Joseph Nuesse, *The Social Thought of American Catholics, 1634–1829* (Washington, 1945).

21. Stewart to Alexius J. Elder, S.S., Baltimore, November 3, 1832 (Archives of St. Joseph's Central House, Emmitsburg).

22. *United States Catholic Miscellany*, January 28, 1824.

23. Gustave de Beaumont, *Marie ou l'esclavage aux États-Unis: Tableau de mœurs américaines* (Paris, 1835), II, 192.

24. [Thomas Hamilton], *Men and Manners in America* (Philadelphia, 1833), II, 108–9. Hamilton's friendly tone toward the Catholics was quite an exception to that shown by the majority of the numerous visitors from Great Britain in these years, for as one writer who studied their travelogues has said: "It can be seen that the British were willing to believe the worst about the Catholics" (Max Berger, *The British Traveller in America, 1836–1860* [New York, 1943], p. 144).

25. Ray Allen Billington, *The Protestant Crusade, 1800–1860* (New York, 1938), p. 438. The full text of the constitution is printed in an appendix, pp. 437–39.

26. Roy P. Basler (ed.), *The Collected Works of Abraham Lincoln* (New Brunswick, 1953), I, 338.

37. Peter Guilday (ed.), *The National Pastorals of the American Hierarchy, 1792–1919* (Washington, 1923), p. 87. The complete text of the pastoral is contained in pp. 80–119.

28. Hugh J. Nolan, *The Most Reverend Francis Patrick Kenrick, Third Bishop of Philadelphia, 1830–1851* (Washington, 1948), p. 294. Nolan has a detailed account of the question in his chapter, "The Native American Riots of 1844," pp. 288–342.

29. Cf. Henry J. Browne, "Public Support of Catholic Education in New York, 1825–1842: Some New Aspects," *Catholic Historical Review*, XXXIX (April, 1953), 1–27.

30. John R. G. Hassard, *Life of the Most Reverend John Hughes, First Archbishop of New York* (New York, 1866), p. 276.

31. Billington, *op. cit.*, p. 232.

32. The nativists, of course, fulminated against high government officials consulting Bishop Hughes on matters relating to the war. They were gleeful when news came through that the San Patricio Battalion, said to have been composed of Irish Catholics, had deserted to Mexico. But the propaganda value of the San Patricio Battalion collapsed when it was later learned that, of the sixteen deserters hanged at San Angel in September, 1847, only seven were Catholics and that the deserters numbered Americans, Germans, and other nationalities and were by no means confined to Irish Catholics (cf. Edward S. Wallace, "Deserters in the Mexican War," *Hispanic-American Historical Review*, XV [August, 1935], 374–83).

33. Alexis de Tocqueville, *Democracy in America*, ed. Phillips Bradley (New York, 1945), I, 300–301.

34. *United States Catholic Miscellany*, August 1, 1835.

35. Quoted in Guilday, *The Life and Times of John Carroll*, I, 97.

36. Arthur M. Schlesinger, Jr., *The Age of Jackson* (Boston, 1945), p. 137.

37. The episode of the so-called "Catholic ticket" in the state elections of New York in November, 1841, on the question of state aid to private schools was a temporary expedient brought on by the attitudes of the candidates of the two regular parties rather than an entrance into politics as such.

38. Guilday, *National Pastorals*, pp. 142–43.

39. Harriet Martineau, *Society in America* (London, 1837), III, 237.

40. On Walsh and Carey cf. Nuesse, *op. cit.*, pp. 212–49.

41. Peter Guilday, *The Life and Times of John England, First Bishop of Charleston, 1786–1842* (New York, 1927), II, 524–27.

42. Hughes to Seward, New York, August 29, 1840, quoted in Browne, *op. cit.*, p. 20. An example of the sensitivity of most Catholic clergymen about revealing their political views is found in Martin J. Spalding, who in August, 1840, was induced by some

friends while on a visit to Nashville to attend the southwestern Whig convention, where he heard a great oration delivered by Senator John J. Crittenden of his native state. Thirty years later Crittenden's daughter asked Spalding—by that time Archbishop of Baltimore—to describe the scene for her. He replied: "As I am not a civilian, but a clergyman, I feel some reluctance in complying with your request. . . . I went, not as a politician, for I took no interest in politics, but as a Kentuckian, anxious to hear a brother Kentuckian speak, and I was well repaid" (Spalding to Mrs. C. Coleman, December 26, 1870, in J. L. Spalding, *The Life of the Most Rev. M. J. Spalding, Archbishop of Baltimore* [New York, 1873], p. 93). At the time of the Nashville convention Spalding was Vicar General of the Diocese of Bardstown.

43. Crèvecœur, *op. cit.*, p. 44.

44. Madison to Carroll, November 20, 1806, in "Letters from the Archiepiscopal Archives at Baltimore, 1787–1815," *Records of the American Catholic Historical Society of Philadelphia*, XX (1909), 64. On the same day Madison sent a private letter to Carroll in which he stated that he shared the latter's opinion entirely concerning the inadvisability of recommending certain priests for the episcopal office in Louisiana (*ibid.*, pp. 64–65).

45. Peter Guilday, *A History of the Councils of Baltimore, 1791–1884* (New York, 1932), p. 178.

46. Guilday, *National Pastorals*, p. 192.

CHAPTER III

1. Mark Twain, *The Innocents Abroad* (New York, 1929), II, 349. This book, which established the author's national reputation, was first published in 1869.

2. John Henry Newman, *Apologia Pro Vita Sua* (New York, 1913), p. 7. The original edition of this work appeared in the spring of 1864.

3. Lincoln to Joshua F. Speed, Springfield, August 24, 1855, in Roy P. Basler (ed.), *The Collected Works of Abraham Lincoln* (New Brunswick, 1953), II, 322–23.

4. Taney to J. Mason Campbell, Faquier White Sulphur Springs, August 28, 1856, Carl Brent Swisher, *Roger B. Taney* (New York, 1936), p. 473.

5. Cf. Leo Francis Stock (ed.), *United States Ministers to the Papal States: Instructions and Despatches, 1848–1868* (Washington, 1933), pp. 413–36, for the dispatches of Rufus King, American Minister to Rome, indicating the unfavorable impression made by the anti-Catholic bias and King's protests against American misrepresentations of the government of Pius IX.

6. The total number of Catholic immigrants for the five decades between 1850 and 1900 was estimated by Gerald Shaughnessy to be 4,805,000 (*Has the Immigrant Kept the Faith?* [New York, 1925], pp. 145, 153, 161, 166, 172).

7. Cf. Henry J. Browne, "Archbishop Hughes and Western Colonization," *Catholic Historical Review,* XXXVI (October, 1950), 257–85; James H. Moynihan, *The Life of Archbishop John Ireland* (New York, 1953), pp. 21–32; and J. L. Spalding, *The Religious Mission of the Irish People and Catholic Colonization* (New York, 1880).

8. Francis Patrick Kenrick, *Theologia moralis* (Philadelphia, 1841), I, 257.

9. In a recent work on Kenrick's theology of slavery the author says: "Certainly no theologian could have permitted slavery as it frequently existed in practice in America. There was equivocal use of the word slavery that should have been more clearly pointed out" (Joseph D. Brokhage, *Francis Patrick Kenrick's Opinion on Slavery* [Washington, 1955], p. 242).

10. Regarding Carroll's methods of manumission, his biographer stated: "Charles Carroll of Carrollton, that representative southern abolitionist, would no more have considered setting free his slaves, without making elaborate provision for their future, than he would have thought it a kindness to open Cousin Rachel's wicker cage of tropical finches, setting them at liberty to fend for and warm and feed themselves in the cold Maryland winter" (Ellen Hart Smith, *Charles Carroll of Carrollton* [Cambridge, 1942], p. 267).

11. Albert S. Foley, S.J., *Bishop Healy: Beloved Outcaste* (New York, 1954), pp. 4–7.

12. Clement Eaton, *Freedom of Thought in the Old South* (Durham, 1940), pp. 228–29. Eaton says: "Irishmen were used in the South to perform dangerous labor, dig ditches, handle the bounding cotton bales in loading ships. The loss of a fifteen-hundred-dollar negro was a serious misfortune, but the loss of an Irishman was lightly regarded."

13. John T. Gillard, S.S.J., *Colored Catholics in the United States* (Baltimore, 1941), p. 99. Gillard confessed that these figures were only rough approximations.

14. Mother St. John Fournier to the Society for the Propagation of the Faith, 1873, in Sister Maria Kostka Logue, *Sisters of St. Joseph of Philadelphia* (Westminster, Maryland, 1950), p. 136. A school for free Negroes begun in New Orleans in 1825 by a zealous laywoman, and later taught by sisters, had better luck and lasted into the 1840's (cf. Roger Baudier, *The Catholic Church in Louisiana* [New Orleans, 1939], pp. 364–65).

15. Archives of the Diocese of Natchez, Elder to the Society for the Propagation of the Faith, 1858, photostat copy, kindness of Bishop Richard O. Gerow.

16. R. H. C., "Thoughts and Suggestions on the Catholic Question in America," *Metropolitan*, V (April, 1857), 141. In all likelihood "R. H. C." was Richard H. Clarke, a New York lawyer, who did a good deal of writing in these years and was the author of the two-volume work, *Lives of Deceased Bishops of the Catholic Church in the United States* (New York, 1872), revised and enlarged in three volumes in 1888.

17. *Pastoral Letter of Archbishop and Bishops of the Province of Baltimore . . . May, 1858* (Baltimore, 1858), p. 12.

18. *Pastoral Letter of the Third Provincial Council of Cincinnati to the Clergy and Laity* (Cincinnati, 1861), p. 6.

19. Kenrick to Eliza Allen Starr, Baltimore, November 11, 1862, in James J. McGovern (ed.), *The Life and Letters of Eliza Allen Starr* (Chicago, 1905), p. 163.

20. Kenrick to Starr, Baltimore, August 6, 1861, *ibid.*, p. 148.

21. James Cardinal Gibbons, "My Memories," *Dublin Review*, CLX (April, 1917), 165.

22. Randall to Seward, Rome, June 11, 1862, in Stock, *op. cit.*, pp. 251–52.

23. Hughes to Lynch, New York, August 23, 1861, in Lawrence Kehoe (ed.), *Complete Works of the Most Rev. John Hughes* (New York, 1865), II, 515. The full text is given here, pp. 513–20. In making Lynch's letter of August 4 public without his permission, Hughes blamed the severed telegraph connections between North and South and explained that if the "innocent lightning of the North were permitted to carry a message into Southern latitudes," he would first have wired the bishop for his permission (p. 513).

After learning that his letter had been published in New York, Lynch gave the full text to the Charleston *Catholic Miscellany*, which carried it in its issue of September 14, 1861.

24. James Parton, "Our Roman Catholic Brethren," *Atlantic Monthly*, XXI (May, 1868), 572. Parton remarked: "It may be that the exploits of some of our Protestant chaplains in the way of 'living on the country' contrasted with the strict observance, by Catholic chaplains, both of military and ecclesiastical rule, had some effect upon observant Protestant minds" (*ibid.*).

25. Dagmar Renshaw Lebreton, *Chahta-Ima: The Life of Adrien-Emmanuel Rouquette* (Baton Rouge, 1947), p. 222, quoting an undated manuscript in the archives of the Archdiocese of New Orleans.

26. Purcell kept up his campaign for the elimination of the slave system and when he learned of a priest in Kentucky who was still advocating slavery, he remarked in a Christmas issue of his paper: "He ought to hide in the Mammoth Cave and associate with the fossils. . . . A Catholic Priest, in the holy times of Christmas, advocating slavery! . . . . What a subject for meditation before the altar on Christmas morning. If slavery must have its advocates, let them be found amongst the laity, and not amongst the Priests" (*Catholic Telegraph*, December 23, 1863).

27. Quoted in Ellen Ryan Jolly, *Nuns of the Battlefield* (Providence, 1927), p. 188.

28. Odin to Spalding, New Orleans, September 7, 1864, in Vincent de Paul McMurry, S.S., "The Catholic Church during Reconstruction, 1865–1877" (unpublished master's thesis, Catholic University of America, 1950), p. 56.

29. Lynch to the Society for the Propagation of the Faith, Charleston, June 17, 1867, *Annales de la propagation de la foi*, XL (1868), 87.

30. *Concilii plenarii Baltimorensis II . . . Acta de decreta* (Baltimore, 1868), p. 245. At the close of the council the bishops issued a pastoral letter to the clergy and laity on October 21 in which they treated the subject. They expressed their regret that "a more gradual system of emancipation" had not been adopted, but they stated: "We urge upon the Clergy and people of our charge the most generous co-operation with the plans which may be adopted . . . to extend to them that Christian education and moral restraint which they so much stand in need of (Peter Guilday [ed.], *The*

National Pastorals of the American Hierarchy, 1792–1919 [Washington, 1923], p. 221).

31. Durier to Mother M. Florence Walter, Natchitoches, November 18, 1889, Sister Mary Generosa Callahan, C.D.P., *The History of the Sisters of Divine Providence, San Antonio, Texas* (Milwaukee, 1955), p. 178.

32. Spalding to John McCloskey, Baltimore, October 9, 1865, in McMurry, *op. cit.*, p. 197.

33. John B. Tennelly, S.S. (ed.), *Our Negro and Indian Missions: Annual Report of the Secretary of the Commission for the Catholic Missions among the Colored People and the Indians* (Washington, 1967), p 22. At the end of 1966 there were 812 priests engaged in work for the blacks, 529 churches, 345 schools with 106,325 students, and a total of 41,178 adult and infant baptisms for that year. Proportionately, Catholics have done better among the Indians, with 135,853 Catholics, or about one-fourth of the Indian population of the United States, for whom there are 394 churches, 253 priests at work, 54 schools with 8,765 students; during 1966 there were 5,446 infant and 1,133 adult Indian baptisms (*ibid.*, p. 33).

34. For the most famous of these conflicts cf. Colman J. Barry, O.S.B., *The Catholic Church and German Americans* (Milwaukee, 1953).

35. Arthur M. Schlesinger, "A Critical Period in American Religion, 1875–1900," *Proceedings of the Massachusetts Historical Society*, LXIV (1932), 533. Schlesinger stated that in the twenty years preceding 1888 there were seventeen Protestant churches that moved out of the district below Fourteenth Street in New York City, although 200,000 more people had crowded into it, and in the decade after 1878 the thirteenth ward in Boston had 22,000 residents "without a single Protestant church" (p. 532).

36. Isa. 17:12.

37. Henry Steele Commager, *The American Mind: An Interpretation of American Thought and Character since the 1880's* (New Haven, 1950), p. 193.

38. *Concillii plenarii Baltimorensis II . . . Acta de decreta* (Baltimore, 1868), p. 263. For the bishops' attitudes on the various societies cf. Fergus Macdonald, *The Catholic Church and the Secret Societies in the United States* (New York, 1946).

39. Gibbons to Simeoni, Rome, February 20, 1887, Henry J. Browne, *The Catholic Church and the Knights of Labor* (Wash-

ington, 1949), p. 372. Pages 365–78 of this work contain a critical edition and translation of the original French document.

40. *Ibid.*, p. 374. A recent writer has termed Gibbons' decision in this instance "one of the stirring examples" of the best kind of practical judgment. In the Knights of Labor case he was said to have shown "a wonderful command of the relevant information, a fine awareness of the moral principles to the practical situation at hand. The Cardinal was on controversial ground, but history has eloquently indicated the justice of his practical judgment" (Joseph P. Fitzpatrick, S.J., "The Practical Judgment," *Thought,* XXX [spring, 1955], 70).

41. "The Catholic Element in the History of the United States," *Metropolitan,* V (August, 1857), 524. The article was unsigned. The most recent scholarly treatments of this subject are John Higham, *Strangers in the Land: Patterns of American Nativism, 1865–1925* (New Brunswick, 1955), and Donald L. Kinzer, *An Episode in Anti-Catholicism: The American Protective Association* (Seattle, 1964).

42. Bancroft to Osgood, Berlin, February 21, 1868, in M. A. DeWolfe Howe, *The Life and Letters of George Bancroft* (New York, 1908), II, 203.

43. John Ireland, *The Church and Modern Society: Lectures and Addresses* (St. Paul, 1905), I, 229. The full text of Ireland's speech is given here, pp. 217–32.

44. Cf. Daniel F. Reilly, O.P., *The School Controversy, 1891–1893* (Washington, 1943).

45. Henry J. Browne, "The American Parish School in the Last Half Century," *Bulletin of the National Catholic Educational Association,* L (August, 1953), 331–33.

46. A. C. F. Beales, "The Struggle for the Schools," in George Andrew Beck, A.A. (ed.), *The English Catholics, 1850–1950* (London, 1950), pp. 389–90.

47. Parton, *op. cit.,* p. 573.

48. Bancroft to Osgood, Berlin, Christmas, 1871, in Howe, *op. cit.,* II, 263. For American press reaction to the Vatican Council cf. J. Ryan Beiser, *The Vatican Council and the American Secular Newspapers, 1869–70* (Washington, 1941).

49. For Spalding's ideas cf. Sister Agnes Claire Schroll, *The Social Thought of John Lancaster Spalding* (Washington, 1944).

50. Frederick J. Zwierlein, *The Life and Letters of Bishop Mc-Quaid* (Rochester, 1927), III, 396. By 1907, however, McQuaid, like a number of others, had come to accept the inevitability of Catholic students in secular universities, and he took steps, therefore, to provide chaplains and religious services for the 300 Catholics who were then attending Cornell (*ibid.*, pp. 405–6).

51. Henry F. Brownson (ed.), *The Works of Orestes A. Brownson* (Detroit, 1885), XIX, 439.

52. "Thoughts and Suggestions on the Catholic Question in America," *Metropolitan*, V (February, 1857), 15. The article was unsigned.

53. John Lancaster Spalding, *Means and Ends of Education* (Chicago, 1897), p. 220. Spalding entitled the sermon of November 16, 1884, "Higher Education." The entire text is given here, pp. 181–232.

54. There have been four volumes published on the history of the university to date: John Tracy Ellis, *The Formative Years of the Catholic University of America* (Washington, 1946); Patrick H. Ahern, *The Catholic University of America, 1887–1896: The Rectorship of John J. Keane* (Washington, 1949); Peter E. Hogan, S.S.J., *The Catholic University of America, 1896–1903: The Rectorship of Thomas J. Conaty* (Washington, 1949); Colman J. Barry, O.S.B., *The Catholic University of America, 1903–1909: The Rectorship of Denis J. O'Connell* (Washington, 1950). For the more recent period, see Roy J. Deferrari, *Memoirs of the Catholic University of America, 1918–1960* (Boston, 1962).

55. Ireland, *op. cit.*, I, 92. The title of Ireland's sermon preached on November 10, 1889, was "The Mission of Catholics in America" (pp. 71–101).

56. D. W. Brogan, *U.S.A.: An Outline of the Country, Its People and Institutions* (London, 1941), p. 65.

57. Recent biographies of these churchmen have treated the questions in detail. Cf. John Tracy Ellis, *The Life of James Cardinal Gibbons, Archbishop of Baltimore, 1834–1921* (Milwaukee, 1952); James H. Moynihan, *The Life of Archbishop John Ireland* (New York, 1953); and Patrick H. Ahern, *The Life of John J. Keane, Educator and Archbishop, 1839–1918* (Milwaukee, 1955).

58. John J. Wynne, S.J. (ed.), *The Great Encyclical Letters of Pope Leo XIII* (New York, 1903), p. 452. The full translation of *Testem benevolentiae* is carried here, pp. 441–53.

59. Gibbons to Leo XIII, Baltimore, March 17, 1899, in Ellis, *op. cit.*, II, 71.

60. Wynne, *op. cit.*, p. 514. The translation of the entire letter of April 15, 1902, is contained here, pp. 513–16.

CHAPTER IV

1. Gerald Shaughnessy, *Has the Immigrant Kept the Faith?* (New York, 1925), p. 172. The tremendous increase in the number of American Catholics in the first half of this century affected almost every phase of Catholic life in this country. For example, in August, 1954, there were 131 Catholic weekly newspapers with approximately 4,000,000 subscribers and 426 magazines with 16,700,000 paid subscriptions. But it is well to keep in mind that the essential progress of the Church is not properly gauged by the increase in Catholic activities. Nearly a century ago an anonymous Catholic writer voiced a salutary warning on that score when he said: "The real prosperity of the Church in any part of the world does not consist merely in large or increasing numbers, in the multiplication of churches and institutions, or in the grandeur and beauty which our growing resources may enable us to bestow upon them. All this constitutes but the shell of religion. . . . It is a grave error, therefore, and a very common one in the United States, to estimate the progress of Catholicity amongst us from this outward stand-point" ("American Catholics, and Catholic Ireland," *Metropolitan*, V [March, 1857], 75).

2. George A. Kelly and Thomas Coogan, "What Is Our Real Catholic Population?" *American Ecclesiastical Review*, CX (May, 1944), 377.

3. *The Glenmary Story* (Glendale, Ohio [1953]), pp. 12–13. For a discussion of the problems of a rural parish, cf. Emerson Hynes, "The Parish in the Rural Community," ed. C. Joseph Nuesse and Thomas J. Harte, C.SS.R., *The Sociology of the Parish* (Milwaukee, 1950), pp. 100–132.

4. According to the *Catholic Directory* for 1956, there was a total of 48,349 priests in the United States, or a ratio of 1 priest for every 696 Catholics. It must be remembered, however, that, of this total, 29,734 belonged to the diocesan clergy whose principal work was centered in the parishes, while 18,615 were priests of

religious orders who are ordinarily engaged in special assignments, such as teaching, preaching missions, etc., although many of the religious also conduct parishes. Moreover, 8,995 American priests were in full-time teaching posts, a figure that included many of the diocesan clergy. While the ratio of priests to people in the United States is fairly good, by reason of the size of the country it is nowhere as satisfactory as it is, for example, in Ireland, where that small country has a ratio of 1 priest to every 560 Catholics.

5. II Tim. 4:9.

6. George A. Kelly, *Catholics and the Practice of the Faith: A Census Study of the Diocese of Saint Augustine* (Washington, 1946), pp. 53–87. Cf. also the same author's *The Story of St. Monica's Parish, New York City, 1879–1954* (New York, 1954), pp. 89–97; Gerald J. Schnepp, S.M., *Leakage from a Catholic Parish* (Washington, 1942); and the two works of Joseph H. Fichter, S.J., *Southern Parish: Dynamics of a City Church* (Chicago, 1951) and *Social Relations in the Urban Parish* (Chicago, 1954).

7. Shaughnessy, *op. cit.*, p. 255.

8. Vaughan to Gibbons, Mill Hill, October 28, 1889, *Catholic Historical Review*, XXX (October, 1944), 292. The full text of the lengthy letter is given here, pp. 290–98.

9. Amleto Giovanni Cicognani, *Sanctity in America* (Paterson, N.J., 1941), pp. 151–56.

10. Louis Bouyer, *Liturgical Piety* (Notre Dame, 1955), p. 1.

11. Gibbons' statement at the outbreak of war, April 5, 1917, is found in John Tracy Ellis, *The Life of James Cardinal Gibbons, Archbishop of Baltimore, 1834–1921* (Milwaukee, 1952), II, 239.

12. Baker to the welfare agencies, Washington, September 24, 1917, in Daniel J. Ryan, *American Catholic World War I Records* (Washington, 1941), p. 28. The full text of Baker's letter is contained here, pp. 27–30. The Bureau of the Census gave the population of the United States on July 1, 1918, as 103,587,955; the *Catholic Directory* of 1919 estimated the Catholic population as 17,549,324 or 16.94 per cent of the entire population. The 1919 figure is given for the latter as a closer approximation because the statistics were gathered the previous year and published in the spring of 1919.

13. Roosevelt to Gibbons, Oyster Bay, January 5, 1917, Ellis, *op. cit.*, II, 500.

14. J. L. Spalding, "Catholicism and APAism," *North American Review*, CLIX (September, 1894), 285.

15. Archives of the Diocese of Rockford, Diary of Bishop Muldoon, June, 1922.

16. Over and above the multiple activities centered in the N.C.W.C., there are numerous national Catholic organizations covering a wide variety of objectives which are entirely independent of the N.C.W.C. The extent of this organizational trend among American Catholics is strikingly illustrated, for example, in the national societies listed in *The 1968 National Catholic Almanac* (Paterson, N.J., 1968), pp. 633–40.

17. Mason to Gibbons, New York, February 25, 1919, Ellis, *op. cit.*, I, 541.

18. John A. Ryan, *Social Doctrine in Action: A Personal History* (New York, 1941), p. 147. On Ryan cf. Francis L. Broderick, *Right Reverend New Dealer: John A. Ryan* (New York, 1963).

19. *Catholic Telegraph-Register*, November 16, 1945.

20. For an attempt to show such an influence cf. Marc Karson, "The Catholic Church and the Political Development of American Trade Unionism, 1900–1918," *Industrial and Labor Relations Review*, IV (July, 1951), 527–42.

21. For a sampling of these studies cf. William S. Ament, "Religion, Education, and Distinction," *School and Society*, XXVI (September 24, 1927), 399–406; Harvey C. Lehman and Paul A. Witty, "Scientific Eminence and Church Membership," *Scientific Monthly*, XXXIII (December, 1931), 544–49; B. W. Kunkel, "The Representation of Colleges in Graduate and Professional Schools in the United States," *Association of American Colleges Bulletin*, XXVII (October, 1941), 449–74; William Miller, "American Historians and the Business Elite," *Journal of Economic History*, IX (November, 1949), 184–208; and R. H. Knapp and H. B. Goodrich, *Origins of American Scientists* (Chicago, 1952). Cf. also John Tracy Ellis, "American Catholics and the Intellectual Life," *Thought*, XXX (autumn, 1955), 351–88.

22. Ronald Chapman, "The Optimism of the 1840's," *Tablet* (London), December 18, 1954, p. 597.

23. D. W. Brogan, *U.S.A.: An Outline of the Country, Its People and Institutions* (London, 1941), p. 65.

24. Philip Blair Rice, "The Intellectual Quarterly in a Nonintellectual Society," *Kenyon Review*, XVI (summer, 1954), 420–

39. Cf. also Francis G. Wilson, "Public Opinion and the Intellectuals," *American Political Science Review*, XLVIII (June, 1954), 321–39; Merle Curti, "Intellectuals and Other People," *American Historical Review*, LX (January, 1955), 259–82; Milton M. Gordon, "Social Class and American Intellectuals," *American Association of University Professors Bulletin*, XL (winter, 1954–55), 517–28; and Wilson Record, "The American Intellectual as Black Sheep and Red Rover," *American Association of University Professors Bulletin*, XL (winter, 1954–55), 536–54.

25. Robert M. Hutchins, "The Integrating Principle of Catholic Higher Education," *College Newsletter, Midwest Regional Unit, N.C.E.A.* (May, 1937), p. 4.

26. Oscar Handlin, *The American People in the Twentieth Century* (Cambridge, 1954), p. 151. On this subject cf. the work of Edmund A. Moore, *A Catholic Runs for President: The Campaign of 1928* (New York, 1956).

27. Cf. Liston Pope, "Religion and the Class Structure," *Annals of the American Academy of Political and Social Science*, CCLVI (March, 1948), 85–86, and the appendix to Herbert Wallace Schneider, *Religion in 20th Century America* (Cambridge, 1952), pp. 227–38. The seminar reports of two of the writer's graduate students, Bosco Cestello, O.S.B., and Oderic Foley, O.F.M.Conv., on Catholics in business and politics were likewise used on this point.

28. James Bryce, *The American Commonwealth* (rev. ed., New York, 1941), II, 763.

29. For a highly critical view of the alleged aggression of the Church in the United States cf. Harold E. Fey, *Can Catholicism Win America?* (Chicago, 1945), a reprint of eight articles that appeared in the *Christian Century* from November 29, 1944, to January 17, 1945.

30. Evarts B. Greene, *Religion and the State: The Making and Testing of an American Tradition* (New York, 1941); Anson Phelps Stokes, *Church and State in the United States* (New York, 1950).

31. Henry Wallace Schneider, *Religion in 20th Century America* (Cambridge, 1952), p. 28.

32. Commager, *The American Mind: An Interpretation of American Thought and Character since the 1880's* (New Haven, 1950), p. 193.

33. Daniel J. Boorstin, *The Genius of American Politics* (Chicago, 1953), pp. 141–46.

34. *New York Times,* May 4, 1948.

35. Boorstin, *op. cit.,* p. 147.

36. Gertrude Himmelfarb (ed.), *Essays on Freedom and Power by John Emerich Edward Dalberg-Acton* (Boston, 1948), p. 40. Acton's statement was made in an address before the Bridgnorth Institute on May 28, 1877.

37. Boorstin, *op. cit.,* p. 148.

38. John Tracy Ellis, "Church and State: An American Catholic Tradition," *Harper's Magazine,* CCVII (November, 1953), 67. Cf. also *New York Times,* January 26, 1948. The chairman of the N.C.W.C. at the time was John T. McNicholas, O.P., Archbishop of Cincinnati. For a more recent statement cf. the toast to "Our Country," given in Rome by Samuel Cardinal Stritch, Archbishop of Chicago, in October, 1953, in *Addresses Delivered at the Dedication Ceremonies of the North American College at Rome, Italy, Wednesday, October 14, 1953* (n.p., n.d.), pp. 17–19.

39. Henry Edward Manning, *The Vatican Decrees in Their Bearing on Civil Allegiance* (New York, 1875), p. 91.

40. Charles C. Marshall, *The Roman Catholic Church in the Modern State* (New York, 1928).

41. Will Herberg, "The Sectarian Conflict over Church and State," *Commentary,* XIV (November, 1952), 450–62; "Religious Communities in Present-Day America," *Review of Politics,* XVI (April, 1954), 155–74; and *Protestant–Catholic–Jew: An Essay in American Religious Sociology* (New York, 1955).

42. John Courtney Murray, S.J., "The Church and Totalitarian Democracy," *Theological Studies,* XIII (December, 1952), 525–63; "Leo XIII: Two Concepts of Government," *Theological Studies,* XIV (December, 1953), 551–67; "The Problem of Pluralism in America," *Thought,* XXIX (summer, 1954), 165–208.

43. Charles W. Lowry, *Should America Be Represented at the Vatican?* p. 8, a privately printed sermon delivered in All Saints' Episcopal Church, Chevy Chase, Maryland, October 28, 1951.

44. Max Salvadori, "American Notes," *World Liberalism,* I (winter, 1951), 20.

45. Peter Viereck, *Shame and Glory of the Intellectuals* (Boston, 1953), p. 45.

46. *New York Times,* December 5, 1954.

CHAPTER V

The writer wishes to thank a number of kind friends who read this chapter in its entirety and offered many helpful corrections and suggestions: the Reverend Raymond G. Decker, Treasurer of the National Federation of Priests' Councils; Sister Mary Bernadette Giles, P.B.V.M., member of the Commission on Human Rights of the Mayor of San Francisco; the Right Reverend Francis T. Hurley, Assistant General Secretary of the United States Catholic Conference; the Right Reverend George G. Higgins, Director of the Social Action Department of the same conference.

1. 10th ed. (New York, 1897), p. 40.

2. As recently as the summer of 1967 there were still forty or more foreign language publications in eighteen different languages being published in the Chicago area alone, not all of which, of course, were Catholic. See John Adam Moreau, "Ethnic Press Holding Its Own in Chicago," *Chicago Sun-Times*, August 27, 1967, p. 14.

3. *The Rise of the City, 1878–1898* (New York, 1933), p. 333.

4. Joseph R. Washington, Jr., *Black Religion: The Negro and Christianity* (Boston, 1964), p. 243.

5. *The Church in Our Day* (Washington, 1968), p. 23.

6. *Ibid.*

7. *Ibid.*, p. 24.

8. *The Secular City: Secularization and Urbanization in Theological Perspective* (New York, 1965), p. 139.

9. Walter M. Abbott, S.J., and Joseph Gallagher (eds.), *The Documents of Vatican II* (New York, 1966), p. 241.

10. *Saint Louis Review*, August 25, 1967, p. 23.

11. Vincent A. Yzermans (ed.), *American Participation in the Second Vatican Council* (New York, 1967), p. 69.

12. *Catholic Standard* (Washington), August 3, 1967, p. 2, for Cardinal O'Boyle's pastoral letter; *Report of the National Advisory Commission on Civil Rights* (New York, 1968), p. 203.

13. Yzermans, *op. cit.*, p. 154.

14. *Ibid.*, p. 157.

15. "A Time to Create," *Commonweal*, October 13, 1967, p. 49.

16. *American Protestantism* (Chicago, 1961), pp. 128–29.

17. Foreword to Robert McAfee Brown and Gustave Weigel, S.J., *An American Dialogue: A Protestant Looks at Catholicism and a Catholic Looks at Protestantism* (Garden City, 1960), p. 12.

18. Edith Lovejoy Pierce, "Pope John XXIII: In Memoriam," *Christian Century*, June 26, 1963, p. 823.

19. Newman, *op. cit.*, p. 37.

20. Brown and Weigel, *op. cit.*, p. 19. Brown's more recent work, *The Ecumenical Revolution* (1967) from the same publisher, shows how far the movement has traveled in the brief span of seven years.

21. *Character and Opinion in the United States* (New York, 1955), pp. 30–31; this is a reprint of the work published in 1920 by Charles Scribner's Sons.

22. In the business world recent evidence has shown that Catholics have been discriminated against on the ground of their religion and, too, that they have themselves discriminated against others. For example, Lewis B. Ward found that among 324 recruiters of college graduates for major American corporations 80 hired only Protestants, 42 hired only Catholics, and 14 hired only Jews. On the other hand, among the large companies covered, those hiring trainees from the "Catholics only" group came second to the "mixed ethnic" group in frequency of large size with 74 per cent, the "Protestants only" with 69 per cent, and the "Jews only" with 57 per cent. "The Ethnics of Executive Selection," *Harvard Business Review*, XLIII (March–April, 1965), 14.

23. *New York Times*, October 18, 1908. The triumph of Taft over Bryan on November 3 of that year by an electoral vote of 321 to 182 naturally elated the Republicans. Theodore Roosevelt remarked in a letter to Archbishop Ireland from Washington on November 20, "I wish I could see you so that we might congratulate each other on our victory, for most emphatically you are one of those who can feel an especial pride in it." Elting E. Morison *et al.* (eds.), *The Letters of Theodore Roosevelt* (Cambridge, 1952, VI, 1368. It was one of the earliest occasions when considerable numbers of Catholic voters in the cities left the Democratic party and voted Republican.

24. Lawrence H. Fuchs, *John F. Kennedy and American Catholicism* (New York, 1967), p. 165.

25. *The Making of the President 1960* (New York, 1961), pp. 261–62.

26. Philip E. Converse *et al.*, "Stability and Change in 1960: A Reinstating Election," *American Political Science Review*, LV (June, 1961), 279.

27. *Ibid.*, p. 280.

28. Fuchs, *op. cit.*, p. 224.

29. *Ibid.*, pp. 31–32.

30. "Religious Affiliations of the Candidates," *Church and State*, XXI (January, 1968), 7.

31. "Characteristics of Members of the 89th Congress," *Congressional Quarterly, Weekly Report*, XXIII (week ending January 1, 1965), 25–29.

32. Robert N. Bellah, "Civil Religion in America," *Daedalus*, XCVI (Winter, 1967), 18.

33. Hughes to the Society for the Propagation of the Faith, New York, February 17, 1844, copy, Archives of the Archdiocese of New York.

34. Dorothy Dohen, *Nationalism and American Catholicism* (New York, 1967), p. 1. While the major thesis of this book, i.e., that there has been too much uncritical support of government policy at times on the part of Catholic churchmen, is basically a sound one, the volume leaves much to be desired by way of a full understanding and interpretation of the historical factors that account for their attitude.

35. "Christian Conscience in America and the War in Vietnam," *Concilium*, Vol. XXIX, Christian Duquoc, O.P. (ed.), *Opportunities for Belief and Behavior* (New York, 1967), p. 61.

36. *The Education of Catholic Americans* (Chicago, 1966). Greeley and Rossi found a significantly higher instance of fidelity to the Catholic faith among those students who had an elementary and secondary training in the Church's schools and then went on to a Catholic college; they were likewise of the belief that neither a religiously oriented home nor the program of the Confraternity of Christian Doctrine for religious instruction of Catholic students could be considered adequate substitutes for the Catholic school.

37. Reginald A. Neuwien (ed.), *Catholic Schools in Action: The Notre Dame Study of Catholic Elementary and Secondary Schools in the United States* (Notre Dame, 1966).

38. "A Program of Continuous Renewal: Statement of the Symposium on Catholic Education," *National Catholic Reporter*, February 21, 1968, p. 6.

39. See Carl J. Ryan, "Cincinnati Takes a Big Step," *Homiletic and Pastoral Review*, LXLV (May, 1964), 2–8, and the same author's "Cincinnati: One Year Later," *ibid.*, LXVI (March, 1966), 498–504. The writer wishes to thank Monsignor Ryan, Superintend-

ent of Schools of the Archdiocese of Cincinnati, for his informative letter of January 24, 1968, and likewise Father Robert Schulzetenburg, Superintendent of Schools of the Diocese of Saint Cloud, for a similar letter of February 2, 1968, in which both writers explained the changes in their respective diocesan school systems.

40. Abbott and Gallagher, *op. cit.*, p. 514.

41. "PL 89-10: The Development of a New Pattern in Federal Aid to Education," *Catholic Educator*, XXXVI (October, 1965), 43.

42. "Church and State: How High a Wall? *Commentary*, XLII (July, 1966), 27.

43. *New York Times*, February 1, 1968, p. 34.

44. *America*, February 3, 1968, p. 138.

45. Prefatory Note to John Tracy Ellis, *American Catholics and the Intellectual Life* (Chicago, 1956), p. 5.

46. See "No Complacency," *America*, April 7, 1956, pp. 14–25.

47. Manning M. Pattillo, Jr., and Donald M. Mackenzie, *Church-Sponsored Higher Education in the United States* (Washington, 1966), p. 139.

48. "Canon Salzbacher's Observations on American Catholic Colleges for Men, 1842," in John Tracy Ellis (ed.), *Documents of American Catholic History*, rev. ed. (Chicago, 1967), I, 261.

49. Abbott and Gallagher, *op. cit.*, p. 674.

50. "Universities: Anxiety behind the Façade," *Time*, June 23, 1967, p. 78.

51. October, 1967, pp. 152–54, 185–86.

52. "Financial Crisis in Catholic Colleges," *America*, September 23, 1967, p. 304.

53. Ellis, *American Catholics and the Intellectual Life*, p. 45.

54. *An Assessment of Quality in Graduate Education* (Washington: American Council on Education, 1966). There have been an increasing number of critical studies on Catholic higher education in recent years, for example, James W. Trent, *Catholics in College: Religious Commitment and the Intellectual Life* (Chicago, 1967), and Andrew M. Greeley, *The Changing Catholic College* (Chicago, 1967). Saint Louis University is also engaged in preparing a comprehensive report on Catholic colleges and universities with a grant from the Ford Foundation.

55. Abbott and Gallagher, *op. cit.*, p. 650.

56. Richard Hofstadter and Walter P. Metzger, *The Development*

of *Academic Freedom in the United States* (New York, 1955), pp. xi–xii.

57. Abbott and Gallagher, *op. cit.*, p. 270.

58. Leonard Swidler, "The Catholic Historian and Freedom," *American Benedictine Review*, XVII (June, 1966), 152. In treating this episode another writer remarked, "Whatever happens at the Catholic University is therefore more than mere incident: it is often a reflection of crucial trends in American Catholicism." Jon Victor (pseud.), "Restraints on American Catholic Freedom," *Harper's Magazine*, December, 1963, p. 33.

59. *AAUP Bulletin*, LIII (December, 1967), 364. On this case, see Joseph Scimecca and Roland Damiano, *Crisis at St. John's: Strike and Revolution on the Catholic Campus* (New York, 1968).

60. *National Catholic Reporter*, October 4, 1967, p. 10.

61. "Academic Freedom and the Crisis in Catholic Universities," in Edward Manier and John W. Houck (eds.), *Academic Freedom and the Catholic University* (Notre Dame, 1967), p. 53.

62. "The University and the Church," *ibid.*, p. 109.

63. "The Freedom of the Priest-Scholar," *ibid.*, p. 173; see the same author's "Q.E.D.," *The Critic*, XXVI (August–September, 1967), 6–8, 79.

64. A further example of the growing literature on this subject is Robert Hassenger (ed.), *The Shape of Catholic Higher Education* (Chicago, 1967), a collection of fifteen essays of which the editor has written five.

65. "Report of the Special Committee on Academic Freedom in Church-Related Colleges and Universities," *AAUP Bulletin*, LIII (December, 1967), 369–71.

66. *The Tower*, April 25, 1967, p. 4; this publication is the students' weekly newspaper.

67. "The Vision of a Great Catholic University in the World of Today," Documentary Service, Press Department, United States Catholic Conference, December 14, 1967, p. 5. Another strong affirmation of the reconcilability of the Catholic Church and higher education under her general auspices was made by Sister Margaret Claydon, S.N.D., President of Trinity College, Washington, D.C., for which see the *Washington Post*, January 16, 1967, p. A 10. A statement dealing with freedom in the context of a Catholic university was likewise issued by the American and Canadian representatives of the International Federation of Catholic Universities

who attended a conference at Land O'Lakes, Wisconsin, on July 21–23, 1967, and issued a statement, "The Catholic University of Today," *America*, August 12, 1967, pp. 154–56.

68. *The Santa Clara*, October 20, 1967, p. 1.

69. Pattillo and Mackenzie, *op. cit.*, p. 105.

70. "Thoughts on the Catholic Intellectual," *Catholic Herald Citizen* (Milwaukee) June 17, 1961, p. 9, supplemented by a photostatic copy of the archbishop's sermon.

71. *Ibid.*

72. Abbott and Gallagher, *op. cit.*, p. 731.

73. John Cogley, "The Future of an Illusion," *Commonweal*, June 2, 1967, p. 310. In the same issue see the replies from ten men and women in academic life who were asked to write a 300-word statement on the possibility of freedom in a Catholic university (pp. 316–21).

74. Abbott and Gallagher, *op. cit.*, p. 205.

75. "Youth Loses Its Faith in America," *Saint Louis Review*, December 1, 1967, p. 16.

76. October 6, 1967, pp. 11–23.

77. John J. McMahon, "Catholic Students Look at Death," *Commonweal*, January 26, 1968, pp. 491–94.

78. Abbott and Gallagher, *op. cit.*, p. 468.

79. "Religious Orders and Renewal," *The Tablet* (London), December 16, 1967, p. 1300.

80. Interview given to Vincent T. Mallon, M.M., Lima, Peru, April 8, 1961, NC News Service, Press Department, National Catholic Welfare Conference, Washington, D.C., April 10, 1961, pp. 3–4.

81. Colman McCarthy, "Renewal Crisis Hits Trappists," *National Catholic Reporter*, December 13, 1967, p. 1.

82. *National Catholic Reporter*, January 11, 1968, p. 11.

83. *Ibid.*, January 3, 1968, p. 1.

84. Edward Carr, "Canada's New Deal in Seminary Education," *Ave Maria*, January 27, 1968, pp. 16–18; for the Garrone document, see the *New York Times*, June 28, 1968, p. 3

85. "The Infidelity of the Future," *Faith and Prejudice and Other Unpublished Sermons of Cardinal Newman*, edited by the Birmingham Oratory (New York, 1956), p. 117.

86. Ronald Berman, *America in the Sixties: An Intellectual History* (New York, 1968), p. 65.

87. A very considerable number of books on seminary education

appeared in the last decade, e.g., H. Richard Niebuhr, Daniel Day Williams, and James M. Gustafson, *The Advancement of Theological Education* (New York, 1957); Stafford Poole, C.M., *Seminary in Crisis* (New York, 1965); James Michael Lee and Louis J. Putz, C.S.C. (eds.), *Seminary Education in a Time of Change* (Notre Dame, 1965); Walter D. Wagoner, *The Seminary: Protestant and Catholic* (New York, 1966); John Tracy Ellis, *Essays in Seminary Education* (Notre Dame, 1967).

88. Abbott and Gallagher, *op. cit.*, pp. 434–57 for the introduction of Bishop Alexander Carter and the text of the decree; pp. 458–61 for Quanbeck's response. Regarding the libraries, Quanbeck remarked, "It is rumored that not all bishops are poignantly aware of the importance of libraries, so some specifics on this topic could be helpful" (p. 460).

89. "New Americans in the Kennedy Image," *America*, March 5, 1966, p. 321.

90. Issue of January 5, 1878.

91. *Newsweek*, December 25, 1967, pp. 45–48; see also Michael Novak, "The New Nuns," *Saturday Evening Post*, July 30, 1966, pp. 21–27, 66–72.

92. See the editorial, "In 1968—Let the Sisters Be," *America*, January 13, 1968, p. 26; also "An Open Letter to Sister Anita," *Ave Maria*, February 3, 1968, pp. 4–5. The latter was signed by thirteen of the nineteen Jesuits of the theological faculty of Alma College, Los Gatos, California, in support of the Superior General of the Immaculate Heart of Mary Sisters and her community in their "Documents of Renewal" passed by their general chapter.

93. *The Future of Man* (New York, 1964), p. 12.

94. Evans, *op. cit.*, p. 1300.

95. Peter Nichols, *The Politics of the Vatican* (London, 1968), p. 188.

96. Yzermans, *op. cit.*, p. 11.

97. *Ibid.*, p. 157.

98. *Ibid.*, p. 69.

99. *Ibid.*, p. 657.

100. On the episode one of the more perceptive works on the council, written in the form of a diary, stated: "The systematic opposition to the schema can now be seen proportionally: it is very weak, about 10 percent of the assembly. In one fell swoop the Council broke out of its impasse. The cleverness of the question is

remarkable. To mention conformity with Catholic doctrine is not so bad as it sounds. The allusion had the purpose of reassuring the minority, who have repeated *ad nauseam* that the schema is unorthodox." Henri Fesquet, *The Drama of Vatican II: The Ecumenical Council, June, 1962–December, 1965* (New York, 1967), p. 614.

101. Abbott and Gallagher, *op. cit.*, p. 674.

102. "The Theological Setting of Vatican II," *The Pilgrim Church* (New York, 1967), p. 16.

103. "Reform in the Church," *Perspectives*, V (January–February, 1960), 4.

104. *National Catholic Reporter*, February 14, 1968, p. 10.

105. "Priests' Councils: Goals and Guidelines," in Vincent A. Yzermans (ed.), *The Time to Build* (Huntington, Ind., 1968), pp. 13–14.

106. News Release, NC News Service, Press Department, United States Catholic Conference, Washington, January 5, 1968, p. 1.

107. Decker, *op. cit.*, pp. 17–18. On this subject, see the writer's article, "On Selecting American Bishops," *Commonweal*, March 10, 1967, pp. 643–49.

108. *Commonweal*, February 16, 1968, pp. 582–92.

109. A summary of the interview appeared in *The Tablet* (London), January 27, 1968, p. 92.

110. *Ibid.*, February 10, 1968, p. 136. The article that Father Schillebeeckx contributed to *Worship*, XLII (March, 1968), 134–49, under the title "Catholic Life in the United States," was much less sensational in tone.

111. "Bishops Back in the Rearguard of Change," *The Times* (London), December 29, 1967, p. 7.

112. Robert G. Hoyt, Jr. (ed.), *Issues That Divide the Church* (New York, 1967).

113. *The True Story of the Vatican Council*, 2d ed. (London, [1877]).

114. "Testimony of a 20th Century Catholic," *America*, December 2, 1967, p. 688.

115. "Catholicism in the United States," in James Ward Smith and A. Leland Jamison (eds.), *Religion in American Life*, I, *The Shaping of American Religion* (Princeton, 1961), p. 120.

116. Bosc, *op. cit.*, p. 323.

117. *The Church after the Council* (New York, 1966), pp. 31–32.

Important Dates

1494 First Mass celebrated in the New World

1542 Fray Juan de Padilla, protomartyr of the United States, murdered by Indians on the plains of Kansas

1565 First Catholic parish of the United States founded at St. Augustine, Florida

1609 The founding of Santa Fe, future headquarters of the missions of New Mexico

1611 Pierre Biard, S.J., and Ennémond Massé, S.J., open the way for missionary efforts among the Indians of Maine

1622 Pope Gregory XV establishes Congregation de Propaganda Fide, under the jurisdiction of which American Catholics remained until 1908

1634 The "Ark" and the "Dove" reach Maryland with first settlers for Baron Baltimore's colony

1642 Virginia outlaws priests and disfranchises Catholics

1646 St. Isaac Jogues, S.J., is murdered by the Iroquois near Auriesville, New York

1647 Massachusetts Bay Colony enacts an anti-priest law

1649 Maryland's general assembly passes an act of religious toleration for all Christians

1654 The Puritan regime repeals the act of religious toleration in Maryland

1671 Sieur de Lusson and Claude Alloüez, S.J., at Mackinac Island take possession of the western country for France, in the name of God and Louis XIV

1673 Louis Jolliet and Jacques Marquette, S.J., conduct an expedition down the Mississippi River

1680 Indian rebellion destroys the missions of New Mexico

1683 Governor Thomas Dongan and New York assembly enact religious toleration for all Christians

1687 Eusebio Francisco Kino, S.J., enters Pimería Alta to inaugurate the missions of Arizona

1692 The Church of England established by law in Maryland; De Vargas reconquers New Mexico and the friars return to reopen the missions

1699 The seminary priests of Quebec begin their missions in the Mississippi Valley

1704 Destruction of Florida's northern missions by Governor James Moore of South Carolina

1716 Antonio Margil, O.F.M., launches his missionary career in Texas

1718 Disfranchisement of Catholics in Maryland

1727 Ursuline Sisters arrive from France to open first Catholic school in New Orleans

1733 Property secured by Joseph Greaton, S.J., for St. Joseph's Chapel, Philadelphia, the center of first public Catholic worship from the penal days to the American Revolution

1741 Theodore Schneider, S.J., and William Wappeler, S.J., arrive in Pennsylvania to minister to German Catholic immigrants

ca. 1745 The Jesuits establish a school for boys at Bohemia Manor, Cecil County, Maryland

1755 The Catholic inhabitants of Acadia expelled to the American colonies

1763 The Jesuits banished from Louisiana and the Illinois Country; further decline of the Catholic missions when Spain cedes Florida to England and the latter gains all east of Mississippi River from France; Bishop Richard Challoner, Vicar Apostolic of the London District, reports on his American jurisdiction to the Holy See

1767 The Jesuits are expelled from all the dominions of Spain

1769 Junípero Serra, O.F.M., founds the first of the California missions at San Diego

1773 Charles Carroll of Carrollton publishes "First Citizen" letters against Daniel Dulany and the royal government in Maryland; the Society of Jesus suppressed by Pope Clement XIV

1774 The Quebec Act passes the British Parliament, revives open hostility of Americans toward the Catholic Church, and furnishes a major reason for rebellion against the crown

1775 The Continental Congress denounces Catholicism to George III and to the British people, but speaks softly on the subject to the French Canadians; Washington suppresses the army's celebration of Guy Fawkes Day; Stephen Moylan named muster master-general of the American army

1776 Charles Carroll appointed with Benjamin Franklin and Samuel Chase as commission of Congress to seek the aid of Canada with Father John Carroll accompanying the commissioners; Virginia the first state to vote full religious freedom in its bill of rights, followed by religious freedom for Christians in Pennsylvania and Maryland; Charles Carroll signs the Declaration of Independence for Maryland; John Barry's "Lexington" takes the "Edward," the first capture in actual battle of a British warship by a regularly commissioned American cruiser

1777 New York's constitutional convention bars Catholics from office through an oath foreswearing all foreign powers, "ecclesiastical as well as civil"

1778 France signs a treaty of alliance with the United States; Father Pierre Gibault assists George Rogers Clark to take Vincennes

1784 John Carroll appointed by the Holy See as superior of the American Catholic missions

1785 Lay trustees secure legal incorporation of St. Peter's Church, New York

1787 Daniel Carroll of Maryland and Thomas FitzSimons of Pennsylvania sign the Constitution of the United States

1788 Laymen gain legal incorporation of Holy Trinity Church, Philadelphia, the first nationalist congregation of the Catholic Church in the United States

1789 Pope Pius VI erects the Diocese of Baltimore and names John Carroll the first bishop

1790 Carroll consecrated in England as first Bishop of Baltimore

1791 French Sulpicians open first seminary in United States, St. Mary's in Baltimore; Georgetown Academy begins classes; Bishop Carroll holds first synod of his clergy

1793 The Holy See erects the Diocese of Louisiana and the Two Floridas

1806   Francis Cooper takes seat in New York legislature after repeal of oath against foreign ecclesiastical powers

1808   Baltimore made the first metropolitan see of the United States with Bardstown (Kentucky), Boston, New York, and Philadelphia as its first suffragan dioceses

1809   Mother Elizabeth Bayley Seton establishes the first native American sisterhood at Emmitsburg, Maryland

1810   First meeting of the American hierarchy

1812   The first two native Catholic sisterhoods in the new West founded in Kentucky

1813   New York Court of General Sessions renders decision favorable to Anthony Kohlmann, S.J., in case involving secrecy of the confessional

1814   Opening of St. Joseph's Orphanage, Philadelphia, the first Catholic asylum for children in the United States

1820   John England, Irish-born, arrives to inaugurate twenty-two year rule as first Bishop of Charleston, South Carolina

1821   Dedication of the Cathedral of the Assumption, Baltimore, the mother cathedral of American Catholics

1822   Bishop England founds the *United States Catholic Miscellany*, the first Catholic newspaper in the country properly so-called; founding in France of the Society for the Propagation of the Faith to help the Catholic missions of the world

1828   First hospital west of the Mississippi opened in St. Louis through generosity of John Mullanphy and staffed by Sisters of Charity from Emmitsburg, Maryland

1829   American bishops hold the First Provincial Council of Baltimore

1830   A group of Protestant ministers launch the *Protestant*, an anti-Catholic weekly, which spearheads the nativist movement

1834   The Ursuline Convent at Charlestown, Massachusetts, is burned by a nativist mob

1836   Publication of the *Awful Disclosures of the Hotel Dieu Nunnery of Montreal* by Maria Monk; President Jackson nominates Roger Brooke Taney as Chief Justice of the United States

1840   Pierre-Jean De Smet, S.J., makes his first trip to the far

Important Dates

West in behalf of the Indian missions; opening of New York controversy over public funds for private religious schools

1844 Philadelphia rioters provoked by nativists burn two Catholic churches and kill thirteen persons; Orestes A. Brownson received into the Catholic Church

1845 Isaac T. Hecker becomes a Catholic; founding of the first American conference of the Society of St. Vincent de Paul in old cathedral parish, St. Louis; beginning of the potato famine in Ireland

1848 Diplomatic relations established between the United States and Papal States; first permanent American Trappist foundation made in Kentucky

1850 Holy See creates three new ecclesiastical provinces with archbishops in Cincinnati, New Orleans, and New York

1852 The First Plenary Council of Baltimore

1853 Know-Nothing demonstrations against Archbishop Gaetano Bedini, papal nuncio

1855 Founding of the German Catholic Centralverein; New York legislature passes the Putnam Bill, a Know-Nothing measure against right of Catholic bishops to hold church properties

1856 Buffalo convention of Catholic societies for western colonization

1857 Opening of American College at Louvain

1858 Founding of the Paulist Fathers, the first native religious community for men

1859 The North American College opens in Rome

1861 Archbishop Hughes commissioned by Lincoln and Seward to go to France in effort to maintain its neutrality in the Civil War.

1865 Founding of *Catholic World;* publication of Brownson's *American Republic*

1866 The Second Plenary Council of Baltimore

1869 Forty-nine American prelates in attendance at the Vatican Council

1875 John McCloskey, Archbishop of New York, becomes first American cardinal; instruction of Congregation de Propaganda Fide concerning danger to religious faith of children in public schools and the need for parochial schools

1876 Founding of the *American Catholic Quarterly Review;* publication of James Gibbons' *Faith of Our Fathers*

1884 The Third Plenary Council of Baltimore

1886 James Gibbons, Archbishop of Baltimore, named the second American cardinal

1887 Gibbons in Rome for red hat lauds Church-State relations in United States, defends the Knights of Labor before the Holy See, and opposes condemnation by the Holy Office of Henry George's works; founding of American Protective Association

1889 Opening of the Catholic University of America

1890 Archbishop Ireland delivers address on public and private schools before the National Education Association in St. Paul

1891 Mother Katharine Drexel founds the Sisters of the Blessed Sacrament for work among the Negroes and Indians; publication of the Lucerne Memorial charging neglect of immigrant Catholics by American bishops

1992 Dr. Edward McGlynn absolved by Archbishop Francesco Satolli, papal ablegate, of censures incurred over his doctrines on private property and single tax theory based on works of Henry George

1893 The Apostolic Delegation established in Washington; College of Notre Dame of Maryland, Baltimore, first Catholic college for women in United States, opened

1899 Pope Leo XIII's apostolic letter, *Testem benevolentiae*, concerning the errors of Americanism

1904 Founding of the National Catholic Educational Association

1905 Founding of the Catholic Church Extension Society for the home missions

1907 Publication of the first volume of the *Catholic Encyclopedia*

1908 Catholic Church in the United States removed from the jurisdiction of the Congregation de Propaganda Fide

1911 Establishment of the Catholic Foreign Mission Society of America (Maryknoll)

1915 Birth of the second Ku Klux Klan

1917 Establishment of the National Catholic War Council

1919 Publication of the *Bishops' Program of Social Reconstruction;* founding of the National Catholic Welfare Conference

1921 Congress passes first immigrant restriction law based on national percentages; death of Cardinal Gibbons

1925 The Supreme Court declares Oregon school law unconstitutional as interfering unreasonably with liberty of parents and guardians to direct education of children under their control and as violating the rights of denominational and private schools

1926 The twenty-eighth International Eucharistic Congress held in Chicago

1928 Governor Alfred E. Smith of New York, first Catholic presidential candidate of a major political party, defeated by Herbert C. Hoover

1939 Pope Pius XII's encyclical *Sertum laetitiae* to Church of the United States on sesquicentennial of its hierarchy; Myron C. Taylor named personal representative of President Roosevelt to Pius XII

1945 Four American churchmen named to College of Cardinals

1948 Protestants and Other Americans for Separation of Church and State (POAU) formed with the aim of opposing federal aid to private religious schools and an American representative at Vatican City

1951 President Truman nominates General Mark Clark as American ambassador to Vatican City; nomination withdrawn at Clark's request because of widespread opposition to any American representation at Vatican City

1954 Establishment of the Sister Formation Conference

1955 Death of Mother Katharine Drexel; publication of John Tracy Ellis' essay, "American Catholics and the Intellectual Life," touches off widespread discussion in Catholic higher education circles

1956 Holy See erects the new Dioceses of Atlanta, Jefferson City, and Springfield-Cape Girardeau to bring the total dioceses in United States to 134

1957 Highest award of Department of Health, Education and Welfare presented to Daughters of Charity of Saint Vincent de Paul "for devoted services to the patients . . . . and contributions to the success of the unique program at this hospital" (United States Public Health Service Hospital, Carville, Louisiana, for lepers); Joseph E. Ritter, Archbishop of Saint Louis, and Metropolitan Church Federation (Protestant) become participants in a zoning law suit filed by a Jewish congregation against the city of Creve Coeur, Missouri, for refusing to permit the building of a synagogue, thus violating the First and Fourteenth Amendments, which guarantee free exercise of religion and rights of religious groups to acquire land for religious purposes; Joseph R. Harris of Philadelphia becomes first Negro elected president of the National Federation of Catholic College Students

1958 POAU urges that Catholic candidates for the presidency be scrutinized with particular care in regard to denominational boycott of public schools, demand for public funds for sectarian schools, and appointment of an American ambassador at Vatican City; Cardinal Samuel Stritch, Archbishop of Chicago, named Pro-Prefect of Congregation de Propaganda Fide; Christopher Dawson named first occupant of the Chauncey Stillman Chair of Roman Catholic Studies in the Divinity School of Harvard University; discrepancy in religious statistics illustrated in report of *Official Catholic Directory* (May) of 36,023,977 Catholics in the United States, whereas Bureau of Census estimated (March, 1957) that there were 43,635,000 Catholics on basis of calculations and projections of findings of a sampling of persons over fourteen in 35,000 households across the country

1959 Catholics become the largest religious group in the United States Congress with twelve senators and ninety-one representatives, followed by the Methodists with ninety-nine in the Congress; Aloisius Muench, Apostolic Nuncio to Germany, becomes the first American cardinal in the Roman Curia

1960 John F. Kennedy becomes the first Catholic elected to the presidency; Bishop James E. Walsh of Maryknoll is sentenced to twenty years of imprisonment by Shanghai Intermediate People's Court for alleged counter-revolutionary activities and attempts at espionage

1962 Congressional Medal awarded posthumously to Thomas A. Dooley, M.D. (d. January 18, 1961) for medical services rendered to the people of Laos; Gustave Weigel, S.J., of Woodstock College appointed by Pope John XXIII as one of five Catholic observers at third general assembly of World Council of Churches at New Delhi; Lawrence J. Shehan, Archbishop of Baltimore, sets up an archdiocesan Commission for Christian Unity; Joseph F. Rummel, Archbishop of New Orleans, announces integration of schools of his archdiocese, which brings opposition and leads to excommunication of three Catholic segregationists; opening of Vatican Council II at which nearly 200 American bishops are in attendance

1963   Rector of the Catholic University of America affirms ban on Godfrey Diekmann, O.S.B., Hans Küng, John Courtney Murray, S.J., and Gustave Weigel, S.J., to speak in student-sponsored series of lectures, leading to a prolonged controversy in Catholic higher education circles; Elizabeth Seton, foundress of first native Catholic sisterhood (1809) becomes the first American to be beatified; widespread discussion over views of Dr. John Rock, a Catholic, clinical professor of gynecology in Harvard Medical School, on birth control methods; Missouri Catholic parents make massive protest against refusal of state legislature to authorize tax-supported bus rides for parochial school children with latter withdrawn from parochial schools and sent to public schools; Supreme Court rules devotional prayers and Bible reading in public schools unconstitutional; beatification of John N. Neuman, C.SS.R., fourth Bishop of Philadelphia; assassination of President John F. Kennedy at Dallas, Texas; announcement of Stephan G. Kuttner as first occupant of chair of Roman Catholic studies at Yale University; Archbishop Karl J. Alter announces dropping of first grade in parochial schools of the Archdiocese of Cincinnati, along with pay raises for all teachers and reduction of classroom sizes; vernacular introduced in notable portions of the Mass; Archdiocese of Santa Fe joins the New Mexico Council of Churches

1965   *Pacem in Terris* Convocation at United Nations draws *ca.* 2,000 delegates from twenty countries; nearly 400 priests and scores of sisters, brothers, and Catholic laity march at Selma, Alabama, in support of Negroes' right to vote; visit of Pope Paul VI to United Nations; Catholic Traditionalist Movement headed by Gommar A. De Pauw issues manifesto; controversy over administration's policies breaks at Saint John's University, Jamaica, New York; promulgation of Declaration on Religious Freedom, of which John Courtney Murray, S.J., the principal author, by Vatican Council II

1966   William H. DuBay suspended as a priest of the Archdiocese of Los Angeles following refusal to cease publicizing proposals for establishment of a priests' union and other changes; formation of the Association of Chicago Priests; establishment of the National Conference of Catholic Bishops with John F. Dearden, Archbishop of Detroit, as the elected president; replacement of the National Catholic Welfare Conference by the United States Catholic Conference

1967 Four American churchmen appointed to the College of Cardinals, bringing representation of the United States to nine, the largest number of American cardinals to date; Holy See erects the Dioceses of Fresno and Monterey, bringing the total of American dioceses to 154

Suggested Reading

GENERAL WORKS

The interested reader will find all the principal works on American Catholic history published down to 1959 in the author's *A Guide to American Catholic History* (Milwaukee, 1959). For the texts of important source materials revised and enlarged *Documents of American Catholic History*, edited in two volumes by John Tracy Ellis (Chicago, 1967), provides the only general work of its kind and introduces the reader to the larger collections of sources for the various periods of the Church's history. In the revised edition the collection comes down to October, 1966. As for general histories of American Catholicism, the best over-all account for the period up to 1866 is still John Gilmary Shea's *History of the Catholic Church in the United States* (4 vols.; New York, 1886-92), although it is poorly arranged and, of course, now outdated in many particulars by later research. In more recent years there have been two one-volume histories, one of which is Theodore Maynard's *The Story of American Catholicism* (New York, 1941), a highly readable book which in the main furnishes a good survey if it is used with the cautions noted in a critical review that appeared some months after its publication (*Catholic Historical Review*, XXVIII [April, 1942], 94–103). The second work, *The Catholic Church in the United States* (St. Louis, 1950) by Theodore Roemer, O.F.M.Cap., lacks the lively style that characterizes the Maynard volume, and while it is on the whole factually accurate, its omission of most of the controversial issues produces an unbalanced effect. In this instance readers will likewise be benefited by a critical review (*Catholic Historical Review*, XXXVI [January, 1951], 467–70). Henry J. Browne's lengthy essay, "Catholicism in the United States," in James Ward Smith and A. Leland Jamison (eds.), *The Shaping of American Religion* (Princeton, 1961) (pp. 72–121), combines the sure hand of the trained historian with the author's imaginative approach to afford the reader a sound interpretation. Andrew M. Greeley, *The Catholic Experience: An Interpretation of the History of American Catholicism* (Garden City, N.Y., 1967), is the work of an able sociologist who, as the writer of the foreword has said, "makes no attempt to be the disinterested chronicler" (p. 10). Greeley himself asks that his interpretation be ultimately judged "not on any individual judgments . . . but rather on the utility of the whole model for understanding and ordering the many complex elements which make up American Catholic history and on the usefulness of this interpretation to stir up others to similar and more refined works of interpretation" (p. 13). That more works of interpretation are needed, there is no doubt; but the highly subjective approach used here will hardly satisfy the historically minded. John J. McGrath, *Church and State in American Law: Cases and Materials* (Milwaukee, 1962), brings the Church-State problem down to the decision of the Supreme Court in June, 1962, in regard to the prayer of the New York Board of Regents—a handy source book. All aspects of the Church-State question, insofar as it relates to the Catholic Church in the United States, were treated in the monumental work of Anson Phelps Stokes *Church and State in the United States* (3 vols.: New York, 1950). For certain correctives, however, see John Tracy Ellis, "Church and State in the United States: A Critical Appraisal," *Catholic Historical Review*, XXXVIII (October, 1952), 285–316. In this connection the learned and urbane essays of Evarts B. Greene in *Religion and the State: The Making and Testing of an American Tradition* (New York, 1941) offer one of the most balanced treatments of this controversial topic. For a brief survey of the problem see John Tracy Ellis, "Church and State: An American Catholic Tradition," *Harper's Magazine*, CCVII (November, 1953), 63–67. The best account of the conciliar meetings and legislation of the American hierarchy throughout the nineteenth century is that of Peter Guilday, *A History of the Councils of Baltimore, 1791–1884* (New York, 1932). The Latin texts of the legislation may be read in the volumes issued for the respective councils, while the hierarchy's joint pastoral letters and annual statements from 1792 to 1951 are contained in the two volumes, *The National Pastorals of the American Hierarchy, 1792–1919*, ed. Peter Guilday (Washington, 1923) and *Our Bishops Speak*, ed. Raphael M. Huber, O.F.M. Conv. (Washington, 1952). On the subject of Catholic population trends through the colonial period and down to 1920 the work of Gerald Shaughnessy, S.M., *Has the Immigrant Kept the Faith?* (New York, 1925), is the only reliable guide, which may be supplemented for the years since 1920 by the annual volumes of the *Official Catholic Directory* (New York, 1921––). There is no adequate history of the American Catholic press, for Paul J. Foik, C.S.C., *Pioneer Catholic Journalism* (New York, 1930) comes down only to 1840 and Apollinaris W. Baumgartner, O.F.M.Cap., *Catholic Journalism: A Study of Its Development in the United States, 1789–1930* (New York, 1931) offers hardly more than an outline. For a general survey of the Church's charitable organizations and institutions the only work available is the volume of John O'Grady, *Catholic Charities in the United States* (Washington, 1930), although the history of one of these national organizations has been thoroughly done in Daniel T. McColgan's *A Century of Charity: The First One Hundred Years of the Society of St. Vincent de Paul in the United States* (2 vols.; Milwaukee, 1951).

The best periodical in the field is the *Catholic Historical Review* (54 vols.; 1915–69), a quarterly which contains many articles embodying material not to be found elsewhere, for example, John J. Meng, "A Century of American Catholicism as Seen Through French Eyes," XXVII (April, 1941), 39–68, as well as careful editions of source materials such as Henry J. Browne, "The Letters of Bishop McQuaid from the Vatican Council," XLI (January, 1956), 408–41. Two other publications devote their space principally to American Catholic history, one of them the *Records of the American Catholic Historical Society of Philadelphia*, which from time to time publishes research studies such as that of Andrew H. Skeabeck, C.SS.R., "Most Rev. William H. Gross, Missionary Bishop of the South," LXV (March, 1954), 11–23 to LXVI (September, 1955), 131–55. The second is the annual volume of the United States Catholic Historical Society of New York, *Historical Records and Studies*, which has carried important essays like Raymond J. Clancy, C.S.C., "American Prelates in the Vatican Council," XXVIII (1937),

7–135. In more recent years the quality of this annual volume has been improved with articles like one by James E. Roohan, "American Catholics and the Social Question, 1865–1900," XLIII (1955), 3–26, and in the same issue Francis X. Curran, S.J., "The Buffalo Mission of the German Jesuits, 1869–1907," pp. 95–126. Important source materials have included, for example, "The Archdiocese of New York a Century Ago: A Memoir of Archbishop Hughes, 1838–1858," ed. Henry J. Browne, XXXIX–XL (1952), 129–90 and "Tour of His Eminence Cardinal Francesco Satolli, Pro-Apostolic Delegate through the United States," ed. Colman J. Barry, O.S.B., XLIII (1955), 27–94. *Mid-America*, a quarterly edited at Loyola University, Chicago, and the *Review of Politics* of the University of Notre Dame likewise publish some American Catholic material, and in the latter the articles by Thomas T. McAvoy, C.S.C., and Aaron I. Abell have been noteworthy respectively for interpretative studies of the Catholic minority and of American Catholic social history.

CHAPTER I. THE CHURCH IN COLONIAL AMERICA, 1492–1790

For the colonial period of American Catholicism numerous and extensive collections of sources are available. For example, the declining days of the Spanish missions of Florida are pictured in *Here They Once Stood: The Tragic End of the Apalachee Missions*, ed. Mark F. Boyd, Hale G. Smith, and John W. Griffin (Gainesville, 1951). The printed source material on the Church in the Southwest and California is far richer, and here the works of Herbert Eugene Bolton are of prime importance as, for example, his edition of *Kino's Historical Memoir of Pimería Alta* (2 vols.; Cleveland, 1919) and *Historical Memoirs of New California by Fray Francisco Palóu, O.F.M.* (4 vols.; Berkeley, 1926). Likewise for this region a definitive edition of the papers of the great California missionary, Junípero Serra, O.F.M., has been projected in four volumes, the first of which appeared in *Writings of Junípero Serra*, ed. Antonine Tibesar, O.F.M. (Washington, 1955), a collection that is of great value. The old narrative work of Zephrin Engelhardt, O.F.M., *The Missions and Missionaries of California* (5 vols.; San Francisco, 1908–15) also contained many documents. It still remains the best over-all account, although it is gradually being superseded by more

Suggested Reading

recent research of the Franciscan historians of the Academy of American Franciscan History in Washington and of the Old Mission, Santa Barbara, California, e.g., Maynard Geiger, O.F.M., *The Life and Times of Fray Junípero Serra, O.F.M.* (2 vols.; Washington, 1959). For Florida, one of the best narratives of the missionary period is Maynard Geiger, O.F.M., *The Franciscan Conquest of Florida, 1573–1618* (Washington, 1937). No area of the Spanish dominions that once embraced sections of the present United States has received of recent date treatment with a thoroughness and scholarship equal to Carlos E. Castañeda's *The Catholic Heritage of Texas* (6 vols.; Austin, 1936–50) which spans the years from 1519 to 1836. For New Mexico, France V. Scholes, *Church and State in New Mexico, 1610–1650* (Albuquerque, 1937) is serviceable as a careful analysis of the relationship of the two governing elements and their frequent conflicts. Bolton's biography of Eusebio Francisco Kino, S.J., *The Rim of Christendom* (New York, 1936) is an excellent study of the famous pioneer of the Arizona missions, and the same author's early essay, "The Mission as a Frontier Institution in the Spanish American Colonies," *American Historical Review*, XXIII (October, 1917), 42–61, retains significance for the entire Spanish borderlands.

In the literature on the French Catholic missions the vast collection, *The Jesuit Relations and Allied Documents*, ed. Reuben Gold Thwaites (73 vols.: Cleveland, 1896–1901), is of paramount importance as source material. A handy one-volume selection from the Thwaites' documents bearing the same title is that of Edna Kenton (New York, 1925). One of the few monographs of solid character dealing with the French missions is John H. Kennedy's *Jesuit and Savage in New France* (New Haven, 1950). For the Church's history in the American empire of France, as well as those of Spain and England, however, the student should not overlook a series of doctoral dissertations done under the direction of Peter Guilday at the Catholic University of America between 1922 and 1940 and which bear the general title "Studies in American Church History."

The area of the thirteen original colonies is treated in four or five volumes of the Guilday series mentioned above, and for this region source materials such as the *Narrative of a Voyage to Maryland by Father Andrew White, S.J.*, ed. E. A. Dalrymple (Baltimore, 1874) and other publications of the Maryland Historical

Society are likewise pertinent. For the checkered history of the principal group of Catholics in the English colonies, the old volume of William T. Russell, *Maryland: The Land of Sanctuary* (Baltimore, 1907) is still of value. On the traditional anti-Catholic bias that permeated the English colonies no one has done a better job than Sister Mary Augustina Ray, B.V.M., *American Opinion of Roman Catholicism in the Eighteenth Century* (New York, 1936). Students of social history will find C. Joseph Nuesse, *The Social Thought of American Catholics, 1634–1829* (Washington, 1945) the most satisfactory survey for the colonial and early national periods.

For a general account see John Tracy Ellis, *Catholics in Colonial America* (Baltimore, 1965), and for the close of the colonial era Charles H. Metzger, S.J., *Catholics and the American Revolution* (Chicago, 1962), is a very useful volume.

CHAPTER II. CATHOLICS AS CITIZENS, 1790–1852

To bridge the transition years between colonial America and the early national period, as well as to highlight the problems confronting the Catholic Church in the new Republic, Annabelle M. Melville's *John Carroll of Baltimore: Founder of the American Catholic Hierarchy* (New York, 1955) will prove of assistance. The Melville book offers a good abridgment and certain correctives to the older biography of Peter Guilday, *The Life and Times of John Carroll, Archbishop of Baltimore, 1735–1815* (2 vols.: New York, 1922). For the outstanding Catholic statesman of the period, Ellen Hart Smith's *Charles Carroll of Carrollton* (Cambridge, 1942) is equally good.

The literature of American Catholicism is, perhaps, strongest in biography. Among the biographies of prominent ecclesiastics of this period the following are the best: J. Herman Schauinger, *Cathedrals in the Wilderness* [Benedict Joseph Flaget, S.S.] (Milwaukee, 1952); Peter Guilday, *The Life and Times of John England, First Bishop of Charleston, 1786–1842* (2 vols.; New York, 1927); Hugh J. Nolan, *The Most Reverend Francis Patrick Kenrick, Third Bishop of Philadelphia, 1830–1851* (Washington, 1948); Mathias M. Hoffman, *The Church Founders of the Northwest* [Bishops Loras of Dubuque and Cretin of St. Paul] (Milwaukee, 1937); John R. G. Hassard, *Life of the Most Reverend John*

Suggested Reading

Hughes, First Archbishop of New York (New York, 1866); and Michael J. Curley, C.SS.R., *Venerable John Neumann, C.SS.R., Fourth Bishop of Philadelphia* (Washington, 1952). Of the Catholic laity of these years good biographies include Sister Mary Virgina Geiger, S.S.N.D., *Daniel Carroll: A Framer of the Constitution* (Washington, 1943); J. Herman Schauinger, *William Gaston: Carolinian* (Milwaukee, 1939); Carl B. Swisher, *Roger Brooke Taney* (New York, 1935); and two studies on the most famous Catholic controversialist of the century, Brownson: Arthur M. Schlesinger, Jr., *Orestes A. Brownson: A Pilgrim's Progress* (Boston, 1939) and Theodore Maynard, *Orestes Brownson: Yankee, Radical, Catholic* (New York, 1943). To read of two prominent converts who became founders of religious congregations, one should consult the biography by Annabelle M. Melville, *Elizabeth Bayley Seton, 1774–1821* (New York, 1951), the thoughtful essays of Joseph McSorley, C.S.P., *Father Hecker and His Friends* (St. Louis, 1952), and Vincent F. Holden, C.S.P., *The Yankee Paul: Isaac Thomas Hecker* (Milwaukee, 1958). The anti-Catholic movements of the years up to the Civil War received scholarly treatment in Ray Allen Billington's *The Protestant Crusade, 1800–1860* (New York, 1938). In that connection the half-dozen doctoral dissertations directed by Richard J. Purcell at the Catholic University of America during the 1930's and 1940's will likewise be found helpful for reading about nativism in American school textbooks and in various localities of the country. In the same category are L. D. Scisco, *Political Nativism in New York State* (New York, 1901) and W. Darrell Overdyke, *The Know-Nothing Party in the South* (Baton Rouge, 1950). American Catholicism is deficient in interpretative studies, but two essays by Thomas T. McAvoy, C.S.C., on Catholics as a minority group up to the Civil War offer new insights: "The Catholic Minority in the United States, 1789–1821," *Historical Records and Studies*, XXXIX-XL (1952), 33–50; and "The Formation of the Catholic Minority in the United States, 1820–1860," *Review of Politics*, X (January, 1948), 13–34.

Since the original edition the following have been published: Robert Trisco, *The Holy See and the Nascent Church in the Middle Western United States, 1826–1850* (Rome, 1962), is an able work done chiefly from unpublished materials in Roman archives that shows the emergence of the Church in the Middle West, where Catholicism has been, perhaps, more progressive and venturesome than in any other region. The following five biographies—two of bishops and three of laymen—help to fill in the student's knowledge of the mid-century Church: Burt Brown Barker, *The McLoughlin Empire and Its Rulers* (Glendale, 1959), contains not only biographical essays on the family of John McLoughlin, famous factor of the Hudson's Bay Company, but likewise a good deal of correspondence between them; Michael V. Gannon, *Rebel Bishop: The Life and Era of Augustin Verot* (Milwaukee, 1964), is a first-class biography of the Civil War prelate who ruled the Sees of Savannah and Saint Augustine and who won the name of *l'enfant terrible* at Vatican Council I for his forthright stands on almost all questions. Father Gannon combines excellent scholarship with a highly interesting style; Peter Leo Johnson, *Crosier on the Frontier: A Life of John Martin Henni* (Madison, 1959), is important as a study of one of the leaders of the German Catholics of the Middle West who died as Archbishop of Milwaukee; William M. Lamers, *The Edge of Glory: A Biography of General William S. Rosecrans, U.S.A.* (New York, 1962), provides the story of the Civil War general who become a Catholic at West Point and who remained throughout his life closely associated with the Church; Walker Lewis, *Without Fear or Favor* (New York, 1965), is the most recent biography of Roger Brooke Taney, the Catholic who served until his death in 1864 as Chief Justice of the United States.

CHAPTER III. CIVIL WAR AND IMMIGRATION, 1852–1908

Generally speaking, the period from the Civil War to the twentieth century has been better served than any other by substantial works on Catholicism during an age when the Church was undergoing severe internal tensions. Among the fairly numerous printed sources for these years the following are good examples: Leo F. Stock (ed.), *United States Ministers to the Papal States. Instructions and Despatches, 1848–1868* (Washington, 1933) and *Consular Relations between the United States and the Papal States: Instructions and Despatches* (Washington, 1945); Sister Blandina Segale, *At the End of the Santa Fe Trail* (Milwaukee, 1948), the amazing memoirs of a missionary Sister of Charity in Colorado and New Mexico during the years 1872–94; *The Church and Modern Society* (2 vols.; St. Paul, 1905), which contain the vigorous public addresses

Suggested Reading

of John Ireland, Archbishop of St. Paul; and Félix Klein, *American-ism: A Phantom Heresy* (Atchinson, Kansas, 1951), a translation from the French original of the memoirs of one of the most prominent figures in the controversy that shook the Church in the United States at the end of the last century. In the biographies of leading Catholics of the period the reader will find further documents, as well as detailed accounts of some of the Church's internal conflicts of these years. The following are among the best of these biographies: Sister M. Hildegarde Yeager, C.S.C., *The Life of James Roosevelt Bayley, First Bishop of Newark and Eighth Archbishop of Baltimore, 1814–1877* (Washington, 1947); Frederick J. Zwierlein, *The Life and Letters of Bishop McQuaid* (3 vols.; Rochester, 1925–27); John Tracy Ellis, *The Life of James Cardinal Gibbons, Archbishop of Baltimore, 1834–1921* (2 vols.; Milwaukee, 1952); James H. Moynihan, *The Life of Archbishop John Ireland* (New York, 1953); Patrick H. Ahern, *The Life of John J. Keane, Educator and Archbishop, 1839–1918* (Milwaukee, 1955); and Mary Harrita Fox, *Peter E. Dietz, Labor Priest* (Notre Dame, 1953).

Besides biographies, there are special studies of merit among which are: Madeleine Hooke Rice, *American Catholic Opinion in the Slavery Controversy* (New York, 1944); Peter J. Rahill, *The Catholic Indian Missions and Grant's Peace Policy, 1870–1884* (Washington, 1953); Fergus Macdonald, *The Catholic Church and the Secret Societies in the United States* (New York, 1946); Henry J. Browne, *The Catholic Church and the Knights of Labor* (Washington, 1949); Colman J. Barry, O.S.B., *The Catholic Church and German Americans* (Milwaukee, 1953); John Tracy Ellis, *The Formative Years of the Catholic University of America* (Washington, 1946); and Daniel F. Reilly, O.P., *The School Controversy, 1891–1893* (Washington, 1943). For the nativist movements against the Catholic Church in the late nineteenth and early twentieth centuries the work of John Higham, *Strangers in the Land: Patterns of American Nativism, 1860–1925* (New Brunswick, 1955) is now the best. One of the weakest areas in the literature on American Catholicism is immigration history. Aside from a few studies, among which were two directed by Marcus L. Hansen at the University of Illinois: Sister Mary Gilbert Kelly, O.P., *Catholic Immigrant Colonization Projects in the United States, 1815–1860* (New York, 1939) and Sister Mary Evangeline Henthorne, B.V.M., *The Career of the Right Reverend John Lancaster Spalding, Bishop of*

American Catholicism

*Peoria, as President of the Irish Catholic Colonization Association
of the United States, 1879–1892* (Urbana, 1932), this rich field for
research remains largely untilled.

The first Catholic college in the United States has had several
volumes of its history published in recent years, among them
Joseph T. Durkin, S.J., *Georgetown University: The Middle Years,
1840–1900* (Washington, 1963), which affords an idea of how a
mid-century college under Catholic auspices was conducted; James
J. Hennesey, S.J., *The First Council of the Vatican: The American
Experience* (New York, 1963), is an engrossing story told by an
able historian and constructed largely from unpublished sources.
Biographies which yield a good deal of information on the Church
in the Far West and in the United States in general are: Francis J.
Weber, *California's Reluctant Prelate: The Life and Times of Right
Reverend Thaddeus Amat, C.M., 1811–1878* (Los Angeles, 1964),
John B. McGloin, S.J., *California's First Archbishop: The Life of
Joseph S. Alemany, O.P., First Archbishop of San Francisco, 1814–
1888* (New York, 1966), and David F. Sweeney, O.F.M., *The Life
of John Lancaster Spalding, First Bishop of Peoria, 1840–1916* (New
York, 1965).

CHAPTER IV. MATURING CATHOLICISM IN THE UNITED STATES 1908–56

Works on this period of Catholicism in the United States have
not, as might be expected, been notable either for their number
or significance. There has been, however, a growing emphasis on
the sociology of the Catholic parish, and in some of these monographs there is valuable material for the historian as, for example,
in the two books of George A. Kelly, *Catholics and the Practice
of the Faith: A Census Study of the Diocese of Saint Augustine*
(Washington, 1946) and *The Story of St. Monica's Parish, New
York City, 1879–1954* (New York, 1954), as well as in the works
of Joseph H. Fichter, S.J., *Southern Parish: Dynamics of a City
Church* (Chicago, 1951) and *Social Relations in the Urban Parish*
(Chicago, 1954). Moreover, local Catholic history has been receiving an increasing amount of attention in recent years in the form of
histories of dioceses, parishes, and educational and charitable institutions. A number of these studies are the product of serious and
mature scholarship which shows a healthy break with the past,

when too frequently a filiopietistic approach and an unwillingness to face up to unpleasant facts precluded the possibility of good history. A number of examples of this improved method in local Catholic history might be cited, but one of the most outstanding is Robert H. Lord, John E. Sexton, and Edward T. Harrington, *History of the Archdiocese of Boston* (3 vols.; New York, 1944), a work which constitutes a thorough and scholarly history of Catholicism for the whole of New England down to about the mid-nineteenth century; another superior work is Robert F. McNamara, *The Diocese of Rochester, 1868–1968* (Rochester, 1968).

Another category in which American Catholicism has been greatly impoverished until recent years is memoir literature. Of late there have been a number of items of this kind that are of worth to the historian of the Church in the twentieth century. The best to date are: Maurice Francis Egan, *Recollections of a Happy Life* (New York, 1924), the autobiography of an educator, journalist, and diplomat; William Cardinal O'Connell, *Recollections of Seventy Years* (Boston, 1934), the life story of a churchman who dominated the Catholic scene in New England from 1907 to his death in 1944; John A. Ryan, *Social Doctrine in Action: A Personal History* (New York, 1941), the somewhat impersonal recollections of the outstanding Catholic social theorist of the century; Francis Clement Kelley, *The Bishop Jots It Down* (New York, 1939), the memoirs of the founder of the most successful Catholic society for the home missions in this country and himself a missionary bishop in Oklahoma from 1924 to his death in 1948; Thomas Merton, *The Seven Storey Mountain* (New York, 1949), the best seller autobiography of a young Greenwich Village sophisticate who found peace of soul in a Trappist monastery in Kentucky; and John LaFarge, S.J., *The Manner Is Ordinary* (New York, 1954), the reminiscences of the scion of a famous American family whose Jesuit career of over a half-century has embraced a wide variety of assignments, from prison chaplain and missionary among the Negroes of southern Maryland to editor of *America*, the Jesuit weekly, and who was a prime mover in the Catholic Interracial Council and the Catholic Association for International Peace.

In lieu of an adequate account of the Catholic Church in relation to World War I, Michael Williams' *American Catholics in the War: National Catholic War Council, 1917–1921* (New York, 1921), contains a fairly broad outline of the principal Catholic activities during the war years. On the question of Catholics and American intellectual movements during the late nineteenth and twentieth centuries, there is no monograph comparable to that of Nuesse on social thought for an earlier period. George N. Shuster, *The Catholic Spirit in America* (New York, 1927) and John A. O'Brien, *Catholics and Scholarship* (Huntington, Ind., 1939) are, however, helpful for explaining the background to the problem and for their emphasis on the causes of Catholic weakness in this area. Some of the most provocative studies under this heading have appeared during the last decade in magazine articles, of which that of John Tracy Ellis, "American Catholics and the Intellectual Life," *Thought*, XXX (Autumn, 1955), 351–88, was one.

Two biographies published within the past ten years are Francis L. Broderick, *Right Reverend New Dealer: John A. Ryan* (New York, 1963), a life of one of the foremost Catholic progressive thinkers of this century, and Charles J. Tull, *Father Coughlin and the New Deal* (Syracuse, 1965), which deals with perhaps the most controversial Catholic priest of the first half of the century.

CHAPTER V. THE CHANGING CHURCH, 1956–68

Much of the literature on American Catholicism during the late 1950's and the 1960's has a sociological tone, with a good deal of emphasis on Catholics' improved social and economic status and the consequences of it. John Tracy Ellis, *Perspectives in American Catholicism* (Baltimore, 1963) contains twenty-three essays, sermons, and reprints of articles, both critical and popular, on various aspects of the Church's life. In *The Catholic Church in a Changing America* (Boston, 1962), Francis J. Lally sought in eight brief, popular, and urbane essays to interpret Catholics as their non-Catholic fellow citizens saw them after the election of John F. Kennedy in November, 1960, and to determine what were the principal factors in the change of image. Georges Tavard, a French priest who has lived in the United States since 1952, interpreted the American Catholics for readers in his native country in *Les catholiques américains: Nouvelles frontières* (Paris, 1966), a slender volume that drew on history, sociology, and theology.

More specialized approaches that either afford good background reading for contemporary history or that carry their narrative into the 1960's are Aaron I. Abell's *American Catholicism and Social Action: A Search for Social Justice, 1865–1950* (Garden City, N.Y.,

Suggested Reading

1960), praised for its assembling of factual data but criticized for its lack of a unifying theme; the same author's edition of a collection of sources, a number of which are relevant for the period after 1956, *American Catholic Thought on Social Questions* (Indianapolis, 1968), was published posthumously; Philip Gleason, *The Conservative Reformers: German-American Catholics and the Social Order* (Notre Dame, 1968), and David J. O'Brien, *American Catholics and Social Reform: The New Deal Years* (New York, 1968), are able studies; Dorothy Dehon's *Nationalism and American Catholicism* (New York, 1967) strikes on a theme worthy of investigation, namely, the superpatriotism of many Catholics, but her effort to weave the account around six bishops between Carroll and Spellman too frequently betrays a lack of understanding of the historical factors that explain these prelates' views. Two of the most prominent types of books on Catholicism in recent years have been collections of papers read at symposia and collections of articles previously published by the respective authors and brought together in book form. In the former category there is *Roman Catholicism and the American Way of Life* (Notre Dame, 1960), edited by Thomas T. McAvoy, C.S.C., which contains eighteen essays of varying subject matter and quality but with the Catholic immigration of the twentieth century their main theme. In the second category are the two volumes by Walter J. Ong, S.J., *Frontiers in American Catholicism: Essays on Ideology and Culture* (New York, 1957) and *American Catholic Crossroads* (New York, 1959), wherein the author seeks through an investigation of cultural factors to account for Catholics' separateness as well as to emphasize the need for their breaking through their isolation and assuming an active role in national life.

On the general subject of Catholic education the following works aim either to present historical background for the Church's schools as they are in the 1960's or to give scientific analyses of contemporary institutions and the most pressing problems that they face. In the former classification is John Tracy Ellis, *Essays in Seminary Education* (Notre Dame, 1967), Neil G. McCluskey, S.J., (ed.), *Catholic Education in America* (New York, 1965); and Robert F. McNamara, *The American College in Rome, 1855–1955* (Rochester, 1956). Notable among the analyses are Andrew M. Greeley, *The Changing Catholic College* (Chicago, 1967); Robert Hassenger (ed.), *The Shape of Catholic Higher Education* (Chicago, 1967);

American Catholicism

Academic Freedom and the Catholic University, edited by Edward Manier and John W. Houck (Notre Dame, 1967); and James W. Trent, *Catholics in College: Religious Commitment and the Intellectual Life* (Chicago, 1967).

The developing field of ecumenism among Catholics is represented by several books which, like some of those in education mentioned above, are not strictly speaking historical in character but which are highly useful to the historian of contemporary Catholicism. For example, there are the six candid and critical essays in *American Catholics: A Protestant-Jewish View* (New York, 1959), edited by Philip Scharper, which provide Catholics with a good introduction through which they might learn what educated Americans not of their faith have thought about them; *Faith and Understanding in America* (New York, 1959) by Gustave Weigel, S.J., probably the ranking figure in the early years of the ecumenical movement as far as Catholics are concerned; and the book that has become, so to speak, the magna carta of the movement, Robert McAfee Brown and Gustave Weigel, S.J., *An American Dialogue: A Protestant Looks at Catholicism and a Catholic Looks at Protestantism* (Garden City, N.Y., 1960).

Among the studies that touch on relations of Church and State are: *Democracy and Catholicism in America* (New York, 1958) by Currin V. Shields, a non-Catholic writer, who says his book was written "for Americans who are members of community groups devoted to common causes" (p. v); John Courtney Murray, S.J., *We Hold These Truths: Catholic Reflections on the American Proposition* (New York, 1960), thirteen essays by the foremost American Catholic theologian of the twentieth century; and Jerome G. Kerwin's useful small volume, *Catholic Viewpoint on Church and State* (Garden City, N.Y., 1960). Of value for a political element hostile to the Church is a journalist's account, David M. Chalmers, *Hooded Americanism: The First Century of the Ku Klux Klan, 1865–1965* (Garden City, N.Y., 1965). An excellent scholarly introduction for trends among progressive Catholics at the mid-century is Robert D. Cross, *The Emergence of Liberal Catholicism in America* (Cambridge, Mass., 1958). Other works of value for these years are the historical section of Daniel Callahan's *The Mind of the Catholic Layman* (New York, 1963); for recent Catholic immigrant groups in New York City, such as the Puerto Ricans, Italians, and Irish, Nathan Glazer and Daniel Patrick Moy-

Suggested Reading

nihan's *Beyond the Melting Pot* (Cambridge, Mass., 1963); and for the texts of the 341 interventions of American bishops at Vatican Council II, supplemented by good historical introductions to the different series of documents, is *American Participation in the Second Vatican Council* (New York, 1967), edited by Vincent A. Yzermans; a sociologist's account of the Church and the American Negro is William A. Osborne, *The Segregated Covenant: Race Relations and American Catholics* (New York, 1967).

There were not many significant biographies or autobiographies of Catholics whose lives continued into the 1960's, but the following are worthy of mention. Dorothy Day's earlier autobiography, *The Long Loneliness* (New York, 1952), is supplemented by *Loaves and Fishes* (New York, 1963), in which she continued her story of an extraordinary career that pioneered in the Catholic Worker Movement for the poor long before the anti-poverty campaigns of the 1960's had gotten underway. Sister Consuela Marie Duffy, S.B.S., provides a documented life of the great apostle to the Negro and Indian Americans in *Katharine Drexel: A Biography* (Philadelphia, 1966), while in the field of politics Lawrence H. Fuchs's *John F. Kennedy and American Catholicism* (New York, 1967) furnishes, perhaps, the most perceptive study to date of the relationship of the young president's religious faith to his political life. In the same field is Richard D. Lunt's *The High Ministry of Government: The Political Career of Frank Murphy* (Detroit, 1965), the biography of a Catholic who served in prominent posts from Governor of Michigan through Governor of the Philippines to Associate Justice of the Supreme Court. On the subject of the Catholic social worker and champion of racial justice are the memoirs of George K. Hunton as told to Gary MacEoin, *All of Which I Saw, Part of Which I Was* (New York, 1967). Three biographies of American cardinals of the period are Thomas T. McAvoy, C.S.C., *Father O'Hara of Notre Dame: The Cardinal-Archbishop of Philadelphia* (Notre Dame, 1967); Robert I. Gannon, S.J., *The Cardinal Spellman Story* (Garden City, N.Y., 1962), a life of the cardinal whose death in December, 1967, was said to have closed an era of American Catholicism; and the biography of Aloisius Muench (now in press) by Colman J. Barry, O.S.B., which tells the story of a churchman who was Bishop of Fargo, Apostolic Nuncio to West Germany after World War II, and who died in February, 1962, as the first American cardinal of the Roman Curia.

307

Index

Index

Index

Index

Index

Index

Index